ROTATION
PLAN

Daria Klimentová

Daria Klimentová

WITH GRAHAM WATTS

AGONY AND ECSTASY:
MY LIFE IN DANCE

metro

Published by Metro Publishing,
an imprint of John Blake Publishing Ltd
3 Bramber Court, 2 Bramber Road,
London W14 9PB, England

www.johnblakepublishing.co.uk

www.facebook.com/Johnblakepub   facebook

twitter.com/johnblakepub   twitter

First published in hardback in 2013

ISBN: 978 1 85782 883 2

British Library Cataloguing-in-Publication Data:

A catalogue record for this book is available from the British Library.

Design by www.envydesign.co.uk

Printed and bound in Great Britain by CPI Group (UK) Ltd

1 3 5 7 9 10 8 6 4 2

© Text copyright Daria Klimentová and Graham Watts 2013

Papers used by John Blake Publishing are natural, recyclable products
made from wood grown in sustainable forests. The manufacturing processes
conform to the environmental regulations of the country of origin.

Every attempt has been made to contact the relevant copyright-holders,
but some were unobtainable. We would be grateful if the
appropriate people could contact us.

For Sabina with love.

Acknowledgements

$\mathcal{S}$everal people have helped us with this project, particularly in terms of verifying facts and providing missing detail relating to Daria's dancing career, and also with their general encouragement throughout our work.

We are grateful to the following for their help in this regard: Laura Bösenberg, Rosanna Bortoli, Vladislav Bubnov, Anna Campbell, Ian Comer, Eve Farraud, Andrea Grofová, Dima Gruzdyev, Christopher Hampson, Caroline Jowett, Ludmila Klimentová, Natalia Kremen, Martin Kubala, Jan Kunovský, Sonja Lampert, David Makhateli, Karen McLernon, Lee McLernon, Dave Morgan, Johana Mücková, Vadim Muntagirov, Neil Norman, Zuzana Rafajová, Tamara Rojo, Michelle Salis, Jane Simpson, Jaroslav Slavický, Roslyn Sulcas and Kamila Tomaszewska.

Cecilia Watts and Tamara Watts helped to proofread drafts and provided advice on consistency and style.

We are also grateful to the many staff at English National Ballet for enabling our regular meetings at the company's headquarters in Jay Mews.

If we have forgotten anyone, we hope to be forgiven! All our friends, colleagues and families have been unwaveringly supportive throughout.

Daria Klimentová and Graham Watts
2013

Contents

Foreword

I first met Daria when I went to Glasgow, aged 19. Galina Samsova had been a judge when I won the Paris Competition and she invited me to perform as a guest with Scottish Ballet. In this respect, I followed Daria since she had come to be in Scotland by similar means when invited by Galina after winning a competition in South Africa.

On arriving in Scotland, I prepared for my own upcoming debut in the ballet by watching the company perform *Swan Lake*. Almost from her first steps on stage, I was immediately in awe of the dancer in the lead role of Odette/Odile. Here was a true prima ballerina with an impeccable quality of which I had not seen before. She was dancing in a style that was new to me, and I found it mesmerising. I was also surprised at how young this dancer was to be able to perform with such assured maturity. At the time, I was quite ignorant of classical ballet – but she seemed to know everything! I suddenly realised how much I had to learn. Having come straight from Spain, I had not experienced the Vaganova School of Ballet, which characterised the formation of dancers from Eastern Europe. Daria came from this tradition in which classic technique was absorbed every day from a very young age. I came to realise that she is a quintessential Vaganova ballerina. She has all their traits, from the alignment of her head and body, the gorgeous arms, hands and feet and an incredible quality of line and technique.

So, my first encounter with Daria was to be in awe of her ability but, then, the very next day, when we met and talked for the first time, I was amazed by how refreshingly direct she was. Instead of the pride that might be expected of such a consummate ballerina, she was constantly making jokes and putting herself down. She was (and still is) very funny in an unusually serious and dry way. I found her self-deprecation to be appealing, since it is traditionally alien to the art of being a prima ballerina. Most ballerinas are typically quite aloof. They are polite but not necessarily warm, yet Daria was honest almost to the point of being rude. I appreciated her integrity and truthfulness, and still do. We just got on from the very beginning and have remained firm friends ever since.

When I joined Scottish Ballet on a permanent contract, Daria had already moved to English National Ballet, but I was soon to make my way south to London to join the same company. When I arrived at English National Ballet, one year after Daria, she had already become established as one of the company's prima ballerinas, alongside Lisa Pavane. She was always easy to get on with and assisted me greatly settling in to this new company – with its speed and constant activity – in a new and exciting city. But, for all Daria's helpfulness and advice, she is always interested to learn from others and this thirst to improve continues to remain with her.

Above all else, Daria is a prima ballerina whom I admire. We have a strong bond of mutual respect, and we both know that we can speak our minds without fear of what the other might think. This is vital in a profession where honest communication is so important. Like all ballerinas, we want praise for our art but neither Daria nor I like, or seek, adulation. Both of us dislike the fawning flattery and idolization that sometimes comes with the territory.

As well as being an incredible ballerina, Daria is a free woman who is always going to live her life in her own way, and she is never going to allow anybody to judge her for it. This is a quality which I greatly appreciate.

Since our first meeting in Scotland, 20 years ago, she has taken many photographs of me, both on and off the stage. Her personal merits of honesty and directness flow through into an exceptional skill as a photographer. At some time in the future, but not for a while I hope, she may have the time to develop huge success in this second career.

Although we are both still dancing, my new role as Artistic Director at English National Ballet means that I am now her boss! There will be many challenges ahead, but I have inherited some wonderful dancers, not least that same ballerina I watched in awe at Scottish Ballet so many years ago.

As you will read, Daria has had a wonderful and varied career stretching well over 1,000 performances. She is still dancing at the very top of her ability, but now adding maturity and experience to that outstanding technique. One of my ambitions as Artistic Director is to help Daria maintain her performances at this level within English National Ballet for future seasons to come...

Tamara Rojo
Artistic Director, English National Ballet
2013

Introduction

*I*t began with a private message on Facebook. 'Do you write books?' This innocent enquiry was followed by a brief meeting with Daria that came in the margins of the National Dance Awards in January 2012. I was Chairman of the event – my first in this capacity – and it had gone well, not least because Daria – ever the most popular of ballerinas – had won the coveted accolade of Dancer of the Year. Perhaps it was the joy of the moment, but we agreed – without a moment's thought – to write this book together.

Our method was simple. To begin with, each week that we were both in the country, I would travel to ENB's headquarters in Jay Mews (or occasionally to the London Coliseum in St Martins Lane, London) and ask her questions. Hundreds – maybe thousands – of questions, and each weekend I would try to make order out of her responses. By August, I had compiled the very rough draft of her life story and began the process of reading each chapter to Daria on an iterative basis. We must have used virtually every office in ENB's building – anywhere that was free – and I watched Daria sew many pairs of pointe shoes as she listened to me read. It was almost so domesticated that all we needed was the cosy fire and the cat!

I was privileged to take custody of a battered grey exercise book, the pages falling apart, which contained (in Czech) the whole list of works that Daria had danced since a child. I soon became expert in understanding the names of ballets and roles written in the Czech language. But, with lots of further research, this amazing record has led to perhaps the most detailed career record of any ballerina, ever published. Reading through it gives so many insights into the way ballet has developed over the past 20 years. I was also given access to Daria's papers in her home in Horní Počernice and I spent three enjoyable days there researching the Czech side of her life. There was one remarkable moment when I discovered information about Daria's great uncle Josef, which she had not previously known, and the day that I was able to reveal the outcome of that research was like our own private episode of *Who Do You Think You Are?*

It has been a happy journey and a very rewarding one. Not only have I come to know so much about this wonderful ballerina's life and work, but we have arrived at a firm friendship that I will always cherish.

Graham Watts OBE
2013

Chapter 1

Horní Počernice

I have been a performer for as long as I can remember. As a ballet dancer, I've played principal roles in nearly 1,100 shows over 23 seasons. Before that – as a young girl – I was competing in gymnastic competitions all over what is now the Czech Republic and Slovakia. But, for all my adult life, I have only been comfortable in the spotlight when I'm playing a role; when I'm dancing. Then – and only then – can I lose myself. Perhaps that is why I have also chosen another professional life as a photographer: putting other people into the picture and remaining behind the lens myself.

On this evening – Sunday, 14 October 2012 – I'm sitting on a platform facing an audience of Czech people at the Žofín Palace (*Palác Žofín*) in central Prague. The room is already full and more chairs are being carried in to cope with the overflow. As befits the palatial setting, these chairs have golden, baroque frames with luscious red seats – each one like a mini-throne – and the room has the kind of ornate decoration and large chandeliers that I am more used to seeing on the set of *The Sleeping Beauty* or *Swan Lake*. But tonight's event is not a ballet.

A Tribute to Daria Klimentová is part of the 49th International Television Festival known as Golden Prague, organised by Czech Television (*Česká televise*) and will feature the Czech premiere of the BBC TV film *Agony and Ecstasy*, which captures the drama of my preparations for the opening night of a season of *Swan Lake* at the Royal Albert Hall in London, as well as showing extracts from two Czech TV documentaries about my life, made by Martin Kubala. The film screenings are to be preceded by speeches about aspects of my career and conclude with me fielding questions from the floor. In the palace's sumptuous entrance foyer there is an exhibition of my photography.

Just walking to the platform is an ordeal. Everyone wants to stop me for a chat or an autograph. They are kind, and I am humbled and touched by all the affection and support that is still showered on me by the people of my homeland, even though it is more than 20 years since I danced here regularly. But, on this occasion, I'm not wearing a tutu. I have to be Daria Klimentová and I don't like it. In truth, lovely though it is to have such support and appreciation, speaking in public is a challenge that I have always found difficult to face. It might be hard to believe it of someone who performs for a living, but I'm a quiet person who much prefers solitude to being the centre of so much attention. I have danced for princes and princesses; for politicians, pop stars, film stars, even for 'James Bond'! But, although I was never fazed by the prospect of dancing before Princess Diana or Madonna, the idea of just mixing with an audience and talking to them openly about my life fills me with dread.

Thankfully, I don't have to face this evening alone. I am with four people who have worked closely with me across the different stages of my career. There is Vadim Muntagirov, my current dance partner (and the reason I'm still dancing at 41), a brilliant young virtuoso Russian dancer, who is already becoming a major international star; one of my teachers from the Prague Conservatoire, Jaroslav Slawický – who speaks affectionately and at length about my early career; the film director, Martin Kubala; and lastly, the chairman of the dance section of the UK Critics' Circle, Graham Watts, the man I have chosen to help me write this book. In his speech, Graham tells the audience that the Czech nation has exported many wonderful things to the United Kingdom and ends by thanking them for lending me to the British people for over 20 years.

Graham was right to place his emphasis on the word 'loan' because I'm certain that the story of my life in dance will end where it began – and that will be in Prague (or as Czech people know it, *Praha*), the magical, romantic capital of the historic region of Bohemia.

Prague is an enchanting treasure trove of beauty and culture, loved especially for the unblemished medieval charms of its cobbled streets, walled courtyards, ancient bridges and countless church spires. The city is overlooked by the imposing ninth-century castle sitting high above the Vltava River. It is funny looking back to when I was a tiny child, sitting on my dad's shoulders, walking through Prague and watching the many swans gliding along the Vltava. I never realised then that I would spend a large part of my adult life trying to perfect the balletic artistry of becoming just like them!

The Old Town (*Staré město*) contains some of the most important and everlasting symbols of Prague's fame, many of which were built in the 14th century, around the reign of King Charles IV, the Holy Roman Emperor and second King of Bohemia. Charles was born as Wenceslas and he is often wrongly identified as the Good King Wenceslas of the popular Christmas carol, which tells of the monarch's benevolence in giving alms to a poor peasant on the Feast of Stephen. But that legend refers to another Wenceslas, known by Czechs as Svatý Václav (Saint Wenceslas), who was the Duke of Bohemia and lived some 400 years before Charles IV.

Every Czech person loves the Charles Bridge (*Karlův most*), an everlasting symbol of Prague, adorned by 30 baroque statues of the saints lined up along both sides, which connects Prague Castle (*Pražský hrad*) with the Old Town and the only means of crossing the Vltava until the 19th century. The bridge was dedicated to Charles IV, who laid the foundation stone at 5.31am on 9 July 1357 (although it then took nearly 50 years to build). The precision of the exact time of this event was no accident since it forms a palindrome when written down numerically in old Czech style: 1357 (year) 9 (day) 7 (month) and 5.31 (time). A lucky formula that has served the bridge well since, unlike the Judith Bridge, which stood on the same spot and was destroyed in 1342, the Charles Bridge has survived many potential disasters over its six-century existence, including the catastrophic flooding of 2002, which engulfed Prague and much of central Europe, and was to have such a major impact on my family's life.

Prague possesses a remarkably diverse architectural realm with stunning examples of Renaissance, Baroque and Gothic styles represented in the many buildings inside Prague Castle, the traditional seat of Bohemian and Czech Kings and now the home of the President. At nearly 600m (1,968.5ft) long, it is the world's largest ancient castle and dominates my city's skyline. A short walk away, at the other end of the Charles Bridge, is the Old Town Square, housing the Town Hall with its famous Astronomical Clock. And further along the riverbank there is the golden roof of the National Theatre (*Národní divadlo*), one of many significant cultural institutions in Prague and a special landmark in my own personal story.

The many cultural significances of Prague led to the city being designated as a World Heritage Site by UNESCO in 1992, which happens also to be the year in which I left home to pursue my life in dance.

Although I have lived for almost 20 years in the United Kingdom, my spirit has remained steadfastly Czech, and I am proud to know that Prague is still my home. This wonderful city has existed for more than a Millennium and at the time of my birth – 23 June 1971 – it was the capital of Czechoslovakia (*Československo*). The nation was young, created in the aftermath of the First World War when it declared independence from the Austro-Hungarian Empire. From 1948, Czechoslovakia was a communist state and in 1960 it became the Czechoslovak Socialist Republic (or ČSSR).

At the beginning of 1993, by which time I was already dancing overseas, the two parts of Czechoslovakia split into the Czech Republic (*Česká republika*) and Slovakia, with Prague becoming the capital of the former, a land of almost 11 million people.

Over the course of my life to date, my homeland has become a new nation. It has moved from the dark side of the Iron Curtain into the light of freedom; from occupation and a one-party state to elections and democracy; from under the oppression of the Soviet Union to being part of the European Union.

I was born on the eastern outskirts of this beautiful city, in a suburb known as Horní (which means, Upper) Počernice – there is also a Dolní (Lower) Počernice. Two years before I was born, the village had been upgraded to a town by order of the Central Bohemian Regional National Committee and – in 1974 – it was incorporated formally into the City of Prague as a suburb with the not so romantic identity of Prague 9. Since 2002, the number of districts in Prague has doubled and my village now goes under the formal name of Prague 20. To keep everyone confused, the street signs still refer to the district as Prague 9 but, of course, everyone still calls the area

Horní Počernice. It is a part of Prague that still bears its own very special identity.

If modern Prague was divided into a jigsaw with each piece representing a district, Horní Počernice (Prague 20) would be one of the outside pieces on the eastern side, roughly central in terms of the north and south of the city. It is approximately to Prague as the London Borough of Bexley is to Greater London (although with less than one-fifteenth the quantity of Bexley's population).

It is said that there has been a settlement in this area between the rivers Rokytka and Svépravického (although the latter is now no more than a hard-to-find stream) since around 4500 BC. The first recorded mention of Horní Počernice dates back to 1357 but, 500 years later – in the census of 1843 – the population of the village was just 735 people. The current municipal district is the product of a merger of three villages and two hamlets – Horní Počernice, Chvaly, Čertousy, Xaverov and Svépravice – which occurred shortly after the Second World War when this wider area had grown to around 9,000 inhabitants.

Today, Horní Počernice is an area of about 17km² (7 square miles) and is home to some 15,000 people. Although the municipality is, strictly speaking, an outlying administrative district of Prague, Horní Počernice effectively remains a small town in its own right, with a mayor and the equivalent of a town hall. It has its own flag with three horizontal stripes, from top to bottom of black, red and silver (although for practical reasons this is usually symbolised in grey) and a coat of arms. This heraldry shows a black horse with a golden bridle, reins and hooves, jumping to the right over three golden ears of corn with the background shield divided diagonally into halves of white over red. The stallion symbolises the centuries-old tradition of horse breeding in the area and the three golden ears of corn stand for the three villages that merged to form Horní Počernice. The district is now twinned with Brunsbüttel in the Schleswig-Holstein region of northern Germany; Mions in the Rhône department of eastern France; and Bořetice, a small wine-growing village situated within the southern Moravian forests of the Czech Republic.

Horní Počernice has few landmarks of special interest but there is a beautiful baroque chapel and Chvalský Fortress, which holds an annual festival based on the burning of witches that remains a major event for local people. There is a lovely forest area with a lake where everyone picks mushrooms and blackberries, and – in stark contrast – Horní Počernice also has one of the Czech Republic's largest industrial parks (the VGP Park), which was commenced in 2006 and grows larger by the year.

Today, driving across Prague to Horní Počernice, it is remarkable how the signs for Kentucky Fried Chicken and the golden arches of McDonald's, which are now all too prevalent as if these are American Highways, suddenly stop at the outskirts of the village as one enters an area that seems magically protected from the advances of modern-day consumerism. Horní Počernice has a single supermarket and an old-fashioned restaurant or two. The houses in the streets where I grew up have been modernised but they haven't changed in character. It all seems exactly as it was.

In truth, Horní Počernice remains little more than a large village on the outskirts of Prague but it is the place that I truly regard as my home; and to where I return, like a homing pigeon, as many times as I can.

My parents were both children of the Second World War. My father, Zdeněk Kliment, was born in 1943, in Jirny, a small village about an hour away from the centre of Prague; and my mother, Ludmila, arrived a year later, in the kitchen of her parents' home in Horní Počernice. Neither of my parents talked to me much about their early

7

years, although I learned more from my maternal grandma, who was also named Ludmila, because I spent a great deal of time with her during my childhood.

Ludmila Lampírová was born in 1910, before the First World War, the Russian Revolution and the consequent flames of communism that engulfed Eastern Europe. At the time of my grandma's birth, Prague was part of the Austro-Hungarian Empire, although a strong movement for Czech nationalism had been rising steadily through the 19th century. Ludmila was the youngest of five children. Throughout my childhood, she would often spend time telling me stories about the Second World War and how it affected everyone's lives so significantly.

The German Army entered Prague in March 1939 and Hitler proclaimed both the historic areas of Bohemia and Moravia as a German Protectorate. The ethnic composition of the city at that time was a mix of Czech, German and Jewish people. But, of course, the Nazi occupation meant the swift and merciless eradication of the entire Jewish population. On 27 May 1942, Prague was the scene of the assassination of Reinhard Heydrich, Hitler's Reich Protector in Bohemia and Moravia, and a despicable man who bore much personal responsibility for inflaming the Holocaust. While in Prague, he suppressed Czech culture and executed many patriots. He was killed by British-trained Czech and Slovak soldiers in Operation Anthropoid, but the Nazis wrongly accused the people of two villages northwest of Prague: Lidice and Ležáky. Both villages were destroyed on Hitler's personal order and 184 men from Lidice (every adult male over 16) were shot, with hundreds of women and children deported to the concentration camps; all 33 men and women of Ležáky were executed and 11 of the village's 13 children were gassed in the Chełmno concentration camp in occupied Poland. Ležáky was wiped from the map, never to be rebuilt.

My family did not escape the atrocities wrought by the Nazis.

Grandma Ludmila's brother, Josef Skřivan, was born in Prague on 10 August 1902. After working as a clerk in a draper's shop, he became a professional actor, enjoying a successful career as a serious character actor on stage; appearing in theatres in Prague, Pardubice and especially at the Provincial Theatre in Brno, where he played over 150 roles, including such iconic Shakespearian characters as Cicero in *Julius Caesar*, Iago in *Othello*, Claudius in *Hamlet* and the title role of Richard III, as well as appearing to great acclaim as Don Quixote and Cyrano de Bergerac. As a ballerina, one of my earliest major roles was as the heroine Kitri in *Don Quixote*, a part that I had coveted from my student days. I wonder if there was a subliminal link back to Josef, this great uncle that I never met but heard so much about from his sister, my grandma.

Great Uncle Josef was a handsome man with strong features offset by the magnetic appeal of soft brown eyes. He had thick black wavy hair and often wore a thin moustache, as was fashionable before the war. He became a regular star of the Brno Radio, appearing in a host of shows in the 1930s, and he was also a stage director of some renown in Brno, directing a seminal performance of *The Tempest* in 1941.

Josef Skřivan made his screen debut in 1928, starring as Field Marshal Schwerdtner in a silent movie entitled *Jménem Jeho Veličenstva* (*On Behalf of His Majesty*) and he progressed to become a comedy film star in Czechoslovakia. His most popular films were in support of the famous Czech clowns, Jiří Voskovec and Jan Werich (who were, I suppose, a kind of Czech Laurel and Hardy, albeit rather more satirical). He starred in three of their films, beginning with *Pudr a benzín* (*Powder and Petrol*/1931) and *Peníze nebo život* (*Money or Your Life*/1932), both directed by Jindřich Honzl; and then the optimistic farce *Hej-rup!* (literally translated as Hey-ho – but more often known as *Workers, Let's Go*/1934), directed by Martin

Fric. Josef also starred as the French painter, Grikova, in the well-known children's film *Ztratila se Bílá paní* (*She Lost the White Lady*/1937).

Jiří Voskovec fled to the USA in 1939, where he continued his film career and he is perhaps best known as the 11th juror in the Henry Fonda film *12 Angry Men* and for his role with Richard Burton as the East German Defence Attorney in *The Spy Who Came in from the Cold*. Jan Werich – who also fled to the West in 1939 – was originally cast to play the villain, Blofeld, in the James Bond film *You Only Live Twice* but he was replaced by Donald Pleasence after a few days' filming because the producer, Cubby Broccoli, felt that he didn't look sufficiently villainous enough. Broccoli thought that he looked too much like Santa Claus!

Although I never met Great Uncle Josef, I saw all of these old Czech films when I was growing up in Horní Počernice. In fact, you can still see them occasionally in the Czech Republic on daytime and late night television.

Josef continued to act on stage after the Nazis occupied Prague but, in 1940, he had a near-fatal bicycle accident that required complex plastic surgery to reconstruct a part of his face. Grandma Ludmila told me that her brother was a communist and, of course, it was extremely dangerous to hold such beliefs while under Nazi occupation. She said that Josef hid these political allegiances from all but his closest friends and family.

Grandma told me that Josef won a prize for his acting – perhaps a lifetime achievement award or something like that – but another actor was jealous of his success and he informed the Germans about Josef's communist sympathies. However, I have recently learned that Josef used his fame as an actor to mask his role in the Czech Resistance and the theatre in Brno was the cover for a hotbed of patriotism and rebellion. By a quirk of coincidence, this theatre in Brno has a major significance in the world of ballet since it was here – on 30 December 1938 – that the very first choreographed version of Prokofiev's rich score for *Romeo and Juliet* was premiered with Žora Semberová as Juliet. I would like to think that Great Uncle Josef was in the audience on that momentous evening. Incidentally, that first Juliet, Žora Semberová, passed away in Australia on 9 October 2012 – at the grand old age of 99 – while I was finishing this book.

On 3 October 1941, Josef was arrested by the Gestapo at a nursing home in Brno, where he was recuperating from further facial surgery. He was imprisoned and tortured for six months. Many of the actors and stage crew from Brno were arrested and the theatre was closed in April 1942.

Josef was taken to the Auschwitz concentration camp in the spring of 1942, just before the Heydrich assassination, where he went into the gas chamber at some time between 25 October and 4 November of that year. He was just 40.

An eyewitness account of Josef's last days by a man named Aleš Podhorský was published in a Czech theatre magazine in 1965. It would appear that Josef was initially kept safe thanks to the protection of one of the camp's guards – who was a fan of his films – but, one day, Josef injured his hand and was unable to go out to work with the other prisoners from his block. A patrol of guards, not including Josef's protector, was ordered to round up anyone unable to work and add them to those queuing for extermination. So, it would seem that an injured face got Josef caught and an injured hand put him into the gas chamber. A part of me would like to believe that death may have been a blessed relief after a year in the hands of the Nazis.

In my house in Horní Počernice, I still have a scrapbook of photos and critical reviews of Josef's performances. My grandma was understandably very proud of her brother's achievements, and I think that her stories about Josef had a significant subliminal impression on me as a child and probably have some relevance in my own choice of career as a performer on stage. A particularly touching tribute to him was that a theatre company in Brno took his name, performing as the Josef Skřivan Theatre Company for more than 30 years, from the early 1950s until the mid-1980s.

Like most people in Czechoslovakia at that time, and despite Josef's fame as an actor, my grandmother's family was poor. Ludmila's husband, Antonín Lampír – my maternal grandfather – who had a business fixing machine engines, died in 1968, before I was born. Ludmila and Antonín had three children: the eldest, also called Antonín, was born in 1937; Ludmila, my mother, followed in 1944; and the youngest, Jan, came along in 1946. The eldest brother, Antonín, was always teasing my mum. A teacher who spoke several languages fluently, including English, Spanish, German and Russian, Antonín was a very active man. He played a lot of sports and – unusually for people in Czechoslovakia – he was able to travel a great deal throughout the world during the days of communist suppression.

At the age of 72, sometime in 2009, Antonín was cutting the branches of a large tree in his garden when he fell several metres and landed on his head. Surprisingly, he got up, brushed himself down and walked back to the house but his wife, Libuše, was worried and insisted that he went to hospital, where it was discovered that Antonín had internal bleeding on his brain.

He fell into a coma for eight months and everyone thought it would be the end for such an elderly man. But, having been very active, Antonín fought back out of the coma, eventually defying the medics by returning to consciousness. He couldn't walk or talk for a long time but – at 75 – he is now fully recovered. The only notable change is that

Uncle Antonín's temperament is now very different. He used to be a very loud man, fond of parties and socialising. He loved nothing more than to have people around to visit, but now he is the exact opposite and wants only quiet and solitude. However, it has been an amazing recovery: Antonín should have died but, after almost a year in a coma, he is not only alive but teaching languages again. I really hope that the strength in his genes flows through my mother's side of the family and into mine.

Grandma Ludmila was a teacher, specialising in Czech history and language, but she retired early and used to help me with my own studies in the Czech language, especially when I was at ballet school. My mum was never sure if I was going to make a successful career as a ballet dancer, so she sent me to my grandma for extra lessons. I used to go to her house every weekend but Grandma Ludmila was not like a teacher; she was far too kind. She used to say to me, 'Oh, you must eat first before lessons,' and then after feeding me she would say it was time to lie down and have a rest!

I liked it a lot because I always wanted to be quiet during my childhood. I didn't like noisy groups of children and I preferred to be on my own. My mum was so much more active and energetic, and she was bossy, too! There was always so much happening at home, and I really craved my restful afternoons at Grandma Ludmila's house when I was supposed to be studying. I have always known that I am much more like my grandma than my mum!

We lived in a two-bedroom apartment in Horní Počernice, but Grandma Ludmila had a house with a lovely garden and visiting her was like heaven for me. I would find little flowers and insects and stare at them for hours. I spent a lot of time at Grandma's house, which was only a ten-minute walk from my family home. It wasn't that I had to be looked after by her in what we might now refer to as childcare; I just loved the peace and quiet so much that I always wanted to visit her, so

I went to her house whenever I was able to go: certainly every week, sometimes every day.

When Grandma Ludmila was 92 she fell downstairs and broke her hip. It was an accident from which she couldn't recover and she died, very peacefully, on 4 December 2002. I was glad that she lived long enough to come and see me dance and to know that I had become successful in my chosen profession as a ballerina. She lived to a grand old age but Grandma Ludmila slept a lot; perhaps that's the secret of a long life! She loved to sleep and so do I. Grandma Ludmila would have a snooze every afternoon and on those days when my mum thought I was cramming in the extra studies and learning more about the Czech language, we used to lie outside together in her garden and doze the whole afternoon away! My grandma's legacy to me is that I still want a snooze every afternoon. I need at least nine hours' sleep at night and, if I get the chance, I will also have a nap after lunch, wherever I am and certainly always before a show. I certainly have Grandma Ludmila's sleeping genes!

Mum had a full-time job in the 1960s but only for about a year. She worked in a laboratory, where police would bring debris from an aircraft crash and scientists then attempted to piece together what had happened to cause the accident. Throughout my childhood, she was always a housewife but she earned some extra money making clothes from wool with a special kind of machine. She has managed to carry this talent forward to the present day and has a speciality in making unique legwarmers for dancers, which was initially my idea because she had so much material and was going to throw it all away. I persuaded her to put the wool to good use and her legwarmers are always greatly prized, not only by the dancers in English National Ballet, but by principal dancers all over the world.

I used to spend some parts of the weekend with my paternal grandparents. My father's father was František Kliment. He was born in 1904 and worked as a cobbler in the town of Jirny about 7km (4.3 miles) from Horní Počernice, where my mum's family lived.

František died in 1981, when I was ten and about to go to the Prague Conservatoire (*Pražská konzervatoř*), which is home to the National Theatre ballet school. It was my first experience of death and the first and last funeral that I have ever attended. Even though I was never particularly close to my grandfather, the whole event traumatised me. He was in an open coffin and the sight of his corpse, the speeches, the crying and that sad music was so upsetting that I vowed never to go to another funeral. And for over 30 years I have stuck dogmatically to this resolution. I have an amazing family who completely understand my phobia, and my mum has also come to share this horror of funerals. No one has ever blamed me for feeling like this.

The first opportunity to skip a funeral came when my paternal grandmother, Růžena, died in 1986, five years after her husband, František. I was already 15 but to save me from the trauma, my mum and dad didn't have a funeral service for Růžena. She was cremated and my dad simply collected her ashes without any ceremony.

Růžena Homolová was born in 1907 as one of 13 children. She couldn't read or write. I remember that when my father was working in Libya, to make money for the family, Růžena regularly asked me to write her letters for her to send to him.

My father had a brother named Jiří (although the family always called him Jirka) but there had been an elder child, also called Zdeněk. However, my dad never knew this older brother because he hung himself at the age of 14, a teenager growing up in Nazi-occupied Prague. I have no idea why he did this, and no one on my father's side ever discussed the tragedy while they were alive, but I can only assume that Uncle Zdeněk's suicide made him just another casualty of the terrible war that ravaged Europe. After his suicide, František and

Růžena decided to have another son – my father – whom they also named Zdeněk. I realised only when preparing this book that I lost an uncle on my father's side and a great uncle on my mother's side in the same year (1942), nearly 30 years before my birth.

Given how I have turned out, it is ironic that my parents met at a dancing party! It was the kind of afternoon event where there is coffee and tea, and a band plays waltzes and other social dances. I don't know if it was love at first sight but they got married very early, aged 20 and 21, although in those days this was not unusual. I discovered that the speed of their wedding was motivated by Ludmila wanting to escape from home because grandfather Antonín was very possessive and unreasonably strict. If she was standing talking to Zdeněk in the garden then her dad would be calling every minute from the window, telling her to come inside. Getting married very quickly was Ludmila's only means of escaping such rigid control!

Mum has always been an attractive and sexy woman. She was as fashionable as living under communism would allow, invariably wearing high heels. Mum has naturally black hair but all her life she has dyed it blonde and worn it short. She has also been blessed with the classic hourglass figure of a slim waist and big boobs. Drivers would frequently beep their horns at her in the street. I can remember them doing so even when I was a teenager walking with her. She was much more temperamental than my dad and she needs to have people around her, to have fun. She is someone who loves to give. Dad was more studious. He used to read all the time but he was naturally fit and athletic. He played a lot of football in the 1960s.

Three years after their wedding – in 1967 – Mum gave birth to my brother, Radomír, but she had been praying to have a 'girl with long hair and long legs'. She tried to get pregnant again almost immediately and, finally, four-and-a-half years after my brother, I was born in the long, hot summer of 1971.

Little Daria became known in the family as Darinka or Darina, although my mum's pet name for me was always *kočička* (which means kitten). As a baby and toddler, I was certainly not as playful as a kitten. Quite the contrary since I was a very quiet and passive baby, not temperamental at all. I slept so much that Mum was constantly afraid that there was something wrong with me or that I had died in my sleep. She would wake me up all the time just to check that I was still alive. Perhaps that's why I need to sleep so much now!

Mum used to tell everyone that I didn't cry for the first time until I was 15 and that she had to teach me how to smile as a teenager in order for me to be photographed. She also used to tell everyone that wherever she left me, she would be sure to find me hours later. It is true that I was a very placid and serious child. People around me thought that there was something wrong and that I must have some innate sadness, but I was rarely unhappy. It was just the way I was: a very quiet and phlegmatic little girl who kept everything bottled up inside.

My brother, on the other hand, was exactly the opposite. Radomír took after Mum. He was slim and small with black hair, and always loud and boisterous. Moody and demanding, he could also be very loving. He was always either laughing or crying. One day Radomír would give you everything he had, but the next he would want it all returned, before trying to take the shirt from your own back.

A lot of my earliest memories are about fighting with my brother. I was a studious girl who liked to spend time alone in my bedroom (which I shared with Radomír throughout my childhood) or at my grandma's house. I was not an extrovert in any way whatsoever. Radomír was constantly teasing me; pinching me when I wasn't looking; pushing me; and hiding my things. He would never hurt me but Radomír made me so angry that I would want to retaliate and hurt him. All our problems started with him teasing me and often he would not stop for hours until I just couldn't take it any longer. The anger about his constant practical jokes would build and build until I would erupt. I'm sure that he always thought that I wouldn't hurt him but sometimes even he got a surprise! Once, I took a chain, something like a bicycle chain only smaller, and I hit him with it on his back and caused a nasty scar. On another occasion, I actually took a knife to him but he still carried on goading me; I was getting so mad, thinking that he wouldn't stop and I would have to stab him, but thankfully he relented! Perhaps he remembered the incident with the chain.

My dad was always my biggest fan. He was very protective of me, especially if there were any other males around, but unlike my mum's father, he was never unduly strict. He would come and see me in every performance, in the school and eventually in the theatre. The schools I attended after my local kindergarten in Horní Počernice were very far from where we lived – at least 90 minutes' drive away – and Dad would drive me, every single day, and sometimes he would stay there for three hours or more, just sitting in the car, patiently reading and waiting to take me home. I don't recall him ever complaining but he spent so much of his life waiting in the car for me. Dad didn't like to show his pride in me too overtly. He encouraged me, especially in the beginning with my gymnastics, and he would help to train me at home. He even put a bar across the doorway so that I could practise. We would do exercises together to flatten our stomachs and we would often go swimming, just the two of us.

Later on, when I started at ballet school, he made a mirror that covered the whole of my bedroom wall and fitted a *barre* for me to practise my exercises. He would think that he was secretly watching me practise from the balcony outside, but I always knew that he was there. I was so happy that I could see him, watching and caring about what I was doing, but we would never, ever talk about it. Dad would never discuss his hopes or aspirations for me, but I knew that he cared very deeply. To be honest, my own serious and timid nature meant that I was happier for those things to remain unsaid.

Chapter 2

Sparta Prague

*W*hile I was at kindergarten in Horní Počernice, a group of men in overcoats came to look at us. I didn't know at the time, and don't remember much about it now, but they were assessing young children for their potential gymnastic capability. I had never played any formal sport and I had no idea that I had any talent for gymnastics but they chose me, so at the age of five I was selected to become a gymnast. I enjoyed the training and I was always very good at doing exactly what I have been asked to do. After one year, the authorities decided that I had even more potential and so – in 1977 – I was sent for training with the Czechoslovakian gymnastics team, which, at that time, was based in the famous stadium complex of Sparta Prague (*Sparta Praha*).

Throughout Eastern Europe a football club is usually part of a much larger multi-sports institution, a concept that was inextricable from significant state support during the communist era. Founded in 1883, Sparta Prague is the best known and most successful Czech football team, but it has also provided a base for the national squads in many other sports, including the national centres for tennis and gymnastics. Many of the great Czech tennis legends trained at Sparta Prague, such as Martina Navrátilová, Helena Suková, Jan Kodeš and Hana Mandlíková (who is the official face of Sparta Prague today). The name Sparta is taken from the fearsome Greek city-state renowned for its military prowess and a holistic emphasis on rigorous physical training.

The sport of gymnastics was still on a high in Czechoslovakia during the 1970s due to the outstanding successes of our gymnasts over the previous decade, led by the charismatic blonde Věra Čáslavská, who won seven gold medals at the Olympic Games of Tokyo (1964) and Mexico City (1968), all of which were in individual events. To this day, Čáslavská holds two amazing records: she is the only gymnast to have won gold in every individual discipline (all-around, balance beam, floor exercise, uneven bars and vault) and she has won more individual Olympic gold medals than any other gymnast.

In addition to her seven gold medals, Čáslavská holds four Olympic silver medals (both team and individual) and 15 other World and European titles. For Czech people, the most important thing is that Čáslavská brought to an end the Soviet Union's domination of women's gymnastics. She is rightly regarded as a heroine in the Czech Republic, not solely due to her amazing sporting achievements but because of her outspoken opposition to the Soviet invasion of Czechoslovakia in 1968. This stand was exemplified by her dignified, silent protest at the Mexico Olympics when, standing on the podium for the medal ceremonies in the floor and beam events (where Čáslavská had suffered from disputed judging), she lowered and averted her head during the playing of the Soviet anthem. Here in the West, this symbol of defiance was overshadowed by the 'Black Power' gloved fist salute by the US African-American sprinters Tommie Smith and John Carlos, at the same Olympic Games, but Čáslavská's protest was no less significant.

Unfortunately, Čáslavská was not to be followed by other great Czechoslovakian gymnasts, and the country won no medals in the gymnastics events in Munich (1972) or Montreal (1976). The women's events in the former were again dominated by the gymnasts of the Soviet Union, winning four of the six gold medals and a total of ten medals altogether, with its team led by the powerful Ludmila Tourischeva and the mercurial Olga Korbut. Four years later, in Montreal, although Korbut and Tourischeva were still part of the victorious USSR team, the five individual titles were shared by the 15-year-old Romanian, Nadia Comăneci (winning all-around, uneven bars and beam) and Nellie Kim of the Soviet Union (victorious on vault and floor).

I was destined to be part of a new push for Czechoslovakian gymnastics aimed at regaining the medal zone at the Olympic Games in the 1980s. I enjoyed it all very much, especially the floor exercise because it meant performing to music, which is where my love of ballet perhaps has its first origins.

In those days, in communist countries, it was a very big thing to be singled out for selection for the national gymnastics team. I still have, at my home in Horní Počernice, a scrapbook containing pictures that I used to collect of all my idols in the sport. I loved the Czech gymnasts, of course, especially the great Čáslavská in her trademark black leotard and beehive of piled-up blonde hair; but also Hana Líšková, Mária Krajcírová and Jana Kubicková-Posnerová. I also admired the more contemporary Russian and Romanian stars, such as Korbut, Kim and Comăneci. I knew of these wonderful gymnasts and I wanted to be just as successful as them.

Attending the national gymnastics centre at Sparta Prague meant a very long journey to the other side of the city, which took a total of three hours to get there and back every day. I trained for at least four hours on every weekday from the age of five until I was ten. I was Czech Junior Champion, both in individual disciplines and as a member of the mighty Sparta Prague, and I won many medals in competitions all around Czechoslovakia, which I have still got at my house in Horní Počernice. In my own little way, I took after the great Čáslavská since I didn't specialise in any apparatus but spread my enthusiasm for the sport across all four of the women's disciplines (balance beam, floor exercise, uneven bars and vault).

When I was nine, at the time of the Olympic Games in Moscow, the coaches at Sparta Prague told me that they were going to put me in the Czech national squad and train me for the next Olympic cycles. I was definitely being groomed for the Olympic Games in 1988. As a young girl, that was my first big dream and I really saw myself as an Olympian, representing my country. That was what I was being trained for. It was also for me, as well as for every other young gymnast in Eastern Europe, the only potential escape from a humdrum existence and for the state, it was a means of showing that communism was the right way. In Czechoslovakia, the additional unspoken determination was also to do better than the athletes from the Soviet Union!

In fact, there were always two levels of competition. First, there was the communist world versus the capitalist world; and then there was the intense competition within the Eastern Bloc itself: most serious of all was the rivalry between the countries that had been effectively 'taken over' by the Union of Socialist Soviet Republics. Nothing pleased Hungarians, Czechs, Poles, Romanians and East Germans more than to have victory over competitors from the Soviet Union. Later, I was to realise that there was another level of competition that we didn't see because within the USSR there was this battle between athletes from the Ukraine, Belarus, Latvia, Estonia, Georgia and all the other proud republics conquered by the 'hammer and sickle' – the symbol of communism under the Soviet Union – to try and beat their contemporaries from Mother Russia.

My academic life suffered because of gymnastics because I was always training. I hardly had time to do homework because of the extra coaching in the evening, followed by a long drive home. At Sparta Prague, much more emphasis was put on my gymnastics training than the academic study accompanying it. I managed to get through the academic work but I was always average, just doing barely enough to get to the next level. Mum was not very strict at pushing me to do schoolwork because she always felt that I needed to rest, since I was training so much. When there was some spare time to study, she would say to me, 'Go to sleep, you already do too much.' And, of course, when I was going to Grandma Ludmila's for extra study at the weekends, I was really just getting some more sleep.

There were all kinds of stories about what would be done to alter the balance of young girls' hormones during their training and competition cycles, bringing on their periods to coincide with major competitions because the perceived wisdom was that they performed better if their menstrual cycle occurred at that time. Thankfully, I was too young for this and it didn't affect me personally, but I heard all of these stories from the other girls.

We had a very strict coach, a strong blonde woman called Mrs Nekvasilová, who used to hit us girls if we didn't do well in training. She would slap our faces regularly if we couldn't perform to her liking. I remember on one occasion I was really struggling with the uneven bars because I was very tired after a day's training and my arms were losing their strength and grip. So, this coach just came over and slapped me very hard. Even though it is a horrible thing and an unforgivable way to treat any young child, I also recall that somehow I did it properly the next time because I was so scared that I would be punished again. We just accepted that this was how it was; we were so young that we didn't know any other way.

I can also remember cheating once because I was tired. I was supposed to do a particular exercise ten times but I did it only five times. Mrs Nekvasilová asked if I had done it properly and I said 'yes', but she had been watching and had caught me in this white lie, which led to another hard slap. It was painful but, again, I have to admit that I didn't cut any more corners, and I certainly didn't lie again about not doing the exercises. So, as nasty as it was, it seems to me that these methods of coaching actually worked. It is not something I would recommend, however!

I wasn't allowed to have any pets but I would often find a feral cat somewhere and bring it home. Mum would let me keep it for a couple of days and then I would have to let it go. Or, I might sometimes bring a hedgehog into the house that I had found nearby and I could also keep that for a while before letting it back into the wild. I love animals and I have always wanted pets, but I just wasn't allowed to have them as a child.

In desperation to have something, Radomír and I kept snails. We would collect about ten of them at a time and paint numbers on their shells. Mine would be numbered one to five and Radomír would have six to ten. We would have competitions and line them up in a row to race them! We weren't allowed to have them in the house, of course, but Mum let us keep them on the outside balcony of our apartment. We would put them in a cardboard box with holes in it. The snails couldn't open the box but, every so often, I would come home and find that, although the box was still closed, there wouldn't be any snails left. So, Radomír and I would collect ten snails again, paint numbers on the new catch and the whole strange process would start over with the mysterious disappearance of these snails after a few days. Mum used to tell us that the snails were very clever and could work out how to open the lid of the box and climb down from the balcony to freedom. For many years, I believed this or, more fancifully, I imagined that it was some kind of magic that enabled the snails to open the box and escape. It was only years later, when Radomír and I no longer kept our 'pet' snails, that Mum confessed to regularly getting rid of them overnight. As a child growing up, I thought a lot about these 'magic' snails in the streets and fields of Horní Počernice with numbers painted on their shells. I loved to imagine the faces of anyone who found one!

I was rarely in trouble as a child but I did cause a fire in the park once. I don't remember how old I was but it was before I started ballet school (so it must have been prior to being ten). I stole some matches and lit some white, easily-combustible material that Dad used to help start a fire. It got out of control and some adults had to come and put it out. I remember being severely told off for that.

Another incident that I recall from childhood, which was more Radomír's fault than mine, came when our apartment was flooded. At this time, Dad had extra part-time work in a bar and sometimes Mum would help him, and they would both be away at night. On one such occasion, Radomír and I woke up in the middle of the night and we wanted to have a drink. Back then, in communist Czechoslovakia, it was common for the water supply not to be working, so my brother went around the whole apartment and opened the faucets, trying to find some water. But there was none. So, we went back to sleep – only Radomír didn't turn the taps off. When my parents returned home early in the morning, the water supply had come back on some hours before and the whole flat was swimming under centimetres of water. It wasn't my fault but we were both equally blamed.

Growing up as a child in Czechoslovakia during the 1970s and early

1980s was difficult but, at the time, we didn't know any differently. It was a great luxury whenever we were able to get toilet paper. We mostly had to use old newspapers to clean ourselves and there was a special technique, taught from a very early age, about how to make the newspaper softer. Also, it was impossible to get hygienic products for when a girl started to menstruate; there were no panty pads or tampons. You just couldn't buy them, so every girl had to improvise her own solutions to the problem, invariably handed down from mother to daughter.

I have a vivid memory of standing in a queue for two hours because someone told us that a store had some bananas to sell. I'm certain that every young person growing up under a post-war communist regime will have similar recollections. Many food items were rationed anyway. Even if you found a store selling fruit, you were only allowed to buy so much per family. Throughout my entire childhood, I don't think I ever ate a whole banana. My mum would cut one to give my dad, brother and me a piece each. Radomír, of course, would invariably measure our respective portions to make sure that it was a fair division of the fruit, and we were always fighting about which of us had the bigger piece.

Food was never plentiful. Grandma Ludmila's lovely garden meant that she could grow tomatoes and other vegetables, such as potatoes and fruits. Whatever you could grow you could keep, so the whole family would share her produce. My uncle and aunt (Antonín and Libuše) lived with Grandma Ludmila and they often kept pigs in the garden, so they would have pork to share with us as well. Like all families in Horní Počernice, we would go and forage regularly in the forest near our home and we were adept – from an early age – at recognising edible mushrooms and berries. In any event, I didn't need much food. Mum says that I never wanted to eat when I was small, and she was always pushing me to eat more. She is a great cook and her specialities were dumplings, sausages and fried cheese. As I recall, more or less everything was fried back then.

It wasn't just food that was scarce, though. Throughout my whole childhood, I just had a single small box of toys. However, we really appreciated what we had. I didn't ever have a proper doll. Actually, I convinced myself at some point that the whole idea of dolls was boring, although looking back at my childhood I can now see that this attitude was just my defence mechanism. If I'm honest, I really wanted a Barbie doll because a friend had one from somewhere, perhaps it had been brought for her from Germany. You certainly couldn't buy one in Czechoslovakia.

I used to invent my own toys. One particular favourite was to create an imaginary friend out of an umbrella. I would make a head and put it on top of the handle and pretend it was a dancing partner. I could play for hours with something like that. Another favourite game of mine was to draw a face on a wooden spoon and make hair and clothing for it.

I would also play with milk. We didn't have bottles of milk back then in Prague, it would mostly come in a plastic packet. I would play with one as if it were my baby for days and days, until the packet wore out so that the rancid milk would leak! When this happened I'd pretend that my baby was peeing. I loved being inventive but we had to be in order to create our own entertainment in those days.

Since around the age of ten, I've always been fascinated by photography and my dad had this funny little camera with a very simple lens that could not zoom in and out. I was allowed to use Dad's camera occasionally to take my own pictures. I remember being very excited about that instant of the 'click' and the process of lining up exactly the right moment to capture on film. I have always loved cats since I was small and my Grandma Ludmila had this lovely long-haired cat that I would photograph, whenever I could.

I didn't have much opportunity to develop this fascination for taking photographs into a hobby, partly because of my gymnastics (and later, dance) training but also because I was very quiet and undemanding. I never asked my parents to buy me a camera for my birthday. I didn't take photographs often, and I would never show my emotions or ask for anything in particular, so, I just kept my secret passion for photography exactly that.

Of course, everyone knows that we couldn't get jeans or fashionable clothes in communist countries back in those days. My Uncle Jirka (Dad's younger brother) was a lorry driver and he was able to go to Germany and to other western European countries. So, although I never got my Barbie doll, he was able to bring me jeans and – I remember very well – a nice quality leotard for my gymnastics, and later for ballet. It was brilliant for me because all the other girls had to sew up old woollen leotards but, from time to time, I would have this wonderful – and unique – western garment.

Jirka would also bring chewing gum and I used to hide mine in a secret place in the apartment but, wherever that was, Radomír would always find it and steal the gum. He didn't care and he didn't even try to hide the fact that he had taken it. He just used to eat it and leave the empty wrappers lying around. My brother was terrible. I remember having a little box in which I would save keepsakes and all my pocket money, and I would hide it so carefully. But, one day Radomír found it and stole all my money and hid the box somewhere else. For more than a year, I thought that I had just misplaced it; hidden it somewhere so well that I couldn't even find it myself. But, then one day I found it jammed behind a cupboard, empty, and I knew that Radomír had done it. There were so many similar incidents while I was living at my parents' home, sharing a bedroom with my naughty, moody brother.

I never wanted to be a ballet dancer. This is a very big difference between me and all of my contemporaries as prima ballerinas. They tell me that they had always wanted to dance. Perhaps they were taken to a ballet when they were young and the magic grew from there. Maybe it was the music or the image of a beautiful ballerina in a book.

No one in my family had ever seen a ballet and, even though my maternal great uncle was a famous stage and screen actor, no one else on either side of my family had any interest in the theatre. So, it is very much the case that I became a ballet dancer by accident rather than by design.

Chapter 3

Conservatoire
and Competition

*M*y first taste of ballet was the hourly lesson once a week as part of our gymnastics training at Sparta Prague. We didn't do any centre work, which may have seemed more appropriate as training for the floor exercise, but we did standard ballet exercises at the *barre*. I remember learning my ballet positions at the Gymnastic School and I guess that you could say that Sparta Prague – the home of the famous football club – first made a ballerina out of me.

The coaches at the national gymnastics team said that I shouldn't do ballet any more seriously than this one hour per week because it would damage me for gymnastics, where in any event careers usually ended by the early 20s. Čáslavská had won her medals in Mexico at the age of 26, but she was very much the exception and some of her teammates at that Olympic Games had finished competing before the end of their teens.

At the age of nine or ten, I was already in a very highly pressurised environment, and at the time I was being selected for the

Czechoslovakian squad to prepare for the Olympic Games. One of the ballet teachers at Sparta Prague – a gentle, elderly former dancer named Mrs Cézarová – suddenly threw in the prospect of switching my career to ballet. Looked at with the benefit of hindsight, it was an intuitive suggestion since – in retaliation for the US boycott of the Moscow Olympic Games in 1980 – the Czechoslovakian Olympic team refused to participate in the Games of 1984, which were held in Los Angeles. Although, I don't think that I was aware of it at the time, I would have been just too young to compete in the LA Games, but at 17, I would have been perfectly placed for the Seoul Olympics of 1988. Unfortunately, however, no Czech women were able to qualify to compete in those Games. The heyday of Czech gymnastics had gone and so too, thanks to the foresight of Mrs Cézarová, had little Daria.

It wasn't planned and I hadn't thought about it, but my mother never really had much ambition for me to be a gymnast and we knew that once you were heading past 20, this career was over. Mrs Cézarová convinced Mum that I had the talent to be a ballet dancer and this was a profession that would last for much longer. I didn't know it at the time, but this was the woman more than any other who set me on the course towards my life in dance.

I remember them asking me, 'Do you want to do ballet?' and I thought, *'Well, what is this ballet?'* At that time, all I knew were the relatively static exercises at the *barre* and that these were helpful to my gymnastic training. I knew nothing about the repertoire of ballet and certainly nothing of its history. So, I asked Mrs Cézarová, 'Can I swish my legs up high in ballet, like I do in the gym?' and when she said 'yes', I thought, *'Well, OK – I don't mind trying something new.'* It seems hard to imagine now, but I really wasn't that bothered. As long as I could kick my legs up high then ballet was as good as gymnastics as far as I was concerned!

At this point I had never seen a ballet performance, not even on television. My mum made up her mind that ballet would be better for my future, and I was a quiet girl who did as she was told, so I went along with her decision. Looking back at my childhood, I always did everything that I was told and this was just another example of little obedient Daria. In any event, I was only ten, so what else did I know? I wasn't at all sure whether I wanted to do ballet, but I was just a good girl who did whatever her mother said. Actually, if the truth be told, I didn't care so much; I wanted to move my body, and when they said that ballet would give me the same feeling as gymnastics, I was very happy to switch.

We found out about the auditions for the Prague State Conservatoire of Music and Dance (which incorporated the ballet school for the National Theatre) but I was already too late to apply. The main auditions had been held six months earlier and the year had already started. Almost all of the children going to the Conservatoire had come from the preparatory ballet school based at the National Theatre itself, but I had missed this initial training. However, because of my gymnastics background and Mrs Cézarová's recommendation, they held an extra audition for me. At that time the only other ballet school in Czechoslovakia was in Bratislava, now the capital of Slovakia. There were no private schools under communism, as there are now, so the Conservatoire was the only option for anyone who aspired to a career in ballet.

I attended the audition wearing a swimming costume as an emergency because I had no ballet leotard and they would not accept my gymnastics leotard (since it had sleeves). I had received no coaching about how to stand or how to behave during the assessments. I remember that the adults were looking at me, lifting my legs up high, prodding and measuring me. The hyper-flexibility they were seeking was obviously very easy for me because of all my elite gymnastics' training. I had no difficulty in doing anything that they asked of me, so I was accepted, but I had to have a medical certificate before they could formally offer me a place.

The first doctor my mother approached refused to give the certificate because he said that I had scoliosis, which is a common condition where the spine is twisted from side to side. It makes life difficult for a dancer and this particular doctor felt that my back would always be in pain; he believed that I wouldn't be able to sustain dancing for long enough to merit a place at the Conservatoire. To make matters worse, he also said that my feet were turned in and my arch was not strong enough for me to become a professional ballet dancer, even if I made it through the school.

For many young girls in my position, I suspect that this diagnosis would have been the end of any dreams of becoming a ballerina. However, thankfully, Mum was more determined than this and she took me to another doctor for a second opinion. He carried out all the proper tests and said that I was in absolutely perfect condition for ballet! So, he gave the medical recommendation I needed to get into the Conservatoire. If Mum had listened to that first doctor I never would have become a ballet dancer and still dancing 30 years later! As it happened, the original doctor was right about the scoliosis, which I have had to live with as a dancer for my whole career, but he was certainly wrong on every other count. In fact, as the years have gone by, this is not the first time that I have had an initial medical diagnosis that has turned out to be spectacularly wrong.

I started at the Prague State Conservatoire in the week following the auditions. I had no time to prepare and when I joined the first year my classmates had already been together for several weeks. It was 1981 and at just a little over ten years old, I had already changed my career.

My first day was awful because Dad didn't know how to find the ballet school. I travelled by car with my parents and we were very late for the first class, which happened to be in mathematics. Although I was absolutely petrified about arriving late, the mathematics teacher turned out to be a lovely guy. To this day, I remember Mr Horvorka clearly: a small, balding man, who was always smiling. He said, 'Come in and sit down, don't be worried.' I took my place but straightaway he said to the rest of the class, 'OK, well let's try the new girl out.' He asked me to stand up again and answer some questions, as an assessment of what I already knew. As already confessed, I was a very timid girl at this age: I didn't know the teacher or any of my classmates, and here I was under their scrutiny, being asked maths questions – never my strongest suit! But Mr Horvorka seemed to be happy with my answers. In fact, throughout my whole time in his class, he was always happy with my answers, whether or not they were right!

To tell the truth, I was hopeless at mathematics and Mr Horvorka didn't help! He spent much of the lesson telling us stories about the war instead of teaching us maths. Unfortunately, some parents complained that their children were not learning enough and the authorities eventually threw him out of the school. Poor Mr Horvorka! My mum was also unhappy about the standard of my academic education and there was a time when she wanted to take me out of the ballet school because she said that I needed to receive proper teaching, especially since my arithmetic was so bad. But it was this particular teacher who said to her, 'No, please don't do this. Believe me, she is such a talented dancer that she will never need to be good at mathematics!' So, it was thanks to Mr Horvorka that Mum kept me at the ballet school and I became a ballet dancer. He was a lovely guy but it is true that he wasn't teaching us, and I have remained hopeless at mathematics until this day. But he was right; I'm a ballet dancer and all I need to do is to be able to count my beats to eight! He gave Mum good advice because I was there to study ballet and not mathematics. After all, we have calculators nowadays!

My daily travel to ballet school was just as bad as it had been to

Sparta Prague, taking at least 90 minutes in each direction across the city. Dad continued to take me every day by car and, if for some reason, he wasn't available then Grandma Ludmila or Mum would take over. Since they didn't drive, we would have to go by bus and two changes by tram. Today, there is a metro line going out east from the city centre that ends close to Horní Počernice, and it is only a 40-minute journey at most, but back then there was nothing like that. I didn't have the option of living-in at ballet school, which was only available to students who came from outside of Prague, and, since Horní Počernice was a district of the city, I had to travel in every day and it remained a big ongoing commitment for my family.

My dad's trade was as a locksmith and metalworker, and for most of my childhood, he worked in a factory. Dad was a hard-working family man, who was very determined to make enough money for us to have all that we needed (and, although he would never admit to it, especially for me to become the best dancer I could possibly be). To achieve this, he often worked in bars to earn extra money in the evenings (such as on the night when Radomír flooded the apartment).

Unfortunately, however, this stressful lifestyle and the easy access to alcohol meant that he had already started to drink heavily when I was a child. I believe that he came under very bad influences with some of the people he was working with – in the bars – at the time. I have vivid recollections of him coming home late at night, extremely drunk and, unfortunately, Dad – normally the most placid and lovely of men – would often get aggressive when drunk. He would never, ever, get angry with me but he would take his aggression out on both my mum and my brother. Mum was bossy and argumentative, and she would complain about his drunkenness and, of course, he didn't like it. So they would fight, although thankfully it was mostly a shouting contest rather than one that descended into any physical violence.

Dad never became an alcoholic, since he could tolerate very long periods of not drinking at all, and it was, of course, very common for men in any Eastern European country to drink to excess. My brother was regularly in trouble as a young man and my father found this hard to cope with. I remember one night when Radomír was about 15, Dad came home and their quarrel escalated into him attacking my brother very violently. Everyone was shocked. After that, I remember sadly that there were a lot more fights, but it never really affected me directly because I always did as I was told. Like many families with such problems, we just didn't talk about these things. They went unspoken and it is still too painful to talk about them, even now, after the passage of 30 years. My mother was far too proud to ever talk to us about this darker side of our life at home.

My parents were always against communism but, of course, they could never voice those opinions openly as I was growing up. They did occasionally talk about their concerns at home, complaining about how things were, but they had to be careful about who they confided in outside of the family. I didn't understand politics as a child, but I remember them being very angry about 'the system'. Unfortunately, I now believe very firmly that, in any free market society, my father would have turned his resourcefulness into being a successful entrepreneur, and I'm sure that he would have made a lot of money. I'm curious about that, and I think that my own desire and ambition to do many things stems from Dad's enquiring and open attitude.

When I was 15, not long after Dad's terrible fight with Radomír, he got the opportunity to go and work for four years in Libya, which was tough but it was good money for us. I didn't see him at all over that time since he couldn't come back home. Mum and Dad had been fighting a lot, so when this opportunity came for him to go and work in Libya, not only was it a financial godsend, but it also helped to fix their marriage, even though they had to be separated for this to happen. Not seeing each other meant that they stopped fighting and stepped back from what I suspect would have been an inevitable divorce, had they remained together in Horní Počernice. When Dad came back from Libya he was better; he had stopped drinking and was lovely all the time without the influence of that pernicious alcohol. Mum always said that the years she had with Dad after he came back from Libya were the very best time of their marriage.

Like so many men in Eastern Europe, my father smoked excessively and both my mum and brother also smoked, although Mum has long ago given up. So, I grew up in a household full of smoke and yet I have never once tried a cigarette, not even so much as a drag. I can't understand why anyone smokes but then I have a personality that is quite opposed to addiction. In fact, I don't think that I'm addicted to anything. I was always training and focused on one thing from the age of five, starting with gymnastics and then moving onto ballet, so I didn't ever get into the business of hanging out with friends after school, 'behind the bike sheds', doing the things that other young people did to while away the time.

Because I started at ballet school three weeks after everyone else, I didn't make friends quickly. The others had already paired off before I arrived. Also, I was so different – I wore ponytails and still had my fringe from gymnastics. I didn't know about buns. I remember on day one of school – after the embarrassment of being late to the maths lesson – at my very first ballet class, the other girls came over and pulled my hair, laughing at the new arrival who clearly knew nothing. Also, I suffered because I didn't have the uniform leotard as everyone else did in those first few weeks. Instead, I wore a multi-coloured Sparta Prague gymnastic leotard with long sleeves, so I really couldn't have done any more to stand out and look different from all the other students. The teachers were immediately onto me to get the regulation clothing and have my hair cut in the correct style. I hated this new enforced look because I had never seen myself without a fringe and I thought I looked so stupid!

At the Conservatoire we had two marks in every assessment: one for technique to measure how good we were at classical ballet; and the other for application, to denote how hard we tried. From the beginning, I always got excellent marks for technique but was never nearly as good in the application assessment. I was always slow, the teachers put me in the corner of the studio, and I would just stand there waiting my turn. I would never just go and practise on my own. I thought that I just needed to do as I was told and nothing more. Looking back, I suppose that I was seen as being a bit lazy and so I was marked down for that in my early assessments. To be honest, I didn't know then that I had to work hard. I have had to learn this over the years. I certainly don't think I was deliberately lazy; it was just that I was so obedient that I did only what I was told. My contemporaries would be put in the queue waiting to demonstrate a passage of steps and – like ballet students, the world over – they would be practising or marking the steps in their heads. But, if I was in the queue, then I just waited my turn!

However, because of my gymnastics training, I very quickly rose to the top of the class. In fact, throughout my whole ballet school career, I remained the best in class from some early point in that first year. At the time, I didn't think about this; in fact, I never knew anything other than this. You don't really see it when you are so young. But, looking back, I can now understand that I was being groomed to be a principal dancer from a very early stage. Even though I never did anything extra, even though I only did what I was asked to do, I still had the best technical marks at every assessment.

I was a pupil at the Conservatoire for some months before our teachers took us to the National Theatre to watch a performance. I often read in accounts of the lives of the great ballerinas that they can recall exactly what ballet they first saw and how this inspired them – I don't recall what the first ballet was that I saw, although I do know that it would have been very Russian in its style. I certainly didn't go, 'Wow, this is amazing!' with any of the early ballets that I saw as a student. I liked the music and the costumes, but I wasn't bowled over by ballet itself. I didn't really think about what the dancers were doing or why; I was much more impressed by the tutus, the glitter and the lights, and the way in which the ballerinas moved to beautiful music. I suppose that I was captivated by the magic of the show rather than by the dancing itself, which I saw as only an incidental part of that appeal. It was the prettiness of the spectacle that attracted me as a young girl.

In fact, looking back, if I'm really honest, I didn't like what I was doing at ballet school for the first couple of years. It seemed so boring, especially compared to gymnastics. But, as the studious and obedient girl that I was, I carried on doing what I had been told, so there was never any question of quitting and going back to Sparta Prague; or even of going on to learn something new about mathematics!

I remember the first time that I tried on pointe shoes, when I was still just ten, early in that first year. These are the shoes with a block at the front that has been stiffened by glue to enable a ballerina to dance on the tips of her toes. In Eastern Europe girls start very early learning to dance in this way (it is called dancing *en pointe*). We were given horrible Czech pointe shoes and I had bleeding toes after that first session, with blood soaking through the shoes and my tights. It was so very painful, and the blood and the agony lasted throughout the whole year. Nowadays, I would find it impossible to stand on those shoes, but back then it was all we had and the blisters and bleeding were just one of many things we all had to accept without complaint.

The origins of ballet education in Prague dated back to 1835 when a school was established within the city's Estates Theatre. It transferred to the Provisional Theatre in 1862 before the Czech National Ballet Preparatory School was formally established by M. Hetzová, six years later. When the National Theatre was opened in 1883, the prep school moved into the theatre, where it existed sporadically up until the early 1950s, often managed by the various artistic directors of the ballet company.

The Prague Conservatoire was founded in 1808 to provide education to orchestral musicians and ranks amongst the oldest of such music schools in Europe. The great composer, Antonín Dvořák, was the headmaster from 1901 to 1904 and the operetta composer, Franz Lehár, was amongst his students at that time. The dancing department of the Conservatoire did not come into being until after the Second World War and it had become an independent conservatoire of dance (in 1980) by the time I had joined.

Ballet training at the Conservatoire followed the Vaganova system, named after the famous Russian pedagogue, Agrippina Vaganova (1879–1951), a former ballerina in the last years of the Imperial Ballet of the Mariinsky Theatre in St Petersburg, who became the most famous teacher at the Petrograd State Choreographic School in Soviet Russia after the Bolshevik Revolution. Her teaching system became the staple for ballet education across the entire Eastern Bloc and also migrated to some parts of the West.

One important aspect of Vaganova training is to retain the same ballet teacher throughout a student's pupillage. Formal full-time ballet training at the Conservatoire doesn't begin until the age of ten and it cannot end earlier than 18. Throughout all eight years of my training, I had the same main teacher, Professor Olga Pásková. The Vaganova method, which progressively develops virtuosity, is a very formal codified arrangement that evolves over the full eight years. I think that this is a very good system because you follow the same direction and learn in the same style. It is much more difficult to switch teachers from year to year, as they often do in the UK, for example. Changing teachers – in any technique – must inevitably mean that the new teacher would want you to do something differently and that tends to be confusing. So, I believe passionately that it is essential to have just one principal teacher through these formative years.

Of course, I did have other specialist teachers for the *pas de deux* classes and for repertoire, and these were a husband and wife team, who were also still soloists in the company: Kateřina Slavická and Jaroslav Slavický (who is now the director of the ballet school). We also had regular guest teachers come from the Vaganova School in Leningrad (now St Petersburg), and I particularly liked the classes given by Boris Bregvadze, a former principal dancer with the famous Kirov Ballet, whose forte was the meaty heroic roles in the soviet repertoire of Vakhtang Chabukiani and Leonid Jacobson. Bregvadze sadly passed away in March 2012, just after his 86th birthday.

Olga Pásková became like a second mother to me. She was in her 60s when I started at the Conservatoire and to us she was already a very old lady. But she was very kind and lovely. We made fun of her a lot because she was so very scatty. She would come to take class with one eye in blue make-up but the other, which may have been black, was already smudged off; or, she might arrive in a dress, for example, that wasn't properly zipped up and so we would make fun about which one of us would have to tell her that day. Quite often, she would fall asleep during class and we would have to carry on regardless. To make matters worse, we had a pianist who was always picking his nose! In those days, the dance studios still had wooden floors, and we had to sprinkle water regularly to prevent us from slipping. Nothing much changed in the ballet school in all the years that I was there.

Professor Pásková could lay claim to teaching a king. In fact, she had something in common with *Anna and the King of Siam* (the story that is the basis for *The King and I*) since the nine-year-old Cambodian prince, Norodom Sihamoni, was sent to train at the Prague conservatoire in 1962. I believe that his mother was interested in establishing a Royal Ballet in Cambodia. Prince Norodom stayed in Prague for 13 years and Olga Pásková was his teacher throughout his time at the Conservatoire. Returning to Prague in March 2010, King Norodom Sihamoni (succeeding on the abdication of his father, King Norodom Sihanouk, in 2004), received an Honorary Doctorate from the Director of the Conservatoire, and at the ceremony for this award he thanked all of his former teachers, especially the late Olga Pásková. Professor Pásková deserves all my heartfelt thanks, too. I recall very proudly that she came to see me dance the lead role in Glen Tetley's *Sphinx* when I was guesting in Prague not long before she died. I loved her, and it was her teaching that gave me the strong basis for a career that has already exceeded 1,000 performances.

One of her clever tricks was that if we were injured and couldn't take class then we had to sit at the side and write out the correct names of all the exercises, in French, which has always been the first language of ballet. At the end of the class these would be handed in and marked. It was a brilliant strategy because it forced us to learn all the correct ballet terminology from a very early age.

As I have said, I didn't enjoy the first two years of ballet school because we concentrated on lots of small exercises without apparent meaning (although now, of course, I know that it all meant a great deal). After my training as a gymnast, doing exciting things like multiple *flick-flack*s, it was very boring doing countless repetitions of *battement tendus*. However, from the third year, we started to learn extracts from the classical repertoire with an emphasis on specific variations, and I began to love dancing much more because of that. Slowly, I became more ambitious and Professor Pásková and her colleagues decided that I was talented enough to be on a trajectory that would lead to soloist and principal roles with the Czech National Ballet, even from that early age. I think that I have always been lucky in my life in some ways; things have been put there in front of me and I have always just gone and done as I have been asked. Learning to be a gymnast or a ballet dancer was never a competitive slippery pole for me. They were just things that I could do, even without particularly applying myself as others had to do. I may have been lucky in my life in this regard, but I suppose it is also true that I have been unlucky with other things.

I have always worked hard but I have never really known what I want. If I was told to do something ten times then I would do it exactly ten times. If I was asked to do two *pirouettes* then I would never dream of doing more than two. It was only later in my life that I realised that the secret to ambition is always to do more than you have been asked to do. The best students today will be trying to do four *pirouettes* – or as many as they can – even if they have only been asked to do two. For me, I would always have been happy just to do two clean *pirouettes*. But, then again, Professor Pásková would always tell me that it is better to do two clean *pirouettes* than a messy three! But now, today's generation of young dancers would far rather lift their legs higher and go for the outrageous extra turn or greater height. I think that's crazy and I wonder how far it will go. *How far can it go?* I'm really not sure that it is for the good of ballet.

I danced in the school shows every year from the age of 12, starting with very small roles and graduating into more significant pieces as the years went by. By the time I graduated, I was already dancing important roles like the *pas de trois* from *Swan Lake* (an important dance for three villagers in Act I). After eight years at the Conservatoire, I graduated with highest honours by giving a performance as the Princess Aurora in *The Sleeping Beauty* at the National Theatre in Prague.

Even though I was always being cast in the more prominent roles for these shows, I still didn't have the confidence to think that I was one of the best dancers in the year. Despite the difficult beginning during my first term after starting so late, I became very close to my classmates – especially Andrea Grofová, who has remained my very best friend since our time together at the Conservatoire – and I was always happy to treat my friends as equals. It was difficult for me to imagine that I was better than them; I certainly didn't want any of them to be jealous of me, and it would have been against my nature to act as if I thought I was a better dancer at that time. I really didn't think about it. I was enjoying my dancing and, of course, I wanted to be a principal dancer, but I never saw ballet school in terms of a competition with my classmates.

Throughout my eight years at the Conservatoire, the fact that I lived at home and came from a family that is not at all balletic meant that I was able to escape from the ballet environment when I went home in the evenings and at weekends. At home we never talked about ballet and I'm very happy for that. I grew up with these two sides to my life. The intense focus on ballet all day, every day, at the national school – although it was a conservatoire that catered for music students as well as ballet – and then a very ordinary young girl's teenage years at home.

It's hard to say that it has ever been exactly normal, but all my life I have been searching for that ordinariness away from ballet. I am very comfortable – and always have been – going home and not talking about ballet. I am glad that I didn't live in halls of residence at the Conservatoire, and I am also glad that I was not one of those many dancers with past generations of relations who were all ballet dancers.

As far as boyfriends were concerned, the boys in our ballet class were off limits. It was much cooler to hang around with the musicians on the other side of the Conservatoire. I never had a relationship with a classmate at school. It was unthinkable. But, in fact, the first boy that I spent time with was not from the Conservatoire at all, although ironically, he was a dancer.

Every Friday, the whole ballet class – all 16 of us – would meet to go dancing! Can you believe it? We danced all week and then on the first night of the weekend, we went dancing for fun! We would go to a club to learn ballroom and Latin dancing. Soon we reached a great standard and were very professional. We even entered competitions.

Stanislav was one of the dancers at the club, which is how we met. I was 16 and he was two years older and already working as a plumber. We became serious enough for Stanislav to meet my parents, but I was busy training at the Conservatoire through the week so we didn't see each other much, although we remained friends for two years before drifting apart

A month or so later, I found myself with another dancer but this time from the world of modern – or contemporary – dance. I knew him through the school because Andrea and I would go to summer courses in modern dance during our holidays. So not only was I training as a ballerina during the week, doing ballroom and Latin at weekends, but I was also spending my holidays doing summer courses. I danced all the time. But these courses taught me about dance beyond ballet. I learned how to tap dance and do flamenco – I really loved dancing while playing the castanets! This new boy was on one such course, which is how we met. He was a couple of years older than me – good-looking, clever, but also very full of himself. I was still very quiet and you know what they say about opposites attracting. But he had a huge ego to go with his good looks, and very quickly I began to feel uncomfortable around him, so this was a relationship destined not to last for long.

I did a lot of competitions during my later years at the Conservatoire. At 16, I was the silver medallist in the Czech National Ballet competition in Brno (dancing in the same theatre where my great uncle, Josef Skřivan, had been director). But I was beaten by a girl from Slovakia; I was very upset about this and, although I didn't show it openly, I was ambitious inside and I hated the fact that I had been beaten into second place by someone from Slovakia. The competition was held every two years and I was determined to win it when it came around again. But, in the event, it was at the same time as I was rehearsing for the Varna competition and I was working so hard for both events and was so tired that I twisted my ankle in preparing for the National Championships. As a result, I couldn't go to the competition, so the girl from Bratislava won again.

In 1988, aged 17, I was entered for Varna (a major ballet competition held in Bulgaria since 1964). The event is held outside in a beautiful open-air theatre, set in a luscious park of several acres that runs down to the sea. It is a major event and the great prima ballerina of the Soviet Union, Galina Ulanova, was chairman of the international jury for many years. Vladimir Vasiliev – one of the greatest virtuoso male dancers of all time – became the first, and only, winner of the Grand Prix award in the inaugural competition of 1964.

The Varna competition has been held every two years and Czechoslovakian dancers had some considerable success in the early events. Marta Drotnerová won the second prize and a silver medal in the inaugural year of Vasiliev's triumph, following up with a gold medal in 1966. She had been trained by E. Gabzdila in Ostrava (a large Czech city, close to the Polish border) and became a leading soloist at the Czech National Ballet, making guest appearances at the Bolshoi Ballet in Moscow. Then came Hana Vláčilová, a pupil of the great Russian ballerina, Natalia Dudinskaya, who won first class distinction in the junior competition of 1972 before going on to win a silver medal in the senior event, four years later. Hana was a beautiful woman, who became a leading ballerina with the Czech National Ballet during the years that I was training at the Conservatoire, and she was a major idol to this aspiring young dancer. The final Czechoslovakian success was by a boy, Lubomir Kafka, who won the Varna gold medal in 1978 and went on to dance with the national company. Dancers from the Soviet Union had routinely dominated the competition but the fact that Czechoslovakia had won two gold medals in the first 14 years had meant a great deal to the development of ballet in my country.

Despite Czechoslovakia enjoying such success in these early years, it had been a barren time at Varna for the nation's ballet dancers in the decade before my appearance. I remember that I was there for three weeks and I had to practise at night-time. One stage rehearsal was at 3am. I went to bed at 11pm and then they would wake me up, and I would go and do a rehearsal in the middle of the night, outside! In those days we were young, we didn't mind and, more importantly, we didn't need to warm up so much. Especially compared to what I need to do now!

Although I got into the finals at Varna, my performance there was not without incident. My first problem was one of expectation! I was dancing with Jan Podařil (whom everyone knew by the nickname 'Honza') from the Prague Conservatoire who wasn't competing but he was there to partner me. In the first two rounds I did a different *pas de deux* with Honza, but I was supposed to do two variations on my own without a partner in the third round, but since the school authorities hadn't considered that there was any chance of me getting further than the second round, we never practised any of the variations! So, when I got through, which nobody had expected, I didn't have anything ready to perform. I had to rush around and quickly prepare two variations to dance in the final.

The second problem was self-inflicted by my own gluttony! Water melons were plentiful and cheap in Bulgaria, and I loved them. I could eat a whole water melon in one go! Unfortunately, I ate one just before my competition final and it gave me a serious bout of diarrhoea. I was already in the costume and they were calling my name ready to go on for my performance, and I had to rush to the toilet. So, there I was, thinking that after three weeks in a strange country and being the first Czech person to get to the final for ten years, I had missed my chance to compete because of my greed for a water melon.

Luckily, the judges took pity on my plight and moved me a few places back so that I had time to get myself together. Despite the diarrhoea and the lack of preparation for the final, I managed to win a major prize and received some scholarship offers to attend summer schools. I remember that I could choose between four different schools in America but my mum was too scared to let me go to the USA at that time (in the late 1980s), so she compromised and allowed me to attend a summer school in Germany.

At 18, I was selected for the Prix de Lausanne – perhaps the most prestigious of all classical ballet competitions, sponsored by the Swiss city of Lausanne every year since 1973 – but the school authorities in Prague wouldn't pay for the airline tickets for me to be able to go. It was hard to be selected from a communist country for these competitions. They wouldn't let just anyone go and it seemed as if a golden opportunity to travel outside of Czechoslovakia would pass me by, but at the last minute my mum was able to borrow the money from a rich Czech émigré, with help from the Conservatoire, to enable both myself and my teacher to go.

The first two rounds of the competition were in Lausanne itself, and I remember having to do a modern variation to jazz, and these contemporary movements were alien to me, so I really struggled with it. I thought there was no way that I was ever going to get it. Somehow I qualified for the finals, which were held in Osaka in Japan. This was only the second time that the final rounds had been moved away from Lausanne (the first being in New York City, four years earlier in 1985).

On the plane to Tokyo, it was the first time in my life that I had ever eaten prawns. Unfortunately, they weren't the best prawns in the world and I got very ill with food poisoning. It was the watermelon all over again! So my first experience of this exciting trip to Japan was being ill and in bed, unable to practise. It was a nightmare. I still managed to compete but I twisted my ankle in the variation and it is amazing that, thanks to YouTube, even now young students come up to me and say that they saw this film of me dancing more than 20 years ago when I fell over! I still managed to finish and win a prize (the Paris Dance Foundation Award), which meant that I got enough money to pay my mum back. With the remaining prize money, I also bought my first video machine.

One of the biggest impacts of leaving the communist bloc to attend these events in Switzerland and Japan was that I got to see how people lived in the West, and it made me realise how much we were controlled by communism. I could now see with my own eyes that the freedom for people in the West was a much better way of life.

One of the nicest things is that all my class were very supportive of me during these competitions, even though it meant there was so much extra attention on me from the faculty of teachers at the Conservatoire. When I came back from wherever I had been around the world, there would be 'welcome back' signs around the changing rooms, with balloons strewn everywhere. It was lovely and, needless to say, many of us are still friends more than 20 years later. The whole world over, down the generations, bonds made at ballet school are rarely broken.

Chapter 4

Under the Golden Roof and Into the Velvet Revolution

I hadn't appreciated that I was on a fast-track to being a soloist (the title of principal dancers at the National Theatre of Prague) from a very early age at ballet school until after I had left the Czech Republic, and I was already dancing principal roles. It just never dawned on me before. At the Conservatoire, I thought it was normal to be trained in this way. I didn't really feel any different to the others, although looking back it was obvious that I was being groomed for solo roles.

All my life I have been modest in my expectations, although this has not stopped me from being very ambitious underneath this external cloak of diffidence. I didn't understand that the reason why I was never given *corps de ballet* work, always solos to learn even from quite a young age, meant that my teachers were preparing me for a solo career. It never occurred to me to ask why I wasn't learning the steps for the last row of the girls in the *corps de ballet*. Perhaps I would have worked harder, had I been doing that. I had always been singled out and so it just seemed that this was how it should be. Believe it or not, the teachers never talked to us about the future; they never looked beyond the school. My dream was to dance in the National Theatre in Prague and, looking back, I realise that becoming a soloist was preordained from an early age, but back then I just didn't know it.

We all had to audition to get into the company during my last year (1989) and I had no idea at the time if I was going to be successful. I don't remember feeling any pressure in those days. I didn't have anything to lose and, over the years, I have come to realise that the more you have, the greater the pressure that creates.

I remember that the audition consisted of ballet class and one variation but I don't remember what I did. As always, I thought that I had done very badly. Despite the competition successes and the fast-tracking, I still never really thought that I was any good in those days, and I always believed the worst about everything. Actually, I *still* think the worst, even now! I certainly wasn't ever aware that they wanted me in the company but I got in.

I don't remember how I was told – I think that they must have posted a list on the noticeboard – but I actually got a *corps de ballet* contract at first, even though I had never done any *corps de ballet* work in the Conservatoire. My final year was a small class: we were 11 girls and five boys but only a handful of us got into the company, including my best friend, Andrea, and two of the boys. Even though my first contract was for the *corps de ballet*, I was to have only the most limited experience at that level.

The ballet company of the National Theatre in Prague, which for ease of reference I shall refer to as the Czech National Ballet, was created in 1883 under the first ballet master, Václav Reisinger. In the early decades the company was dominated by the Italian school of ballet but from the 1920s onwards the Russian school prevailed. The company had always performed the classical ballets (*Giselle*, *Swan*

Lake, Sylvia and *Coppélia*) but the repertoire was updated under the directorship of the Polish dancer and choreographer, Remislav Remislavsky (1923–27) to incorporate some of the major works from the Diaghilev repertoire, such as *Shéhérazade* and *Petrushka*. In the post-war era, the leadership of Saša Machov (1946–51) did much to disentangle the ballet company from the more dominant opera. This period also witnessed the development of indigenous Czech ballets, such as *Vostřák's Filosofská historie* (*The Philosopher's History*/1949) and *Viktorka* (1950).

Through the 1960s, the repertoire was dominated by the Soviet model of big drama ballets and the modern, shorter works encouraged by the long-serving director, Jiří Němeček, whose leadership encompassed two distinct periods (1957–70 and 1979–89).

I started my first season with the National Company, in the last months of Němeček's 23 years as director, being cast in solo roles. My first role as a professional dancer was as one of the girls dancing the mazurka in *Les Sylphides*, a very famous one-act plot-less ballet with choreography by Mikhail Fokine and music by Chopin. The original version had been premiered at the Mariinsky Theatre in St Petersburg in 1907, with Anna Pavlova in the cast.

I was never prepared to do anything like the fourth girl along in the *corps de ballet*, but after a few months with the company there was a flu epidemic and in the morning I was asked to dance in the *corps de ballet* for that evening. So I had to learn the steps during the day for Act II of *La Sylphide* (a two-act Romantic ballet set in Scotland, which is not to be confused with *Les Sylphides*) – and to this day, it is still the most stressful thing that I have ever done!

I had to do two shows and it was a complete disaster having to try and fit in with everyone else. Looking back, I really wouldn't have liked to see that show with the one girl always out of time! The girl behind me would be telling me on which leg to stand and the other girls would all be whispering to me, 'Go there, come here! Now go back!' Without a doubt, nothing has subsequently exceeded this as being the single most traumatising experience of my professional life as a dancer.

On another occasion, I danced *Macbeth*, a neoclassical ballet by Daniel Wiesner in the middle of which they needed eight girls dressed as birds to form a circle. I did quite a few of those performances, actually! But there I could do whatever I wanted – we ran on stage and did a circle for so many counts and then some *pas de chats* but it didn't all need to be in precise harmony – I didn't have to be exactly in time with the girls next to me, and so it wasn't so bad.

My worst nightmare as a ballet dancer would be to dance in the *corps de ballet* of swans in Act IV of *Swan Lake*. I have some similar experiences, such as doing the three Bayadères (or temple dancers) in Act III of *La Bayadère* (a famous ballet by Marius Petipa, set in ancient India to a score by Leon Minkus, which premiered in St Petersburg in 1877), or dancing as the Lilac Fairy in *The Sleeping Beauty* and keeping in time with the six other fairies. It was stressful enough, just staying in harmony with a few other girls. I didn't need to be in the *corps de ballet* to be traumatised by my difficulties of keeping in step with other dancers.

Even dancing the lead Muse, Terpsichore, in *Apollo* (a one-act ballet by George Balanchine made to Stravinsky's score for Diaghilev's Ballets Russes in 1928), I find to be very difficult. It is a nightmare for me to be in the middle of the two other Muses (Polyhymnia and Caliope), doing the same stuff. It is so much more stressful than being on my own, dancing the main role in front of royalty or an audience of thousands.

I had no training for the *corps de ballet* and I have no doubt that it is much harder to be a girl in the *corps de ballet* than to be a principal. And they work so hard. We work very hard rehearsing for principal roles, of course, but it is done in a few hours, here and there. The *corps de ballet* girls are working all day and they stand around for hours, just waiting. If one girl makes a mistake, they all have to repeat it again just because of that one girl. To the audience, if one girl in the *corps de ballet* makes a mistake it is so obvious, but if a soloist makes a mistake, perhaps being just off the music, it is rarely noticeable to anyone but a professional with the most discerning eye. If you want to lift your leg higher as a soloist, you can but in the *corps de ballet*, you cannot look any different from the others.

Although the principal dancer's contract didn't come straight away, the offer arrived after just six months with the company. The key factor was that, after these first few months, the director changed to a younger man – Vlastimil Harapes, who was still a leading dancer in his 40s – and he gave me a soloist's contract as soon as he took over. In most European companies there will be several levels in the hierarchy of dancers' seniority (for example, at English National Ballet there are six levels, from artists up to senior principals), but in the Czech National Ballet there was just the *corps de ballet* and soloists, so a soloist's contract was the highest level.

Harapes wanted to shake up the company and change things, so it was a big deal for him to promote an 18-year-old girl to soloist. In the past, even the best dancers stayed in the *corps de ballet* for a few years before being offered a soloist's contract and, although I knew that I had been groomed on a special programme for leading roles, I also imagined that part of the plan was for me to earn my promotion over time. However, Harapes didn't believe in this old-fashioned hierarchy; he felt that if I was talented enough to already be doing opening nights, then I should have the status to go with it, irrespective of my age. People in the company were shocked and I experienced some envy from older dancers, although a lot of this passed over my head because I was so taken up with my new status.

In 1989/90 – my first year in the company – there were many strikes, with thousands of people demonstrating in Wenceslas Square. I went and participated several times, with all my friends from the ballet company, to support the pro-democracy movement. It was very exciting but we were so scared. There were many policemen with their shields and truncheons, and we never really knew if the situation would take off and escalate into violence but I was always careful and usually made sure that I was at the back, well away from any potential danger. Andrea and I were clever and always planned in advance the way that we could escape, if there was any trouble.

These were exciting times: we hadn't known freedom. The theatres in Prague would cancel shows but the audience would still come in and instead of the performance, there would be a discussion about how to make the country better. I loved it all, although I was very much a bystander. I wasn't an activist – I was too busy dancing. However, I'm proud to have been there, in Wenceslas Square, a part of the Velvet Revolution and to have stood up for freedom and Václav Havel, who was to become the last President of Czechoslovakia (1989–1992) and the first President of the Czech Republic (1993–2003).

Havel was a playwright and a poet, who became a dissident and a politician. Many years later, I got to know him, especially after Czech TV made two long-running documentary films about me, and the film director, Martin Kubala, introduced me to Havel. I came to know his second wife, Dagmar Havlová, very well. She had been a famous actress who has now, since her husband's death, on 18 December 2011, returned to the stage.

Looking back, of course the momentous changes to Czechoslovakia in 1989 were crucially important for my future, since without Havel and the Velvet Revolution there is little chance that I would have been able to leave the country and dance elsewhere. I could never have contemplated a dance career in the UK when I was at the Conservatoire but then, suddenly, it all became possible. Although I won't go to funerals, I watched Václav Havel's State Funeral on television here in the UK, and it was an extremely profound and moving event for all Czech people. I was incredibly humbled and emotional as I saw his cortège travel slowly across the Charles Bridge.

My opening monthly salary in the *corps de ballet* was 1,900 crowns (about £60 at that time). It was so amazing, having my own income. When I was promoted to soloist it went up by another 1,000 crowns. But I was still living at home – there was no way that I could have afforded to live anywhere else. In our first year with the company, Andrea and I planned to save some of our salaries to buy lots of plates and smash them by way of a crazy, anarchic celebration. However, as time went by (and perhaps we grew more responsible about the money we were earning), we went off the idea of smashing our money to pieces and went to Ibiza instead!

The system at the Czech National Ballet was that we gave up to 11 different shows a month, with just one or two performances of each production equalling around 16 performances per month. These would be the same shows performed in the next month and so on, in a kind of rolling programme over the season. It's not like the system in the UK and elsewhere in the West, where companies will give 20 performances of the same ballet before moving on to something else. In Eastern Europe, it didn't work like that.

Each morning we would have to rehearse the ballet we were going to be dancing in two days. It was very hard to adjust from one ballet to another and I remember that I was tired all of the time. I also had the added problem of having to go home every day on a long journey consisting of a three-hour round trip. My dad was now back from

Libya and picking me up, then driving me home again. He hardly ever missed a show while we were both in Prague. Mum would be there for every new production but Dad would be there almost every night that I performed – and he didn't particularly like ballet.

With the popular classic ballets, such as *Swan Lake*, we would probably have two performances every month through the whole of the season, but with only two casts who were able to perform the roles, and another that we would describe as 'in brackets' (i.e. they were dancers shadowing the main casts, learning the roles but not performing them). Because there were so few dancers able to dance given roles it was often the case that, say, one dancer was injured and another was ill, the show had to be cancelled. Over all the time I have been here, I have never known a show to be cancelled in the UK because there are not enough dancers capable of performing in it, but it happened in the Czech National Ballet on a regular basis.

The other aspect of this is that dancers were (and still are) treated with much greater respect in Prague – and, in fact, across the whole of Eastern Europe – than they are here in the UK. The director and ballet staff would consult with dancers about everything: what rehearsals they needed and when they were ready to take a part. And they trusted the dancers. They would take the view that if a dancer had been promoted to soloist status then that dancer would know what was best for their own role development.

In fact, very early on in my first season the two dancers who normally performed the lead role as Princess Aurora in *The Sleeping Beauty* were indisposed, and I was the dancer 'in brackets', so the director asked me if I would do the show on the next evening. Even though I already knew the steps because I had performed a shortened version of the ballet for my graduation a few months before, I didn't feel ready but no one put pressure on me to perform and so the show was cancelled and people were given refunds. There is no way that this would happen with any company in the UK. Some poor dancer would be thrust prematurely into performing a role that he or she was insufficiently prepared for. I have seen careers stunted and ended because of the effect of such bad judgement.

My refusal to dance as Aurora was not held against me and I continued to be prepared for this to be my first principal role with the company, during which time I danced the smaller (but nonetheless important) roles as Princess Florine in the final act Bluebird *pas de deux* and as one of the fairies in the prologue. After eight months of preparation, during which time I was allowed to perfect my own interpretation of the role, I finally got to debut as Aurora.

Although it was my first major ballet, I have never particularly enjoyed *The Sleeping Beauty*. I know that this will surprise so many balletomanes, but I find it boring. And, I have already decided that I will never dance the role of Aurora again. It is such a long ballet with a chunky prologue that explains the back story of Aurora's christening; the gifts she receives from the fairies and the omission of the wicked fairy, Carabosse, from the guest list, which leads to her surprise arrival at the christening party and her foretelling of Aurora growing up to be a beautiful, graceful and kind women, only to be poisoned by the prick of a spindle on her 16th birthday. Of course, the good Lilac Fairy commutes the effect of this poison from death to a permanent sleep until she is awakened by the kiss of a handsome prince.

The only problem with all of this is that the prologue can take up to 50 minutes, and the ballerina portraying Aurora is not required. After the complex, killing *balances* of the Rose Adage in Act I, Aurora is in her '100-year' sleep throughout the next part, and sits and watches sundry nursery rhyme characters dance divertissements in her wedding scene of the final act before at last she gets to perform the concluding *pas de deux*. *The Sleeping Beauty* is a long ballet to watch, but it is a relentlessly long ballet for the poor dancer playing the lead role!

For the first time in my life, I recently asked not to perform a role when *The Sleeping Beauty* returned to the ENB repertoire to begin the 2012/13 season. I thought about it seriously for six months but decided that I no longer feel that it is appropriate for a ballerina in her 40s to be playing a 16-year-old girl. I enjoy dancing roles that require a strong emotional expression and something more than entering your birthday party with a permanent smile glued onto your face. It also hurts my back a lot to dance the Aurora role, much more than as Odette/Odile in *Swan Lake*, for example. We have to say goodbye to all things in due course, and I think that my time for the Princess Aurora has now been and gone.

In any event, we have so many lovely young dancers at ENB who deserve their opportunity to dance the role of Aurora while they are still young. I really want to see the role danced by up-and-coming soloists like Ksenia Ovsyanick (who made a great impression as *The Firebird* in George Williamson's new interpretation of that ballet early in 2012) and Shiori Kase, who was voted as ENB's Emerging Dancer of 2011. I very much enjoy helping young dancers to prepare for these major roles for the first time, not in terms of formal coaching but simply by giving advice and passing on tips. Although I've given up on Princess Aurora, I still plan to carry on dancing the pivotal role of the Lilac Fairy for a while longer.

In many respects, *The Sleeping Beauty* should mean a lot to me since I spent the last year in school learning to perfect the role of Aurora and it formed the basis for my graduation performance in Prague. When I came into the company and the director changed to Vlastimil Harapes, he gave me my first big breakthrough show as Aurora, so having spent the last year of my school rehearsing this role, it then took up much of my first season as a professional dancer.

Although it may seem that the choreography by Marius Petipa is standard for Aurora, there are actually very significant differences between the Russian version that I first learned in Prague and the productions that I have danced here in the UK. I prefer the Russian version to what I have come to describe as the 'constipated' English version generally performed in the UK. In the Russian version, we do *grand jetés* as they should be done, but here they are like limp lettuce leaves by comparison. In the Russian version, the ballerina does the *balances* in the famous Rose Adage with a proper promenade with her four cavaliers and the arms are so very strong and much more important. After you have performed the 'English' version ten times you feel completely constipated – I much prefer the version I grew up with in Prague.

It was my dream from the early years at the Conservatoire to perform the fiery role of Kitri in *Don Quixote* because there was so much opportunity for jumping around and for comedy. I just loved this. And I was lucky enough to dance as Kitri in a very Russian version of *Don Quixote* in my final season at the Czech National Ballet; so unlike other ballerinas, who sometimes wait all their careers to dance the role that they have coveted the most, I got mine within three years of leaving school!

Kitri was very hard for me because you have to have strong virtuoso skills with big jumps, but performed with very correct technique. It was a big struggle for me but I loved that challenge. If I had a much longer run at performing Kitri, I'm sure that I would have been able to perfect the role but, unfortunately, I was only able to perform it five times in Prague because none of my subsequent companies have had the ballet within their repertoire. I have, of course, performed the *pas de deux* separately at galas but only as an extract of the ballet taken out of its context. Like Aurora, Kitri is certainly a role with a prescribed shelf life, suitable only for dancers up to a certain age, and I know now that I will certainly never perform it again.

There was quite a drama in my second season in Prague because I was chosen to dance the title role of Marguerite in the opening of a new ballet, *The Lady of the Camellias* (performed to music by Verdi and choreographed by Robert Balogh), which was to be filmed for Czech television. Harapes selected me for this great honour ahead of all the older principal ballerinas in the company and they certainly didn't like it. I remember one of them saying very loudly to another, deliberately so that I could overhear, 'Oh, I see that the kindergarten girl is going to do the opening night!'

There was a lot of nastiness going on but I was young and didn't really care. In ballet, there is always a lot of jealousy, something I was to find out about later in my career, but to be honest, I wasn't really conscious of it in those early years in Prague.

This ballet was a significant enterprise for Czech TV and we even had a dramaturge assigned to us so that we could work on the narrative from the original novel by Alexandre Dumas, *fils* (*La Dame aux camélias*), and she took us to exhibitions, the cinema and theatre to help find the right emotional expression. Even so, I didn't really appreciate how important the televising of *The Lady of the Camellias* was and how, for example, that one performance by the 19-year-old Daria can still be seen regularly on Czech TV, more than 20 years later! One unforeseen benefit of this performance was the repeat television fees, which probably helped to make this one of my highest-paid performances ever!

In fact, I was literally so careless that I did an unforgiveable thing that can only really be explained by the rashness of youth. Just before the filming of *The Lady of the Camellias* the whole company was given a week's holiday as a mid-season break. The whole point of this interlude was for the dancers to rest but a few of us, including Andrea and myself, went skiing! Now, no serious modern dancer would risk skiing just before a major performance (indeed, the risk of injury is so great that many ballet dancers would never ski) but we did and – especially since it was my first time – as a result, I was in agony during the filming of the ballet. Of course, I never told any of the TV or ballet staff why!

In this second season, I began to enjoy an established partnership with Stanislav Fečo, a young man who had just graduated from the Conservatoire, one year after me, and we performed *The Lady of the Camellias* together. The authorities in Prague were trying to pair us as two young Czech principal dancers and in the next season we did many shows together, such as *Don Quixote*. Stanislav and I became very good friends and I enjoyed dancing with him.

When young, you just aren't worried about anything. You go for coffee with your friends and you're not conscious of any stress: you are young and carefree, just enjoying what you can. I have come to realise, later in life, that the more you achieve, the more this puts pressure on you. If you start to garner praise for your performances, then with every compliment grows expectation and you begin, foolishly but inevitably, to expect praise. You start to take the bouquets, the praise and the good notices for granted and this all becomes something that – if uncontrolled – continues to build as your career grows. The secret is to control it, which is one reason why I have never paid too much attention to compliments, or to critical reviews. In fact, I only read them if someone pushes one in front of me.

My ballet coaches, Kateřina Slavická and Jaroslav Slavický, had a son, Lukáš – who is now dancing with the Bayerisches Staatsballett in Munich and doing very well. He won the Prix Benois de la Danse (one of the most prestigious awards in ballet) in 2003, but I think that Kateřina also wanted a daughter and she kind of adopted me as a surrogate mother. Even though she was my teacher and more than 20 years older than me, we even danced together, performing the duet for two girls in *Paquita*, a ballet originally choreographed by Joseph Mazilier in 1846 about the bravery of a young gypsy girl in Spain during its occupation by the Napoleonic army. I didn't mind all this attention at first, but gradually I came to feel as if I had no independence. Everything was being controlled for me.

In the ballet company, I was being told when to eat and when to sleep. I was always quiet and kept my opinions to myself. And I'm sure that I made it easy for the ballet staff to try and control my life and they thought that I needed their advice because I said so little and was so compliant. One step led to another until the control began to spread into deciding everything for me. I rebelled against this level of control as any 20-year-old would. This claustrophobia, the feeling that I could not control my own life, became one of the main reasons why I decided to leave the Czech Republic. I didn't exactly plan to escape, but the opportunity just fell into my lap.

Chapter 5

Out to Africa

*I*n 1991, during my third season with the National Ballet in Prague, I was invited to go to a competition in Pretoria in South Africa, where I won the gold medal. Later that year, Veronica Paeper, who was the director of the CAPAB Ballet Company (the acronym stood for the CApe Performing Arts Board) in Cape Town invited me back to dance at Christmas as a guest Sugar Plum Fairy in four performances of *The Nutcracker*. She then offered me a contract to dance with the company in the next season.

The company in Cape Town had been established by the South African ballet dancer Dulcie Howes, initially as the UCT Ballet Company in 1934/5. Howes had left South Africa in the 1920s to train with Margaret Craske and Tamara Karsavina, before joining Anna Pavlova's dance troupe and touring throughout Europe in 1927. She returned to Cape Town in 1930 and opened a ballet school, which led to the formation of the UCT Company, four years later.

For any ballet historian, there is an interesting parallel between Howes and Ninette de Valois, the founder of The Royal Ballet. Where Howes danced with Pavlova, de Valois danced with Anna's arch rival Sergei Diaghilev; both took these experiences back to create indigenous schools in their homelands (although de Valois was born – as Edris Stannus – in Ireland), which led to the founding of their own national ballet companies. The formation of UCT Ballet came just three years after de Valois started the Vic-Wells Ballet, which subsequently grew into what is now The Royal Ballet. Like de Valois, Howes remained at the helm of her company for decades and choreographed several ballets. In 1965, the UCT Company became CAPAB and Howes remained its artistic director until 1969, also retiring as head of the ballet school in 1972.

The similarities in the career trajectories of Howes and de Valois have not translated into a similar path for ballet in Britain and South Africa. Despite the fact that Cape Town has had a classical ballet company for almost 80 years, it really has little in the way of any profound ballet culture. What it did have – in the early 1990s – was lots of money! The company greatly benefitted from significant government funding of the arts and by 1990 it had grown to a large ensemble of over 60 dancers.

At the time of Veronica Paeper's initial offer, I couldn't speak English and I really had no intention of taking up the invitation to join the CAPAB Ballet; anyway, I thought that South Africa was so far away from my home. But, over the months that followed the competition in Pretoria, I began to have concerns about the domineering attitude of the management in Prague and this helped to keep in mind the opportunity of transferring my career to a new continent.

So, gradually, I started to look at the option differently and began to see it in a new light. Also, as I procrastinated, the Cape Town company began to offer me more and more money, and the longer I dithered about saying 'yes', the more they came back with. After the money came a car and then a flat, and suddenly I had everything I always wanted. I wasn't holding out on purpose but my indecision turned out to be really good business!

Eventually, in the spring of 1992, I decided that perhaps I should consider going to Cape Town on a sabbatical from the Czech National Ballet for just one season. It seemed to me to be an important part of finding my own independence. I was very friendly with a young man called Ondřej Rudčenko, who was a pianist for the company in Prague, and I confided in him, telling him all about the offer from South Africa and asking for his opinion. Ondřej knew about the problems that I had been having in Prague and he advised me to seize the opportunity with both hands. So, I did.

Then, having accepted the offer to join the CAPAB Ballet (now known as the CAPAB Kruik Ballet) for a year, I discovered that without telling me Ondřej had also applied to the same company and been accepted as a pianist. Instead of being angry that he did this without consulting me, I was actually relieved because it meant that I wouldn't be going to Africa alone, and Ondřej had become a close friend and confidant. I knew that Ondřej and I could support each other, just as friends, and it would help that there was someone else there that I could converse with in Czech. Better still, Ondřej could speak English, which meant that he could help as my translator. It also eased my parents' fears, knowing that I wasn't going on my own.

When I discovered that Ondřej was coming with me everything else just fell into place. I knew that I could learn English and that my increased salary now also extended to a car and a flat, so I thought why not go? What had I got to lose? The contract was just for a year and I knew that I could go back to Prague at any time if it didn't work out.

I didn't have a driving licence, so that was the very first thing that I had to do so that I could make use of the free car. Within weeks of arriving in Cape Town I learned how to drive but just as quickly, I found out that driving a car is not for me and I've never driven again since then! In fact, I have only ever driven a car in South Africa.

All my friends – apart from Ondřej, of course – laughed when they found out that I was going to Cape Town. No one in Czechoslovakia believed that there was such a thing as ballet in Africa. They all felt that the continent and the country of South Africa had no culture and that I was stupid for leaving a preeminent position in the Prague National Theatre to go to such a place. However, I was attracted to the country and I had everything I wanted there, which considering the shortages of things that I had lived through only a very few years before under communism, made it all seem very exciting. I felt that I needed to be more educated – and I especially wanted to learn English – and it all seemed like a very big adventure.

The Cape Town company was run by a mixture of ex-Royal Ballet dancers and South African dancers, who had made it in the UK or elsewhere and then come back home. The audiences were largely expatriate British people now living in South Africa. I enjoyed my time there very much. It was amazing weather, and I made full use of the fact that I could never just have a 'ballet-ballet' life. I took full advantage of the opportunities afforded by my time away from the theatre and studio, and of course my mum came to visit me. I also discovered a love of riding ostriches.

My new director, Veronica Paeper, was born in South Africa and had received her initial ballet training from Dulcie Howes at the UCT Ballet School. She had been a principal dancer, performing with all three of the main South African companies, including CAPAB. In 1972 she began choreographing and, just two years later, was appointed as CAPAB's resident choreographer. When David Poole retired as the director of the company, Veronica took up the post on 1 January 1991.

Soon after we arrived in South Africa, I quickly found a companion. Or, perhaps I should say that one was provided for me. My new man wasn't a dancer and nor was he a native South African. There is a thriving Czech community in Cape Town and they soon found out about this Czech ballet dancer and invited me to all kinds of events and parties. Because I couldn't speak English at first, it was a great safety blanket for me to be a part of this Czech Diaspora. Through this community, I met a lovely Czech family very early on in my time in South Africa. They invited me to lunch one day and Mario was there. It was not so much an attempt at matchmaking, just that they felt this young friend of theirs might be a good companion to show me the wonderful sights of the Cape. So, he took me to the summit of Table Mountain and elsewhere, and I was quite happy to have this handsome guide – even if we could only communicate in sign-language!

Mario was of Portuguese extraction and he looked the part: dark, swarthy with black curly hair. He was not really my type at all, and I certainly didn't envisage any likely romantic attachment. Not only that but he worked as an accountant, so we certainly didn't have mathematics or book-keeping in common! We were, as they say, 'just good friends' for a long time. We had a lot of fun and – even with the language barrier – we quickly found that we had the same sense of humour. Eventually we just slipped from easy companionship into a relationship quite surreptitiously.

At that age, I certainly wasn't looking for a man to marry and ballet was the most important thing for me. But at home I had always had a life away from ballet with my family, and I needed someone to be able to take me away from ballet in Cape Town and that was Mario! He had the advantage over the friend who came with me from Prague because – as a ballet pianist – Ondřej was always in the studios and the theatre. Ondřej has remained a good friend since our mutual escape to Africa. He is now the pianist at Hamburg Ballet and, whenever I dance with the National Ballet in Prague, he will sometimes fly from Germany to see me, which is an allegiance that I will always cherish. Although we haven't seen each other a great deal since those days in Cape Town, we have often met up for coffee and a chat if we have both been in Prague at the same time.

I didn't live with Mario in South Africa. I'm quite private, so I kept the relationship at arms' length. I continued to want to have my separate life away from ballet and Mario helped with that during my time in Cape Town. We would spend all my spare time seeing the attractions around the Cape. Sometimes, Mario and I would go to Hermanus, a small town on the southern coast of the Western Cape, where we would hire a cottage for the weekend. We'd go to Grotto Beach or watch the southern right whales from the cliffs above. Strangely, for a performer, I don't like crowds or too many people in a room at once, so it was always just the two of us. I think that Mario came to see every single show that I performed in Cape Town.

I managed to learn respectable English while I was in South Africa, helped by a course of study that I carried out by distance learning from a Czech University. I can remember that it was four books, one for each year, and I studied it through to the end on my own. I took the books with me to South Africa and continued studying after I arrived in Scotland. I would practise every evening, continually writing down English phrases. Since I didn't speak Portuguese, I had to communicate with Mario in English, so it all became very important to me. I had a dictionary and I would run to translate every word that I didn't know.

Through the same Czech woman who introduced me to Mario, I also met a woman who owned a zoo and, because I have always loved animals so much, whenever I could, I went to this zoo – not every weekend but many times during my year in South Africa. The zoo had a little two-year-old chimpanzee called Louis and I would spend whole days there playing with him. Looking back over 20 years, strangely, the games with Louis are some of my fondest memories from that year in South Africa.

The quality of the ballet in Cape Town was much better in those days. There was more public money invested in ballet back then and they could afford to run a proper company. Although the CAPAB Kruik Ballet had around 60 dancers when I was there, the company, which became Cape Town City Ballet in 1997, had only enough money to retain around half that number in 2012, which obviously makes life more difficult. They have to recruit amateur dancers from ballet schools just to be able to do the classics.

I left Prague just after the Velvet Revolution and arrived in Cape Town just in time to witness the end of apartheid. My year in Africa was immediately before Nelson Mandela became President (in 1994). It was a tumultuous, exciting, historic time to witness at first hand. One of my first experiences in South Africa was watching a crowd of black South Africans standing on a bridge and throwing stones at all the people passing underneath, including me! There was more than one occasion when I narrowly missed being caught up in riots while travelling through the Cape. It was, however, still the time when white people had more money and they spent it on the things that they liked, including ballet.

The dancers in the company were mostly white but in 1993 there were already some black and coloured dancers, including one soloist. The company was not run on the lines of apartheid and the dancers were well integrated. In 2012, I went back to Cape Town three times to dance the leads in both *Giselle, Swan Lake* and *The Nutcracker*. Veronica Paeper came backstage to see me – more than 20 years after I had danced for her company – and it was a great surprise to meet her again. It was even more surprising to hear her apologise for being horrible to me when I danced there. I told her, 'Well, if you *were* horrible to me, then I can't have understood anything about it at the time!' But meeting her again after the passage of all those years brought back memories that I had forgotten about in the intervening two decades of dancing in the UK.

Surprisingly, I had found life more relaxed in my three seasons as a soloist with the Czech National Ballet than I did in Cape Town. I had to work harder in South Africa, and I remembered that Paeper always pushed me to do more. And I recall that on one particular occasion she took me aside to tell me that I was fat.

I was certainly at my biggest during my time in Cape Town and so, although it might surprise anyone seeing me now to hear that I was once described as fat by an artistic director, at the time it was perhaps understandable. As a dancer, if I'm honest, I certainly felt that I was fat when I was 21. I was enjoying life in Cape Town and I put on a little extra weight while I was there. One of the main issues was that the company didn't have many shows, performing only seven or eight times each month and, as a principal dancer, I would perhaps do only three or four of these programmes.

In fact, during the whole season I only did 33 shows in South Africa, all but one of which was in Cape Town: I did four shows of *Hamlet* in one month, three triple bills the next, then two shows of *Coppélia* followed by a batch of Veronica Paeper's own version of *A Christmas Carol*. I really didn't like waiting around and performing so sporadically.

Most ballerinas are generally at their biggest weight – because of hormonal development – between the ages of 18 and 22. South Africa didn't help. If I wasn't dancing very much, I was enjoying life. I was going to the beach and loving the amazing food. I was 21, a young girl, enjoying a healthy, active life and my hormones were working naturally! My top half was certainly bigger than my bottom half.

In the meeting where I was confronted about my size, Veronica

Paeper asked Ondřej to come and translate since my English was still not good. She told me that I had put on too much weight and that I must lose it. She wasn't horrible. In fact she said it all very nicely but – of course – it bothered me immensely and I just thought, *'Oh my God – how am I going to lose this weight?'*

I am 1.62m (5' 4'), which I think is a good height for a ballerina, and right now (aged 41), I weigh 47kg (7st 5lb), which is a perfect weight for me. Since coming to the UK, I have been this weight more or less consistently. I do believe that dancers must be slim. We have to be lifted and we need to look ethereal, as if we are fairies, but I also believe that our weight needs to be natural and not forced. When I was growing up in the Czech Republic, my mum was a great cook and she made fantastic dumplings. Most of the food we ate was fried and, although I was never a huge eater, it did mean that I was at my heaviest between the ages of 18 and 21, which ended with the year that I was in Cape Town. To put matters into perspective, my heaviest weight at that time was around 48kg (7st 8lb). That one extra kilo was the reason for me being described as fat!

However, unlike a lot of young ballet dancers in this position, I was sensible enough not to let it bother me psychologically. I certainly didn't stop eating. In fact, I carried on eating exactly as before but I exercised a lot more and countered the reduction in my performing schedule with more aerobic workouts and a lot more swimming.

Throughout my career, I have had a lot of people suggest that I must be anorexic to be so slim, but it is just so far from the truth. I suppose that I could have become anorexic in response to being told that I was too fat in South Africa, and I'm sure that exactly this kind of shock is what causes eating disorders in so many young dancers, especially during that vulnerable age range of 18 to 22. But the truth is that I was enjoying life to the full, having a great time outside of ballet and I didn't let it affect me. In fact, it wasn't until I met my former director backstage after *Giselle* in 2012 that the memories came flooding back; I had forgotten all about her comments of 20 years before.

Looking back, to have been told that I was too fat at 21 is especially ironic, given that others have subsequently thought I am anorexic! In the first of the Czech TV documentaries about my life, when I am discussing eating issues on camera, the people responsible for the English sub-titles even translated my comments as an admission of being anorexic, which is so far from the truth as to be laughable.

I can see that many young dancers are rounder in their late teenage years and there are young girls wanting to be ballerinas who wrongly believe that they are fat and it affects them greatly, when in fact it is simply a transition that they are going through, just as happened to me in South Africa. I spend a lot of my time now explaining to these young women that maybe in a year's time their body will naturally change to the shape that they will feel more comfortable with and it isn't something that the intervention of not eating properly can alter. It's a natural state and I always advise them to continue eating normally. Sure, they should concentrate on eating healthily and every dancer knows that chocolate is an occasional luxury at best.

During my career, I have known many dancers who have become anorexic due to a horrible self-loathing perception of their body image on stage. Many have got through this and recovered, but regrettably some never do. Some ballerinas go all through their dancing lives starving themselves to look thin. Anorexia can destroy lives. It stops periods, it ages people prematurely and damages those who suffer from it, often internally, meaning that those women who endure such trauma are unable to conceive or bear children. Any eating disorder is a terrible, terrible illness.

It is a fact of life that not all dancers can be the same sylphlike tiny size. Some of our greatest ballerinas have naturally bigger bodies. The strong women can get any concerns about this out of their heads; they get on with being dancers and they have great careers. But others struggle with eating disorders all through their lives because of this perception, often caused by the ill-judged remarks of an artistic director, a ballet coach or other dancers during those formative years in their late teens and early 20s. This never leaves them and I'm afraid to say that there are many well-known ballerinas who have suffered from this dreadful curse. The bottom line is that there is no need to stop eating naturally and properly to be a ballet dancer.

I hope that it is a good message for any young dancers reading this that when I was 20/21, I was told that I was too fat to make it as a principal dancer. I did nothing about it specifically other than to eat more healthily and exercise more; I didn't change the amount I ate and my life remained as it was. The irony is that now I am in my 40s, I have a bigger complex about the fact that people think that I am anorexic, since I don't want to look too thin. I don't think it looks good on stage, especially at my age! Audiences don't want to see dancers who look anorexic.

Although I danced only 32 shows in Cape Town during the whole season I spent there, I had to learn roles in ballets that were created on me, like *A Christmas Carol* and Titania in *A Midsummer Night's Dream* (both choreographed by Paeper). The latter was filmed for South African TV, just as I had created *The Lady of the Camellias* in Prague to be filmed for Czech TV. So by the time I was 21, I had created two ballets that had been filmed on national TV networks. I count myself as being very fortunate in this regard because many wonderful dancers never, ever get this opportunity. Another highlight of the season was an opportunity to dance the whole of *Raymonda*, a three-act ballet to Alexander Glazunov's luscious score, in South Africa in Norman Furber's version of Marius Petipa's famous 1898 ballet about the romance during the time of the Crusades between Raymonda and the medieval knight, Jean de Brienne.

I hardly travelled with the company while I was in South Africa. Only one of my performances was not in Cape Town, being held in Mossel Bay, a harbour town situated over 400 km (248 miles) east of Cape Town. Audiences in South Africa were very appreciative and, because there were so few shows, performances were invariably sold out. There was also not much choice, so if you wanted to see ballet it had to be performed by the Cape Town Ballet company. This became one of my great frustrations in South Africa. Although I loved the country, I really missed seeing other companies perform and having the opportunity of widening my cultural horizons because I truly believe that, as a performer, I must be able to keep feeding myself with other artistic influences in order to enrich what I am able to produce on the stage.

I got used to a certain amount of minor celebrity in Cape Town. Interviews and press attention had been a part of my life since the Prix de Lausanne – when I was just 18 – and I was steadily getting used to it, although it is a part of the role of being a prima ballerina that I have never enjoyed. Starring in the TV adaptation of *The Lady of the Camellias* in Prague had also been a big thing in my native country. Ballet was not headline news in South Africa and it was – and still is – very much the preserve of the white population. However, it was big enough to attract the TV cameras and this led to a significant amount of press attention.

Along with the fame comes the fans, and I have been amazed at the strength of feeling that ballet dancers can command. All ballerinas have their special fans. At one end of the scale this might mean just waiting at the stage door for an autograph, but it progresses to invitations to dinner and expensive presents. I have had lots of lovely pieces of jewellery given to me over the years, especially earrings, although I feel sorry for the expense since I've never had my ears pierced. I always thought that it would hurt too much, which is ironic when one thinks how much pain I have had to endure as a ballerina! So, I have a lot of beautiful earrings that I can't wear.

A charming Japanese man would come to see my performances all over the world, even arriving in Australia when the company toured there. He would just wait at the stage door and ask for my autograph on every programme. It was very lovely to have that depth of undemanding support.

I am happy losing myself on stage in expressing a role and can do anything while in the thrall of performance but as myself, away from the stage, I have always felt that to be the most difficult aspect of my life in ballet. I can't lose myself when I am being Daria Klimentová.

In 2012, while I was preparing this book, an invitation came to return to Cape Town and I jumped to take it. When I went back to perform *Giselle*, it was the first time that I had returned since leaving the country in 1993. I had really loved the place and the people, and had always promised myself that I would return one day but it seemed that this day would never come.

It was odd going back: I had goose bumps when I arrived at Cape Town airport. The audience was amazing – they were standing after my shows. It's hard to make the audience in London stand up to applaud, but in Cape Town it was a standing ovation every night. It felt beautiful that they appreciated what we did. I performed in the same theatre as I had done 20 years before, but the company is smaller and the overall standard undoubtedly worse than when I danced there in 1992/3. They know this, but it is very difficult for them to recruit and keep dancers. In particular, it seems that they really don't have any boys who are comfortable and secure in principal roles, and I danced with Vadim Muntagirov, my wonderful partner from English National Ballet, on all three return visits to date. Cape Town is a gorgeous city to visit and I hope to dance there many more times before I call it a day on my career as a ballerina.

At the end of my year in Cape Town, I had become hungry to again be a part of a world-class ballet company in a European country. Even though I was supposed to be returning to Prague, I started sending my videos to various companies in Europe and America. Ondřej, the pianist, suggested that it would be wrong for me to go back and I agreed with him; I wanted to expand my experience. I was curious to see other companies, and Cape Town had given me the bug to explore new horizons – I knew that if I didn't find anywhere then my 'safety net' was that I could always go back to Prague, if all else failed.

I sent out several copies of the video of *The Lady of the Camellias* to try and win a new job. Following this, I received an offer from Maina Gielgud, the artistic director of The Australian Ballet, who was very interested in me. I wanted to go to Sydney; living in Australia sounded very exciting at that time and a perfect place to go after Cape Town. But in those days there were problems in recruiting foreign dancers to work in Australia – they could do exchanges but that wasn't going to work for me.

Another who received a video from me was Galina Samsova, who had been director of Scottish Ballet since 1991. I didn't know this at the time but Samsova had also been one of the judges at the Pretoria competition, where I had won the gold medal, (which had led to me joining the CAPAB Kruik Ballet). I had struck lucky.

Chapter 6

A Scotch Symphony

When she received my video, Galina Samsova remembered me from the Pretoria competition and she wrote back straight-away, asking me to move to Scotland. I then remembered her name as one of the judges in Pretoria, so it seemed that I would at least be going somewhere that I would be known. So, for the second time, I got a job without having to do a formal audition!

I had originally taken just a leave of absence from the Czech National Ballet because I planned to return to Prague after one year and, although I did stay in Cape Town for just a year, it wasn't Prague that was to be my next destination but Glasgow.

The South African season finished in May 1993 and by June everyone had started their holidays. I went back to Prague, with Mario in tow, for a month in June to guest with the Czech National Ballet at the end of their season, dancing in the *pas de trois* in Act I of *Swan Lake* and in a Czech ballet entitled *The Princess with the Golden Hair*, which was part of a suite known as *Z pohádky do pohádky* (*From fairy tale to fairy tale*). By this time, my Czech director, Vlastimil Harapes, suspected that I wasn't coming back, and I already knew that my immediate future lay in Bonny Scotland.

Believe it or not, I travelled from Prague to Scotland by bus! I have always been careful with money – I guess that it has much to do with having so little as a child growing up in Czechoslovakia. During my year in South Africa I had earned good money and even though I could easily afford to fly, my mum had always taught me that you have to save your money, just in case. And so the bus seemed to be the cheapest and the best option for travelling across Europe to my new home, and the long overnight journey really didn't seem such a sacrifice. Actually, I rather enjoyed it. Besides, Czech people travelled everywhere by bus, so going to Scotland by road didn't seem such a big deal! Mario and I got on the bus in Prague with our suitcases and off we went to Glasgow.

I stayed with Mario for three years. He gave up his job and left all his friends and everything he had known in South Africa to follow me to Glasgow. He had no promise of work but after a month, he found a job as an accountant for a record company. Looking back, I can see that it was a remarkable commitment for him to move to Scotland with me, but when you are as young as we were at that time, you really don't take these things that seriously. I remember thinking to myself, *'Wow, I'm going to Glasgow,'* but actually I didn't think it was that big a deal. We certainly weren't thinking of getting married or anything like that, but it was nice not to be travelling to a new country on my own. I had travelled to South Africa with Ondřej, and now I was going to Glasgow with Mario – I always seemed to have a man to carry the cases!

I moved to Scotland as a principal dancer for a slight increase in salary and the company gave me a flat for a month until I was able to sort out somewhere to live for myself. But I didn't get off to the best of starts. I remember arriving in Glasgow on the bus and thinking, '*Oh my God, where am I going? Do they really have a ballet company here?*' I had no real understanding about Scotland at all. I came from Prague with all its history, its architecture and culture, and the beautiful National Theatre with its golden roof, and suddenly, as I looked around Glasgow, I missed all of that. I had understood that there was not the same culture in Cape Town, but it had so many other advantages and benefits, and I had always known that it was only to last for a year.

Glasgow was not at all what I had expected. In particular, I struggled so much with the climate and the cold! It was raining and cloudy when I arrived, and I think it stayed like that for the three years that I lived there. In the whole time I was in Scotland, I never ever wore just a t-shirt outside, and I slept in a tracksuit almost every night! Even though we had central heating in our flat, I was always freezing and it was such a horrible, damp cold. After I arrived in Scotland I felt sure that I would not be able to stay there for long.

However, I was to discover that Scotland is one of the most beautiful countries on earth, and I loved finding out more about what the Scots call 'God's own country', although I have come to understand that lots of other nations use the same phrase! We all love our homelands but the Scottish people have particular reason to be proud of their country. On our many tours with Scottish Ballet, I loved exploring the Highlands and the Lochs. I adored being in the midst of such wonderful scenery, such as Loch Ness or Loch Lomond, gazing at the mountains and not being able to see other people. But my English language lessons in Cape Town could not have prepared me for the Glaswegian accent and I spent the first year desperately trying to understand people and mostly not succeeding. However, I did soon come to realise that the Scots are the friendliest, happiest and most sociable people. I don't drink alcohol at all these days and, even when

I was young, it hardly ever passed my lips, but in my years in Scottish Ballet I was very often in the pub, watching Scots have a good time. They certainly know how to party!

Although my first instinct had been that I couldn't stay in Scotland for long, the people and the country made such an impact on me that it took me three years to leave. Scottish Ballet was a medium-sized company with about 55/60 dancers and it had struggled with money problems for a long time. Galina Samsova had recently started as artistic director not long before I arrived, having succeeded Peter Darrell, who had founded the company as Scottish Theatre Ballet.

In fact, Scottish Ballet had the most peculiar origins since Darrell initially formed the company – together with Elizabeth West – in Bristol as Western Theatre Ballet, back in 1957. On her death, in 1962, he became the sole director and, having fought off bankruptcy in its formative years, the company moved lock, stock and barrel to Glasgow in 1969 at the invitation of the Scottish Arts Council to become the brand new national ballet company of Scotland. It was renamed Scottish Ballet, in 1972. Darrell died, in post as artistic director, in 1987 and there were a series of temporary replacements before Samsova arrived, initially as guest director, in 1990.

The company performed the usual classics such as *The Sleeping Beauty* and *Swan Lake*, together with several ballets that were new to me. I was not particularly close to the gossip, and I never really understood that there were severe money problems. I didn't ever do ballet for money, so it never really mattered to me what kind of salary I had.

I liked Galina Samsova a lot because she was Russian and had been a big star in Canada and then at the London Festival Ballet (which later became English National Ballet) and at the Sadler's Wells Royal Ballet (now Birmingham Royal Ballet). I believed that I could learn a great deal from her, but unfortunately, because she was the company's artistic director, she didn't have much time to spend in the studio. She was busy with all the other administrative and directorial stuff, so I grew to be disappointed with this lack of contact, since I had imagined a much closer coaching relationship with her in the studio and I believed that Samsova would make me a better dancer. I now know that my youthful expectations were unrealistic since I didn't appreciate how many things that the director of a company like Scottish Ballet had to do, nor that this precluded much time to invest in the coaching of individual dancers.

Life is full of swings and roundabouts and, although I was sad not to get more of Samsova's time, this was soon compensated by discovering Daniel Job. Daniel was from Belgium and he had trained at the School of American Ballet, as well as with Royal Danish Ballet and at the Paris Opera. As a dancer, he had worked all over Europe, including with the Deutsche Oper Berlin under Kenneth MacMillan and in Marseilles with Roland Petit. He became my coach at Scottish Ballet and he really pushed me hard. In particular – and for the very first time – I found a teacher who could advise me on how to dance to suit my body and in doing so this helped me to improve. Daniel was a teacher who went well beyond the call of duty – there are many of them in ballet – and he would give me many private lessons in addition to the work he was being paid to do. It wasn't just for me either; he did this for many of the dancers at Scottish Ballet. He did it for anyone who needed extra help. Daniel was a great coach and he taught me to get the best out of my body. He is now the artistic advisor at Ballet West in Scotland and still coaching as a guest teacher around the world.

I had only really enjoyed one established dance partnership in my career to date – with Stanislav Fečo, who had been Armand to my Marguerite in *The Lady of the Camellias* in Prague. In South Africa, I had performed with several dancers and I hadn't forged any particular partnership. The same thing happened in Scotland, where I had a lot of different dance partners over the three years. However, I danced mostly with Vladislav Bubnov, an attractive Russian danseur who had been a soloist with the famous Bolshoi Ballet in Moscow before he came to Scotland. Because Vladislav was Russian and I could speak Russian, I suppose that it was natural for Samsova to pair us together. We had a lot of fun and we laughed a lot, particularly since there was a strong cultural and technical connection in our dance training. I don't think that we ever quite reached the emotional heights of making audiences cry as artists, but we had a good time together and I remember that we laughed a lot during rehearsals. Vladislav left Scottish Ballet in 2000 to join the ballet company in Leipzig, before joining English National Ballet, where he stayed for five years. He is now a physiotherapist and ballet coach working in London. He is a fun guy and we are still very good friends.

One major highlight in Scotland was having Galina Samsova's production of *The Sleeping Beauty* made on me and performing the opening night with Vladislav. What was especially exciting about this production was that it was designed by Jasper Conran. He created the costumes, and it was very exciting having him there, designing Princess Aurora's tutus on me. What I remember most about Conran was that he always seemed to be there during rehearsals and was so full of life. I recall that he became very upset with the colour of one particular costume just before the dress rehearsal and decided to spray it a different colour, which held everything up. He always seemed to be flying everywhere, a man of such energy and vitality, who was great fun to work with. Later on he also designed *Swan Lake* for Samsova and Scottish Ballet, but since I was in the second cast for this production, I spent less time with him in the studio.

I also performed both as Kitty and in the title role of André Prokovsky's *Anna Karenina*. Prokovsky was Samsova's ex-dance partner and ex-husband. I didn't work directly with him, but it was his ballet. It was very hard for me to play a role like Anna Karenina because I was just a young girl in my early 20s with little real experience of life. Whereas the heroine of Tolstoy's famous novel was married to an older man, she had a child, a torrid affair that turned society against her and then she committed suicide. At the time, I remember thinking that I had no idea why she would do that! *'How was I to replicate all these feelings and experiences?'* It wasn't a new dilemma for me. After all, as an innocent 19-year-old in Prague, I had played Marguerite Gautier in *The Lady of the Camellias* – a mature courtesan who dies of consumption.

I now feel certain that these are both roles that I could tackle with even greater confidence and ability at this stage in my career, but unfortunately, the chance to dance Marguerite and Anna came when I was too young. As a young dancer, aged 19 and 23 respectively, I readily admit that although I had read the novels by Tolstoy and Alexandre Dumas, fils, and understood the narrative, I really didn't feel the emotion or the expressiveness of these iconic characters at all. If only I could have that chance again.

Among other 'new' works for me to experience in Scotland was my very first taste of George Balanchine's choreography. Balanchine is widely regarded as having been one of the great – if not the greatest – choreographers of the 20th century. A Georgian, born in St Petersburg in 1904, where he trained at the Petrograd Ballet School (he was a student there during the Russian Revolution), he became the leading choreographer of Diaghilev's famous Ballets Russes, where he met and worked with Stravinsky. However, it is for his work in establishing and developing ballet in the USA, specifically at New York City Ballet, for which he is rightly revered. Balanchine developed a specific genre of neoclassical ballet, which builds on the essential traditions of classical ballet in the Russian style but marries this to a dynamic, fast, fluid modern style, which especially appealed to American audiences. He was a prolific choreographer and the catalogue of his official works number some 425 pieces, the last of which (*Variations for Orchestra*, inevitably to music by Stravinsky) premiered in July 1982, some nine months before his death at the age of 79.

His work, *Scotch Symphony*, made in 1952 and inspired both by New York City Ballet's first visit to the Edinburgh Festival and Mendelssohn's eponymous Symphony (written in 1829 and dedicated to Queen Victoria), was unsurprisingly in the repertory for Scottish Ballet and at first I found it incredibly hard to perform. Not only is it a balletic homage to Scotland but also to the Romantic notion of the elusive sylph (a mythological spirit in western folklore). The steps are so fast and not set on a regular count, and the technique was alien to my very formal Russian schooling. However, I came to love performing it, particularly since in my three years in Scotland I didn't do much contemporary or neoclassical work, sticking mainly to the classics.

Gradually, over many years, I have become very comfortable performing Balanchine and, in fact, I have come to adore dancing his choreography and relish the challenge of maintaining my technique at such breakneck speeds. I would happily dance the 'Tchai pas', the nickname for Balanchine's *Tchaikovsky Pas de Deux* (a virtuoso duet regularly performed at galas all over the world), at the drop of a hat!

As I have noted, I only made 33 performances in the whole season in Cape Town, but at Scottish Ballet I had 61 shows in my first year (1993/4). The next year it was 63, so I was working much harder. I did many performances of both Aurora and the Lilac Fairy in *The Sleeping Beauty* (which toured to seven cities in the spring of 1994), together with *Anna Karenina* and *Peter Pan* – a ballet by Graham Lustig, a former dancer with Sadler's Wells Royal Ballet. This toured twice during my time at Scottish Ballet, in which I danced the character of

Wendy, a role I really enjoyed. My career in Scotland developed into a case of doing the same few ballets over and over again, which was very different to the situation in Prague of doing several ballets in a year but just a few times each.

The company toured a great deal, so I was performing all over Scotland, Northern Ireland and England, in places such as Glasgow, Edinburgh, Aberdeen, Stirling, Inverness, Oxford, Newcastle and Hull. This was a first for me since in Prague and Cape Town almost all of my performances had been in the same theatre. To be honest, I hated touring and I still do, which is odd since I have spent most of the last 20 years on tour! It was a shocking experience for me at first. Mario was not able to come with me, and since I'm not a very sociable person, I don't make friends that easily, so for me touring was often a solitary experience. I didn't really make many friends in the company, apart from Vladislav.

We seemed to always be staying in tiny bed and breakfast 'digs' or in small hotels. I absolutely hated it and it was made worse by virtue of the fact that I was always so tired because I wasn't used to doing so many shows in succession. This was the first time in my life (but certainly not the last) that I actually faked illness so that I wouldn't have to perform! I never would have thought that I could ever have done such a thing, but the situation often got so dire that I had no alternative.

To be truthful, I didn't exactly fake an illness as make myself ill. On the first occasion, I washed my hair and then deliberately went outside in the bitter cold without drying it. I knew that this would make me ill and it did. That is how desperate I had become. I caught a cold – thankfully, not too badly – but it was enough to get me out of performing for a week. Looking back, I know that it is a bad thing to admit to having done but it encapsulates how awful I was feeling at the time.

I had doubled the number of shows I was giving and was travelling all over the place to perform. It was a shock to my system. I was very young and I was scared to tell the company the plain truth, which was that I was too tired and too stressed to perform. This was a major difference between the Eastern European companies back then and what I have found in the West. If you were feeling tired or stressed in Prague, then the management would understand and they would give you the night off, even if it meant cancelling a show. Obviously, when the state is paying for mostly everything then that attitude is possible, but here in the West, where money is much tighter, I understand that such a caring and flexible attitude towards dancers is impossible.

Back then, in the UK, I felt that young dancers were treated as if they were children. If you told someone in the company that you were under too much stress to perform, they would probably just pat you on the head and say, 'There, there,' as they pushed you out on stage! Making myself ill was sometimes the only means of escape. Since then, I must say that I have done something similar a few times and it is probably evident that I am far from unique in having taken such action to escape the continuing stresses of multiple performances on tour.

Even though we had never shared a home in South Africa, I moved in with Mario as soon as we arrived in Glasgow. If I'm honest, I wasn't at all ready for any strong commitment, but I felt that I had little choice since he had moved continents to be with me. But what we had in Cape Town didn't last and almost from the very beginning of our time together in Scotland, Mario and I grew steadily apart. In Cape Town we could always go back to our separate homes at the end of the day so, having had that private space, I found sharing a flat with him in Glasgow to be very suffocating. I didn't like it that he was always there, and I seemed to have no escape to just be me. Worst of all, Mario started to become very demanding and possessive – difficult personality traits that I hadn't seen in him during our time together in Cape Town.

Even if I went out for coffee with my dance partner, Vladislav, with whom I had developed a great friendship, Mario would become jealous. It is true that Vladislav was handsome and fun, and, of course, we shared so much in common. It is also true that a ballerina cannot have much to hide from her dance partner; we are emotionally connected and all the lifting and support means that there is not much of a ballerina's body that isn't felt by her partner! All of this might suggest suitable justification for Mario to be jealous of Vladislav, except for one quite important matter, which is that Vladislav was also openly gay. There was no danger whatsoever that we could ever have become an item, but if I went out with Vladislav to lunch, I would come back and Mario would be lying on the sofa with a lit candle next to a photograph of me and he would often be crying. It made me feel very uncomfortable and guilty, even though I had nothing to be remotely guilty about. As Mario grew more possessive the more distant it made me become.

He also started trying to save money by unscrewing light bulbs and switching the heating off, even though he knew how cold I felt. We didn't need to economise, but he was doing it because he felt that he needed to send money home to his mum in South Africa. I remember thinking that it was nice to send money home to his mother, but I wasn't going to freeze because of it. It all hastened the inevitable separation.

I don't recall any specific scene that ended our relationship, it just fizzled out – it was his possessive personality that I couldn't cope with, and I never wanted to have to deal with such jealousy again. It took me a while to pluck up the courage to end things. I thought that it must be my fault and tried to repair things while I carried on suffering. I spent a year trying to mend the relationship with Mario, but at the same time I was a professional ballet dancer and I wasn't going to let jealousy ruin my life. We carried on under this cloud for a long while, but eventually – after about 18 months of living together in Glasgow – we split up, both of us leaving our original flat and moving into separate apartments.

Glasgow was a comparatively small city and I would still see Mario around. I'm pleased that we remained friends, and he still came to watch my shows. After I left Scottish Ballet and moved to London, he remained in Glasgow for a few more years and eventually we lost contact. I often think about the fact that this man moved from his home in Cape Town to Glasgow because of me – I mean, he really changed his life for me in a very unselfish way – and, well, I left him there! I often wonder what happened to him: if he ever got married and had children.

Even though I was unhappy in Scotland to begin with, I didn't start looking for a job elsewhere for three years. I was always cold and the disappointment of not getting enough coaching from Galina Samsova never improved. She brought some very lovely ballets that they didn't have before, but I just didn't get enough of her time, which had been one of the major reasons for going to the company in the first place.

For a while, I toyed with the idea of applying to work with Jiří Kylián, the Czech choreographer, at Nederlands Dans Theater. I had worked with him in Prague on a ballet entitled *Return to a Strange Land* (*Návraty do neznámé Zemé*) and found it to be an incredible experience. Kylián is so enthusiastic in the way that he explains every single step in his work. I felt that he was teaching me emotions rather than the steps. He was very attentive and careful to give you the exact meaning of every little nuance in his choreography. Kylián's work is often described as abstract or non-narrative, and it is true that there are no plots that audiences can easily follow, but there is such a rich panoply of meaning and purpose in everything that he does. As a fellow Czech, I was drawn to Kylián and very tempted to offer myself to NDT, but I decided that my future had to remain as a classical ballerina. Unfortunately, that experience in Prague has remained my one and only experience of working with the greatest of all Czech choreographers.

I was convinced from a very early period that I wanted to be in London. It has always seemed to me that London is the centre of so much, particularly in terms of a rich cultural life, and I was enthusiastic to be a part of it. A woman named Zina, who had been a ballerina at the Czech National Ballet in Prague, was teaching character dances at The Royal Ballet. I knew her well and she was always asking me to go to London. I genuinely believe now, in retrospect, that all the moves that I made from Prague to South Africa and then Scotland were really just stepping stones on my inevitable journey to London.

Chapter 7

New Beginnings: Expectation and Loss

For me, dancing in London meant going to either The Royal Ballet or to English National Ballet. I left it until my third season in Scotland before seeking the move. And I went for the tougher choice first.

I visited London many times while I was in Scotland – again as a true Czech woman, always travelling down by bus – and I immersed myself in the wonderful culture of this great city, seeing as many plays and exhibitions as I could fit in to each visit. On one such trip, I arranged to do class with The Royal Ballet. At that time, the only person in the company that I knew was Hubert Essakow, a South African born in Johannesburg, with whom I had danced *Hamlet* during my time in Cape Town. Hubert left South Africa to become a soloist at The Royal Ballet at the same time as I left for Scotland. I remember when I came to do class with the Royal, Hubert stood next to me and spent the whole time pushing me, saying, 'Come on, go for it!' He was so keen to get me into the company alongside him.

At that time, The Royal Ballet was under the direction of Sir Anthony Dowell, only recently knighted for his services to ballet. He was one of the finest, lyrical British dancers of all time, having danced with The Royal Ballet from 1961 until the early 1990s, forging a remarkable partnership with Antoinette Sibley (she became Dame Antoinette in 1996, a year after Dowell was knighted). He also spent two years on a leave of absence, dancing with Natalia Makarova at American Ballet Theatre between 1978 and 1980. Dowell became artistic director of The Royal Ballet in 1986 and served for 15 years.

Dame Ninette de Valois had founded the company in 1931, originally as the Vic-Wells Ballet based at Sadler's Wells Theatre, eventually becoming the Sadler's Wells Royal Ballet, ten years later. It didn't become The Royal Ballet until the award of a Royal Charter in 1956. De Valois stepped down from the post of director in 1963, although she was to remain closely associated with the company until her death, which fell just short of her 103rd birthday in 2001. She was involved in the company for 70 years and led it for over 30, but Dowell's directorship remains the longest tenure as (artistic) director in the time since the company became The Royal Ballet.

Unfortunately, I didn't see or speak to Dowell on the few occasions when I took class with the company. Instead, I spoke to his assistant director, Monica Mason, who would eventually become the director for a decade, retiring in 2012 after a remarkable 54 years of unbroken service to the Royal, as both dancer and manager. She offered me the opportunity of joining The Royal Ballet, but on a soloist's contract and not as a principal. I was a principal already and had been so almost since the very beginning of my career, dancing lead roles for five seasons in three different companies. At that time, The Royal Ballet had some great ballerinas, led by the home-grown British star Darcey Bussell (now enjoying a whole new career as a judge on the BBC's *Strictly Come Dancing*), and the gamine, ebullient Italian ballerina

Viviana Durante, and I knew that I was not close to approaching their ability at that time. So, although I understood why Monica was only able to offer me a contract as a soloist, I didn't want to take a demotion, even for The Royal Ballet.

Since it was one of the world's major companies this may appear to have been an odd decision (and, in fact, it is common for new dancers to come in as principals from other companies but to join the Royal initially in the lower rank of soloist). However, I simply couldn't face several years of trying to get back to being a principal by dancing the plethora of soloist roles. It is hard work being a soloist and you have to perform almost every night, certainly many more times than the principals. As far as I was concerned, life was too short – it was an easy decision for me to turn the offer down and I knew, even from that early age, that The Royal Ballet was never going to be for me.

So, by a simple process of elimination, this inevitably led me to English National Ballet, known universally as ENB. The company had its origins in the Markova-Dolin Ballet, which had toured Britain in the 1930s as a star vehicle for the two great dancers, Alicia Markova and Anton Dolin. Their company was briefly reformed after the war but I understand that they were keen to drop their names from the title since Dolin was then approaching 50 and Markova was already 40. They knew that they could not perform in every show, which is what their audiences around the country would always expect, so long as their names were in the company title. It was decided that a new name should be based on the forthcoming Festival of Britain and so, in 1950, it came into renewed life as the London Festival Ballet under the artistic direction of Dolin, giving regular performances at London's Royal Festival Hall on the South Bank.

In 1989, the company's growing reputation around the world was recognised by changing its name to English National Ballet, thus conferring the status of becoming the national ballet company of

England. At the same time, ENB's home performing base in London switched to the Coliseum in Upper St Martin's Lane, although for many years the company has also had annual seasons at the Royal Albert Hall, just a stone's throw away from its base at Markova House in Jay Mews, Kensington. The company's own school had been founded in 1988.

The star partnership at ENB at the time that I considered joining was the Estonian couple of Thomas Edur and Agnes Oaks, who were partners, on and off the stage. They had joined together in 1990 – and my first experience of them (and the company) was seeing a performance of *The Nutcracker* at the Royal Festival Hall and I really liked it. I distinctly remember that Tom and Aggie, as everyone knew them, performed a beautiful *pas de deux.* I had heard of them and thought that it would be nice to be in the same company and to learn from these great dancers.

I asked the director, Derek Deane, if I could do class but it transpired that ENB was taking class on the stage at the Royal Festival Hall. So my very first experience of his strict and unbending attitude came in his curt response to my request, when he told me that outsiders were not allowed. Across the world it is quite normal and accepted practice for established professional dancers to ask permission to take class with another company, if they happen to be in a different city, away from their own home base. Everyone knows that ballet dancers have to stay in shape and the daily class, mixing routines at the *barre* and in the centre, is a staple part of every dancer's life. I have often met dancers in their 80s who still take class every day. It is as vital to our daily routine as getting up in the morning and brushing our teeth. And there has always been an informal, unwritten code among ballet companies to allow professional dancers from other companies to keep in shape by taking class whenever they need to. However, at that time, this was not the case at ENB. Outsiders were only permitted to take class if Derek specifically wanted to see them.

I wasn't going to take being ignored as the end of it, and on a subsequent trip to London, visiting the company's headquarters in Jay Mews, I happened to bump into David Wall, a former principal dancer at The Royal Ballet who had joined ENB as ballet master in 1995. Unlike my previous experience, David was very welcoming: he courteously showed me around the building and invited me to take class with the company. I liked the environment and the spirit of the place, plus I found something very warm and supportive about Mr Wall.

I returned to Scotland and immediately sent the Czech TV video tape of me performing *The Lady of the Camellias* in Prague to Derek Deane, and he replied immediately to say that he liked my dancing very much and he also liked Robert Balogh's choreography. Now he was interested. He asked me to come back to London so that he could see me taking class. I went down – again, of course, on my trusty bus – and met with Derek before joining ENB's ensemble for their daily class. It wasn't without incident because, at that time, I wasn't used to doing class wearing pointe shoes and I remember that Rosalyn Whitten, one of the ballet staff – whom everyone knew as Ros – came up to me and said, 'Derek wants you to put your pointe shoes on.' I was surprised because this was a novelty to me. I had danced in the Czech Republic, South Africa and Scotland and had never worn pointe shoes for class before. I thought that it was absolutely terrible but, of course, I did as I was told, put them on and thankfully, got through the class without breaking my foot!

This was my first audition since graduating from the Prague Conservatoire and once again I thought – as I always did when I put myself under pressure – that I had done terribly. In fact, I remember thinking that I must have looked like an amateur dancer. Derek came over to me straightaway and I felt sure that he was going to tell me to leave, as if I were some kind of imposter, but instead he asked me to come to his office.

However, before I got the chance to go into his office for this interview, I heard him screaming at Ros and some of the other ballet staff. He was shouting at them very loudly and angrily, telling them that any dancers who are not in class have to call beforehand to explain what is wrong with them and not just fail to turn up. He was absolutely yelling his head off at them and, looking back with the benefit of hindsight, I would be surprised if it wasn't all done deliberately for my benefit! So, before I actually got to meet Derek to have my interview with him about joining the company, I got to hear him shouting at the staff! I was already nervous enough and so you can imagine how bad this made me feel. Despite all of this, my first impressions of Derek before the interview, in person, were that he was very business-like and important. And he seemed to like me from the beginning.

Derek Deane had been a dancer at The Royal Ballet, joining straight from the Upper School in 1972 and rising to the rank of principal dancer in 1978. He began choreographing very early in his dance career and had some works performed for the Sadler's Wells Royal Ballet – the company that has since become Birmingham Royal Ballet – while he was still dancing, including *The Picture of Dorian Gray* (to music by Carl Davis) in 1987. Two years later, aged 35, he became resident choreographer at the Teatro dell'Opera in Rome before joining ENB as artistic director in 1993.

The interview was just between the two of us. Derek asked me how old I was and how long had I been dancing. I thought that he should have already known these basic things, and I remember thinking, '*I'm only 25... I'm not old yet, am I?*' He was especially concerned to know whether I suffered from a lot of injuries and was unduly worried about my health. He questioned whether I was strong enough for a career at

ENB. I told him that I was fine and – touching wood as I said it – that I had always been relatively injury-free, but he continued to give me the third degree by asking lots of questions about my health and past injuries. In fact, at one point he adopted quite an aggressive attitude and I felt very uncomfortable, as if he was looking at me like a piece of shit on the floor. I began to imagine that he was thinking why on earth I should possibly believe that I was good enough to come to his company. As the interview progressed, I felt terrible and wanted the floor to open and swallow me up, but as he carried on – still in quite a surprisingly aggressive manner – it dawned on me perversely that perhaps he was exactly the director that I needed! Succumbing to the temptation of laziness was my biggest worry in those days, so I began to see that this was a director who would make me work.

So, as I experienced my first dose of Derek's wayward behaviour, in a funny sort of way, it actually sold me on the fact that this was exactly the right company for me! After his aggressive questioning, he suddenly switched back to being nice. He ended the interview by saying that he liked me very much and would let me know as soon as possible whether he could give me a job. Exactly one week later, a letter offering me a contract with ENB as a principal dancer dropped onto my doormat in Glasgow.

At that time, apart from the video film I had sent, Derek had never seen me perform. Later, I discovered that Tom and Agnes (Edur and Oaks) had left the company and gone to Birmingham Royal Ballet, so it would appear that my luck was good, as the timing of my approach to ENB was perfect since there was suddenly a vacancy for a principal ballerina. I hadn't known at the time but Derek was clearly looking for someone to replace Agnes (although, in fact, she and Tom only stayed in Birmingham for a season, returning to ENB as guest principals in 1998).

At the same time as recruiting me, Derek also brought in Zoltan

Solymosi as a new principal from The Royal Ballet. Born in 1967, Zoltan had already danced as a principal at Dutch National Ballet, Bayerisches Staatsballet in Munich, Hungarian State Ballet and La Scala in Milan before coming to London in 1992. Zoltan landed in Jay Mews as my intended new partner at ENB soon after arriving in London.

I didn't own a flat in Scotland, so moving down to London to take up my contract with ENB was relatively straightforward. I had planned it so that I was able to make a very clean break from Scotland. Proving that we had remained on very good terms, Mario hired a car and helped me move to yet another new country by driving to London with all my stuff.

To satisfy my love of animals, he had bought me a pet budgerigar called Pepíček (which is essentially the Czech nickname for Joseph). He was a beautiful, multi-coloured bird and he talked so well. He could say his name 'Pepíček-oo, Pepíček-oo' and I would spend hours just talking to him. I loved my Pepíček but, unfortunately, I had to leave him behind with Mario because he couldn't come on tour with me as a dancer. Soon after I left Scotland, Mario changed flats to live somewhere different and little Pepíček couldn't cope with this extra change of environment and he died. Perhaps he missed me too much?

Arriving in London, I moved straight into the flat of the choreographer, Mark Baldwin. Mark is now well-known as having been the artistic director of Britain's oldest dance ensemble – Rambert Dance Company – since 2002 (having previously danced with Rambert for a decade) but back then, he was director of his own company – the Mark Baldwin Dance Company – and he was a very successful freelance choreographer. He had made two pieces on me for Scottish Ballet: *A Fond Kiss* (to music by Stravinsky, in the spring of 1996, which I performed in six Scottish and English cities); and, later that same year, *Haydn Pieces*, which was the centrepiece of the company's *Sweet Baroque and Roll* tour, taking in Glasgow, Edinburgh, Norwich, Stirling and Aberdeen.

Mark heard that I was moving to London and he had a huge flat in the Barons Court area in the south-west of the city; he was happy to rent two rooms out to me. Being able to agree this arrangement before I moved to London gave me somewhere to live straightaway and – even better – it was close to ENB headquarters.

Mark is a lovely, sunny guy who has the happy-go-lucky South Seas attitude of a man born in Fiji and raised in New Zealand. He has a wonderful eye as a choreographer, which probably has something to do with having studied Fine Art at University in Auckland. Mark was in great demand, making new choreography all over the world, so he was more often away than at home, meaning that I mostly had his huge flat all to myself. I lived with Mark for a year before I managed to buy my own place.

I have been a saver all my life and I had been putting money aside since my competition prizes as a teenager. When I left Cape Town, I received a large capital sum because I was able to take my pension with me, which helped to boost my savings even further. All of this meant that I had comfortably saved enough for a deposit on a new flat in London.

As soon as I arrived in London – in September 1996 – I went straight to work at ENB and quickly discovered that I had never before had to work so hard. It felt like being in an army camp, with highly-disciplined military routines and constant pressure to do things all the time. I had wanted to come to ENB because I thought Derek would make me work, but I had no idea what that really meant. I soon realised that it required more effort than I could ever have imagined! Derek seemed to be at ENB for every one of every day's 24 hours, and he was invariably strict with everyone. We had to do class *en pointe* and every single exercise or rehearsal had to be finished to his satisfaction. I had never taken class wearing pointe shoes in Prague, Cape Town, at Scottish Ballet or in any of the competitions that I had entered, so it was a whole new experience for me. Now, of course, every ballerina wears pointe shoes for their centre work, and this is good because it makes girls stronger, but it caught me out at first when I joined ENB because it was such a novelty. I had reached 25 without having done it and I had to learn a whole new way of taking class.

Everything was also so much faster than I had been used to in any previous ballet environment. The relentless pace of both our company classes and constantly rehearsing different works, including new choreographies, was at a hugely stressful level of intensity. I had been schooled in a slower Russian style of dancing with a big preparation, and all of a sudden I was dealing with this incredibly fast footwork preceded by small preparations. I was practising ballet technique exactly as I had been taught but then being shouted at by the ballet staff for doing the movements correctly since it did not 'suit' ENB style. It seemed to me that everything was twice as fast as I'd ever danced before and it took me three years to get used to this and to begin to feel that I was fitting in to this company's particular ballet style.

I wasn't the only dancer to suffer in this way. Every one of the dancers trained in a Russian style has had problems fitting in with the speed of ENB. Over the many years that I have danced with the company, I have come to realise that there is a compromise to be achieved and, if you can combine the best of the slow *adagio* style and expressiveness in Russian ballet with the speed and attack of the English way, you can make the best of both worlds. But some other dancers schooled in the Vaganova technique have simply not been able to cope.

One issue I have found with Deane's choreography, in particular, is that everything has to be done with a movement. So, as Odette in *Swan Lake,* for example, the swan princess cannot waste a beat of the music by looking at Siegfried in a way that says 'I love you', as might happen in a Russian choreography. Here in England that look would have to be done with a turn or a step. To be fair to Derek, it wasn't just the English way since Rudolf Nureyev (who was as Russian as they come) choreographed like this, too.

If you didn't finish something then ENB ballet staff would castigate you at full volume. The whole staff had been really well trained by Derek and that meant they got top marks for shouting at dancers. I cried a lot in my first month with the company and I wasn't alone. I was certainly by no means the weakest link.

Another dancer who joined at the same time as me was a guy called Laurentiu Guinea, an experienced prize-winning Romanian dancer who also came as a new principal, alongside Zoltan and me. All three of us were initially only given a contract for six months. I suppose it was like a trial, a sort of probationary period that you might have in any employment – I guess that it was a Derek thing, to keep us on our toes. Unfortunately, Zoltan didn't manage to pass through the six months and he left after the Christmas/New Year season at the London Coliseum.

Laurentiu had a noble stage presence and an impressive jump. He was an excellent dancer who was very capable in both the princely roles and in character mode, as for example Drosselmeyer in *The Nutcracker* or Tybalt in *Romeo and Juliet.* He stayed with the company for three or four seasons but it always seemed that he was never good enough for Derek, who was to destroy his confidence over the short time that he was with ENB. At every rehearsal he would bully him relentlessly, and I saw it all because I was dancing with Laurentiu during this time. He was so destroyed by Derek's treatment of him that he left dancing altogether after his time as a principal with ENB, even though he was still comparatively young at the time. He went back to Spain with his wife Monica Puerta, who had been a soloist with ENB, where they tried to build their own company but unfortunately it didn't work out.

I remember being in a rehearsal with Laurentiu and he was standing there in the middle of the stage and Derek was out in the darkened auditorium, yelling at him through a megaphone. Laurentiu simply had to stand there and take it all on the chin. None of us were immune to this treatment, and Derek was like this with everyone at one time or another, but some dancers took it more than most and it was Laurentiu who received the brunt of Derek's anger on a frequent basis at that time. I suffered a fair bit, too. Derek was always happy to have a go at me – in fact, he had a go at every single person in the company – but it was never as bad or as rough as the treatment that poor Laurentiu received.

Derek had his favourites. He loved Erina Takahashi, for example: a Japanese dancer who came through ENB's school to join the company in 1996 – the same year that I arrived – and was promoted by Derek to principal dancer in 2000. But being a favourite provided no cloak of immunity from Derek. Erina was strong and just took everything that Derek had to dish out and she never went off (a dancer's expression for not performing through some indisposition), and that is why she achieved her breakthrough. To make it out of the *corps de ballet* and be promoted to a principal dancer, you have to be strong. It was unbelievable what she had to go through to achieve her success.

My first ballet with ENB was to be cast as Swanilda in *Coppélia*, dancing alongside Zoltan Solymosi, as Franz, on the opening night. It wasn't new to me since I had danced the role of Swanilda before at Scottish Ballet. *Coppélia* is a very warm-hearted take on a slightly macabre fairytale by E.T.A. Hoffmann, which weaves the romantic escapades of Swanilda and Franz into the story of the ancient doll maker, Dr Coppelius, who dreams of bringing Coppélia, his mechanical doll, to life. I was very happy about opening my ENB career by dancing a role in which I felt very comfortable, and I loved ENB's production by Ronnie Hynd, which was so enjoyable to dance. And, even more exciting was that I was cast to perform with a dancer of Zoltan's reputation as a leading ballet, so I was also nervous about dancing with him.

Zoltan was unhappy with me almost from the start, and our first rehearsal was a bad one. I had never met him before and we had just started to do some *pirouettes* together when he immediately shouted out loudly to anyone who wanted to hear, 'This is just NOT going to work!' He was especially concerned that I was different physically from anyone he had danced with before. I'm certainly not built like Darcey Bussell, who is much, much longer than me. So, there was this great tension between us from the very first day. Having looked forward to partnering Zoltan, I was terribly upset since I always want to dance with someone that I get on with personally; but we already had this unhappy relationship without having had the chance to talk much together, which is the worst of all worlds.

After this initial rehearsal the arguing continued, and it must have become obvious to Derek and his management team that the casting had to be changed. And, of course, as the 'junior' dancer it was me that had to be demoted from the opening night cast. I was placed in the second cast with the Australian dancer Greg Horsman and his intended partner – actually, his wife – Lisa Pavane was promoted to take my place on opening night. As far as I was concerned, I hadn't done anything wrong but because Zoltan had complained about me and he was the star who had come from The Royal Ballet, clearly I was the one who had to be moved. What was worse was that no one even talked to me about it; the swap just appeared on the schedule pinned to the noticeboard. It just happened like that, and it's a good example of dancers merely being pawns at the disposal of the management. In those days, I was a shy, quiet girl and I didn't complain about it, even though I was very upset by what had happened. At that stage in my career, it was a big thing to be asked to do an opening night in London, so it was a huge blow to me. But I just accepted the complaint and the consequent decision, and Zoltan and I never spoke of it again.

Zoltan was a lovely dancer but he was very temperamental and I was to discover that things weren't right with him. He only remained at ENB for a few months, until the December of that first season. After the *Coppélia* debacle I was perversely cast with him again, almost immediately, to dance in both *Alice in Wonderland* and as the Sugar Plum Fairy in *The Nutcracker*, but this time he didn't make a murmur about dancing with me. There were a few tensions in the rehearsal room but nothing out of the ordinary, and he was not particularly rude. By this time, I had got to know more about him as we were touring together in the same company, although Zoltan wasn't an easy person to become friendly with. He was so aloof that he would often not even acknowledge me if I passed him in the canteen. I knew from talking to other dancers that I was not alone in suffering this icy treatment.

We danced together in both *Alice* and *The Nutcracker* during the autumn tour around England before the December season in London, where Lisa Pavane and Greg Horsman did the opening night. I danced in that opening performance but in the supporting soloist's role as an Ice Queen. But I was cast to be the Sugar Plum Fairy on the second night. During the tour, I realised that Zoltan was slowly getting more difficult. I wasn't sure what was wrong with him but he would have sudden outbursts of temper that were sometimes uncontrollable. Thankfully, I didn't suffer that many problems with him, although he would have some moments of irritation with me (but most dancers do!). He even took me out to a jazz bar once and we had a good time, but on the stage and in the studio it was not always so smooth.

I danced as his partner in Zoltan's last show at ENB and he was even losing it during the performance. We were supposed to run to each other across the stage for him to lift me, but instead of running towards me, Zoltan cowered in the corner. It was obvious that he had simply forgotten what he had to do and he was just staring at us. After that he left ENB and, following a brief spell with the London City Ballet, he returned to Hungary. I haven't seen Zoltan much since he left ENB but I am very close friends with his brother, Tamás, who has worked with me many times on my Ballet Masterclasses in Prague.

I remember that during my early period with ENB, Ivan Liška, another Czech compatriot and fellow alumni of the Prague Conservatoire, came to London to see me. Ivan had recently become ballet director of Bayerisches Staatsballett in Munich, and I knew that he was keen to offer me a contract to become a principal dancer with his new company. I had been to Munich – while I was still dancing with Scottish Ballet – to have a look at the company and the city. I took class with them and Ivan was keen to have me join them. But I chose London instead because I thought that it was the centre of everything and I just wanted to be a part of this exciting cultural world. Nevertheless, Ivan remained keen and he came to watch me rehearse in London still intent on changing my mind.

We were doing Harald Lander's *Études* and, of course, Derek knew that Ivan was the ballet director in Munich and he must have known – or, at least, suspected – that something lay behind Ivan's request to watch me in the studio. Derek was his usual self in the rehearsal in front of Ivan. I will never forget that horrible experience. Derek was criticising me from the beginning of the rehearsal until the moment that it ended. It wasn't just about correction – all dancers are used to having their technique or movement corrected by ballet staff (in fact, like most dancers, I worry when I don't get corrections) – it was just very harsh and typically blunt. Derek would stop for a second and start shouting at somebody else and, once his attention had moved on from me, I would go and do a few steps on my own or just fetch a cardigan or something but he would immediately turn back to me and start shouting again, saying, 'Don't walk away when I'm talking to you.' It was awful.

When the rehearsal finished, Ivan Liška came up to me and, before I had a chance to speak or apologise, he said, 'Don't worry I know what Derek is like.' I suppose everyone in the ballet world knew what Derek was like. As a former principal dancer at The Royal Ballet, he knew what it took to make every one of his dancers work hard. In particular, Derek knew all about the tricks that dancers can play to avoid doing something – like going to get a cardigan – and he made sure that he stopped them. In a funny kind of a way, even though I suffered at his hands a lot, I could respect and appreciate what motivated him to remain on top of dancers, even if it led to excessive measures.

I learned a lot from Derek. Most of all, I learned how to work hard. Before Derek, I honestly didn't know what it meant to work hard. I always thought I was putting in the effort but now I know that I was just kidding myself. I was very slow and I would always go and stand in the corner until it was my turn to do something in class. But, with Derek there was definitely no slouching about in corners, waiting your turn. I learned from him that you have to be making use of every moment, whether it is in class or in the studio.

Without the aggressive side of Derek, perhaps I wouldn't have achieved so much over the past decade. But, I will never forget that every single day I worked with him, I went to the studios with a lump in my stomach. For the first few months, I kept asking myself what I was doing there and why was I putting myself through all these horrors. But I am a strong person, who is stoical about such things. I don't give up easily on anything, so I persevered and kept on working – often in secret and by myself – to make myself a better ballerina.

For me, working hard meant finishing every class, which I had certainly never really done before. Normally, if I got tired I would stop when the main elements of the class were over. At ENB this was unheard of in those days. There was no stopping until the ballet masters said that the class was finished.

Also, the repertoire was harder and there was more of it. In the first few months, we were performing *Coppélia* and a triple bill on tour throughout the UK, with a typical week usually consisting of the triple for the first three days and then switching to *Coppélia* for the last four days. In none of my other companies had we danced anything like as many performances. In the next batch of performances I was cast to perform the title role in the final act of *Paquita*, in *Études* and *Alice in Wonderland*, as well as continuing with Swanilda in *Coppélia*. And so, in one week at ENB, I could be dancing three or four main roles compared to dancing a principal role perhaps just once a week in any of my three previous companies. Also, of course, I was learning a lot of new repertoire for the first time. It was a very complex set of new experiences for me.

In my first season, I didn't have any friends, just the people I worked with and Mark Baldwin, whose flat I was sharing when in London, but Mark was away most of the time, travelling as an itinerant choreographer around the globe. So, for the first few months it was just work and then home, and almost nothing in between. Then we went on tour in the autumn and this is where I met the man who was eventually to become my husband.

The company's first stop was performing *Coppélia* in Liverpool and one of the stage technicians kept pestering me in breaks between rehearsals. Although I was polite, I wasn't interested in him but it didn't stop his attentions. I discovered later that he was notorious within the company for bothering every new girl, but I didn't know that at the time. My husband-to-be saw this going on and he came over to save me. Basically, he manoeuvred the other guy out of the way and said, 'Hi, I'm Muppet,' after which I was left alone by the nuisance man.

'Muppet' is Ian's nickname. He has been known as Muppet (or 'Mup') since long before I first met him. He didn't really want to bother me but he had come over on purpose to save me from the unwanted attentions of that pesky technician! Muppet is the man who sits behind the lighting desk, making sure that the dancers are correctly lit when we are on stage. Because we don't see the technicians in London – they work at the theatres and we take class and rehearse in the studio – I hadn't previously met him. ENB dancers only get to meet the stage team members when we go on tour. When he walked away after that brief first meeting, I realised that Muppet had deliberately intervened to save me from the attentions of the other guy.

After his little bit of gallantry, I would see Muppet regularly thereafter, both around the theatres and at the stage door, and there was always a little secret frisson between us because of that initial incident. I managed to blurt out, 'Thank you for saving me,' on the next occasion when we spoke and after that we started to talk and slowly got to know each other.

Those first few months in London were marked by the dreadful tragedy of my dear father passing away. He was only 53 when he died on 4 October 1996. I had come home from ENB's studios to Mark's flat in Barons Court, when I received a horrible phone call that I shall never forget. My father would always call me once a week, every week when I was in Scotland. After I moved to London, however, Dad was in hospital in Prague and I would call his hospital, but I would have to wait so long to get through to him. Obviously, in those days we didn't

Above left: As a young child I was placid and serious, but my brother, Radomír, was the complete opposite.

Above right: My dad was always my biggest fan.

Below: My parent's nickname for me was Darinka. Here we are on holiday in Bulgaria in 1977.

Photos © Daria Klimentová

Above left: At the age of five, my school was assessed for potential gymnasts and I was selected to train. At that age, I had no idea that I had any talent for gymnastics.

Above right: After a year, I was sent for training with the Czechoslovakian gymnastics team.

Below left: I never wanted to be a ballerina but when I was ten I switched 'career'. I was happy to change so long as I could swish my legs up high!

Below right: I didn't enjoy the first two years of ballet school, but eventually we started to learn extracts from the classical repertoire, and I began to love dancing much more.

Photos © Daria Klimentová

Above: A picture taken during the Prix de Lausanne international dance competition. I was just 18 years old.

Below: From a young age, I was being trained to dance principal roles. Playing the part of Aurora in *The Sleeping Beauty* – my first big principal role and a ballet I have danced many times since.

Photos © Daria Klimentová

Dancing *The Lady of the Camellias* with Stanislav Fečo.
© *Daria Klimentová*

In the spring of 1992, I decided to accept an offer to dance with the CAPAB Ballet Company in South Africa.

Left: It wasn't all about dancing. Riding an ostrich in Cape Town!

Below: Although life was relaxed in Cape Town, I had to work much harder in the studio and on stage. Me dancing in *Raymonda*.

Photos © Daria Klimentová

Preparing to perform Odette in *Swan Lake*.   © Daria Klimentová

A lot of hard work and dedication goes on behind the scenes of a ballet performance, but there is plenty of fun in the studio, too.

Above left: With David Wall after rehearsing at ENB's studio.

Above right: Rehearsing with Friedemann Vogel.

Below: I like to pass on my knowledge to other dancers, so I set up 'International Ballet Masterclasses' in Prague for future ballet dancers. Coaching a class with Tamás Solymosi.

Photos © Daria Klimentová

There are plenty of rewards for performing professionally as a ballerina.

Above left: Accepting a bouquet of flowers from Vlastimil Harapes.
© *Petr Naš*

Above right: With Graham Watts at The Golden Film Festival's Tribute to Daria, October 2012.
© *Veronika Hráčkov*

Below left: In Taiwan with Martin Kubala filming the first full-length documentary about me!
© *Daria Klimentov*

Below right: Being presented with the Critics' Circle Patron's Award for Lifetime Achievement.
© *Dave Morga*

have mobile phones. A heavy smoker all of his life, I knew that my father had lung cancer and I imagine that, as his health deteriorated, Dad couldn't get close enough to the phone to speak with me. In his last weeks, I could hear how terrible his breathing was. It felt horrible being in London and knowing that my dad was ill in hospital so many hundreds of miles away.

My father had been ill for a year but at first we had hope. I had been at home during August before starting my first season with ENB. My dad was not in hospital at that time, but when I left my parents' apartment in Horní Počernice to return to London, my dad – who had been too ill to get out of his chair throughout my visit – struggled to the window to wave goodbye. It was as if he knew that this would be the last occasion that he would see me. And, unfortunately, he was right.

Dad had come through the chemotherapy and although he lost all his hair, it seemed to make an improvement. My mum said that he would never ever complain. He became ill again in late September, soon after I had moved down to London, and his surgeons decided to operate to remove the tumour. But, when they opened Dad up to see inside, they realised that the cancer had spread and it was just not possible to take it all away and so they just sewed his chest back up without removing anything. The worst of it was that they didn't tell him. So, he felt so much better after this operation because psychologically, he thought that he had been cured because they had taken the cancer away. He really thought that he would get better – it is incredible what the mind can do. But, obviously, the reality was that he was getting worse and worse, until one day I received that tragic phone call.

I had only been in London for a little while and I remember hearing Mum's words and just holding the phone, feeling like I was screaming out loud, but I was so quiet and the scream was all inside of me. It was a terrible shock. Thankfully, this was one night when Mark was at home, and as soon as he saw the terrible state that I was in, he opened a bottle of vodka and we got very drunk together. I don't really drink, but that was that and, with Mark's help, I drank myself into a sad stupor.

At the time I was rehearsing *Études* with Ros Whitten and she was well trained by Derek. I was very tired and slow from being so drunk the night before and when I arrived at the studio I didn't feel like telling anyone that my father had died. Ros yelled at me in the rehearsal and I walked away, crying. She came after me and asked what was wrong; only then did I tell her what had happened. I felt like she didn't really understand what I was going through when I told her that my father had passed away in another country, the day before.

I didn't go back to Prague and, of course, as had now become the tradition in our family – resulting from my phobia since grandfather František's death – there was no funeral service for Dad. Mum wanted to have something for other people but in the end even she decided that it would be too upsetting, so there was just a very simple cremation. She picked up Dad's ashes from the crematorium, which she took back to her apartment to sit on her bedroom shelf in an urn. We have a family plot in a cemetery in Horní Počernice where his ashes were eventually scattered, a long time later.

Some people say that a funeral service helps to be able to say goodbye but it doesn't work for me at all. I would have gone back for his funeral if that was what my father had wanted but he didn't want it and none of my close family, not even my mum, wanted a funeral service just so that we could say goodbye to his ashes. I didn't go back to the Czech Republic for nearly a year after Dad died, which is my longest absence ever from my homeland.

Understandably, my mum was very upset about Dad's death and now, looking back, I know how selfish I must have seemed to her at the time. She was expecting more support from her only daughter at such a sad time and I just didn't give it to her. Because there was no funeral to attend, I was able to use that as an excuse to stay in London. On the other hand, I was in a new city, beginning a new life in a new company, rehearsing new ballets and feeling overwhelmed by the intense pressure from Derek, Ros and the other coaches at ENB.

Every season someone seemed to be sacked and at the time I was terrified that I might be in the next batch to go. And so I resisted any sign of weakness by running home, even though it was where I wanted to be. I already had a problem with accepting death and I had kept to my mantra of never going to funerals, so I feel that subconsciously I created a web of excuses to miss all the formalities that would follow my own father's death. If the truth be told, I was frightened to go home and find the place without him. Work became a convenient excuse not to go back and help.

Mum got very angry with me and I know that it was, of course, much harder for her at that time. She had lived through my father's illness and looked after him. They had gone through so many difficulties and lived apart for so long while he was working in Libya, and his illness came at a point where my mum and dad were just beginning to live happily and be comfortable together. Mum was to tell me that it was the best time of their marriage, but then one year later my dad got ill and was taken from her. It was awful that I didn't really support her more but you learn as you get older, and if I could have this time again I would not have been so selfish. But you can never go back and you make decisions at the time according to how you feel then. You can never have the benefit of hindsight. I would like to feel that a more mature Daria – perhaps, especially now that I am a mother myself – may have behaved differently.

After a while, I managed to persuade my mum to come to London and spend a week with me in Mark's apartment, which I hoped would help to rebuild our relationship again. Unfortunately, this week turned out to be a ridiculously busy time for me as Ros wanted me to stay and do more work every night, so poor Mum, who spoke no English at that time, was stuck in a strange apartment waiting for me to finish. It didn't work out and I think that she was very happy to go back after the week was up. After that, because I didn't return to Prague for almost a year, things remained a little strained between us.

Because of Dad's death and the temporary alienation with Mum, I guess that I became more attached to Muppet. He became my rock. We were 'just good friends', as they say, but he was there for me and that was very important, particularly since I didn't really have any other friends in London, especially when Mark was away.

Although Derek was undoubtedly extremely demanding, if you won him round – as I believe that I did in that first year – he would definitely come to respect you. This was the strong side of Derek as a director. If he trusted you, it meant that he would give you the opening night performances. Derek was not the kind of artistic director who would suddenly pluck a girl from the *corps de ballet*, as so often happens nowadays, to do the main roles or even to star in an opening night. He always looked after his dancers. There would be flowers for the leading girls and champagne for the guys after every performance, and he would arrange taxis home (which is certainly not usual these days, where dancers are just left to their own devices to wander down to the Tube in their exhausted state). If you worked hard, Derek would reward you. He had structure and discipline in his company and I admire him for that, even though dancers often struggled with the robustness of the discipline.

I even went to Derek once and asked for a pay rise and he said immediately, without a flinch, 'Yes, of course you deserve it,' and he actually gave me a big increase. So there were many good things about

Derek. He kept faith with the people he respected, but boy did you have to earn that respect!

After seven years dancing in Prague, Cape Town and Scotland, moving to ENB had been a real wake-up call for me. Looking back at that time, I expressed my feelings to Czech journalist Martina Kubáňiová in an interview in 2004, telling her, 'I had more competition and harder work in London. I really had to pull my socks up, which was difficult because I was used to having things my own way. Everything was me, me, me. It was so simple: there was no one better than I. Then I came to London and, all of a sudden, there were equally good, if not better, dancers than myself.'

At the end of my first year at ENB, I had lost my father and damaged my relationship with my mother over an unwillingness to help her come to terms with this loss. I was struggling with the speed and other differences in learning to dance in ENB style, and also having to learn a whole new repertoire not to mention dealing with the competition of other equally good, if not better, dancers within a regime of much harder work. I had certainly felt the tough love of Derek and his team of acolytes running the company. It had been hard but I had survived it. I was still fighting and I had met my Muppet. The much-needed escape from my life being all about ballet was just around the corner.

Chapter 8

Muppet and Motherhood

Muppet was not a dancer but he understands the artistic temperament well because he has always had to work around it, having had so many key roles behind the scenes in the theatre world for many years. He has produced shows and was a lighting and stage designer and technician. For a while he also had his own company that made and constructed theatrical scenery.

Being 14 years older than me meant that Muppet had been around the company for longer. He knew all the people and he could advise me about what to do and what to avoid. He is very interested in dance and knows exactly what I mean when I tell him about the problems of being Aurora, or my difficulties in performing the fiendishly difficult 32 *fouettés en tournant* in *Swan Lake*, but he was just enough removed from the studio to meet my needs of getting away from dance when I closed the door to our flat. The fact that Muppet wasn't a dancer was very important to me. I have never met a dancer that I felt I could live with in that sense – I just needed someone who could listen to me but who did not have the same problems as another dancer would have. He gave me just the balance that I needed.

I have never called my husband by his first name, which is Ian. He has always been Muppet from the first day that we met. He thinks that Ian is just the worst name in the world, without substance; he feels that it comes out as 'een' when someone refers to him by his given name. Naturally, the nickname comes from Jim Henson's *The Muppet Show*, the apparent reason being that when he was much younger, Ian apparently looked like one of the puppet drummers, particularly since he used to have very long hair. When I met him, he was known as Muppet only in the theatre – his family still called him Ian – but obviously because I met him in that world, the name stuck with me as well.

In fact, because everyone in the theatre called him Muppet and his nickname appeared to be 'Mup', which I heard people calling him all the time, I just assumed that it was actually his name. I wasn't familiar with *The Muppet Show* and, although it wasn't a name I had heard before, I'm from Prague and I was used to hearing lots of strange names in London. So it seemed perfectly reasonable for me to believe that it was a real old English name. I don't remember how I realised that Muppet was not Ian's real name, but it was a long time after we had started dating! At least it was before we got married because I would have had a huge shock being asked to take Ian in lawful matrimony, when I was expecting to marry a Muppet!

After Muppet intervened to save me from the pesky technician on the eve of my first performance as Swanilda, we carried on seeing each other every day around the theatre in Liverpool and we would say 'hi' to each other. I really didn't know many people in the company at that time, so I was a bit of a loner. A few weeks later, when ENB had moved to perform in Southampton, he asked me out to dinner after a show.

It was very nearly our first and last date because I had never seen him smoking before, and after dinner Muppet lit up a cigarette. Cigarettes have been a bad odour throughout my life. My father had only just died from lung cancer caused by smoking cigarettes all his adult life, and I grew up in a house where I was the only non-smoker in a smoking family. Even though I was performing in a profession where many dancers smoke, especially to suppress their appetite, I hated smoke, so I'm sure that I made Muppet aware of my hatred of cigarettes as soon as he lit up on our first date. So, it was the first and the last time that I have ever seen him smoke! I know that he didn't stop smoking but, because of my comments at that dinner, he never again smoked in front of me and he has never smoked at home, even in secret. I never even saw him pop out into the garden at parties – he just never smoked cigarettes when I was around. Eventually, he gave up altogether.

Muppet was the only person who was consistently friendly with me at this vulnerable time in my life. I was in a new city and my father had just died, still only in his early 50s, back in my homeland. My relationship with my mother had deteriorated because of my selfishness in not going home to help her, following Dad's death. I had a new job in a new company and the star dancer, who was supposed to have danced with me, had refused to do so. I suppose it would be a straightforward case study for a psychiatrist to understand why I became comfortable in my attraction to a man who was 14 years my elder.

I particularly liked that Muppet was very caring: he always listened intently to my problems and was forever willing to have a cup of coffee with me, whenever I needed advice or a shoulder to cry on. In my experience, guys seemed rarely willing to listen and they usually wanted something more straightaway. Muppet was different: kind, caring and attentive. He seemed to be in it for the long haul, and I had certainly not met anyone like that before.

However, his smoking habit was not the only thing about Muppet that I had to change before considering him as a partner. He used to wear a long black coat all the time and always with the same uniform of a t-shirt and jeans. I mean, he never seemed to take that coat off. I called it his 'charity shop special' – it was so unfashionable. That had to go!

He also had a very old Jaguar with damaged seats, which I didn't like much either. Approaching his 40s, he was understandably set in his ways, but he knew a lot about art and culture and also about ballet because he had worked in that environment for 25 years before he met me. I also found out that he knew all about the idiosyncrasies of ballerinas since Muppet had dated a few others before me! This was important because it meant that he knew how to deal with ballet dancers since we are not normal people. If a ballerina dates a man who knows nothing about what we do then it can be a huge problem, not just in understanding our foibles about eating, resting and superstitions about performance, but also in terms of seeing a dancer as Juliet, falling in love with another Romeo on stage. Many men can't come to terms with that and become ridiculously jealous, but Muppet had been around dance and dancers for long enough to understand the distinction between our stage and real-life personas. Also, for a long time he preferred to talk and to listen than to rush me into a physical relation, and I admired him for that sensitivity. I always knew that I could change the coat and the car!

When I met him, Muppet lived on a houseboat in Twickenham, which was a home that went well with the battered Jaguar and the ubiquitous coat, and I wasn't at all keen on this living arrangement. It was far too small and cramped for me. Even though we stayed just good friends for a few months, eventually we started to spend more time together and our relationship arrived at a more serious level. I wasn't happy about sleeping on the houseboat, so we needed to consider our future living arrangements. And, of course, the houseboat went the same way as the coat and the car. In any event, towards the end of my first season with the company, I bought my one-bedroom flat in Chiswick, so we had somewhere more convenient (and spacious) to stay! Muppet helped me to make it even more comfortable by bringing his expertise in constructing theatre sets to the practical use of converting an extra bedroom from the attic space.

He also reinvigorated my love for photography that had been sparked in secret as a ten-year-old girl borrowing her father's camera, and it was Muppet who bought me my first camera when we were dating. It was nothing spectacular, just a little digital camera, but I took it into work and was soon clicking away, taking photographs of colleagues dancing and rehearsing. So, Muppet would then buy me a better camera for the following Christmas and then he would add to my photographic collection each time that I was due a present, giving me a better lens or a printer so that I could start to print my own photographs. Eventually, Muppet bought me a Nikon D7000 – which is the camera that I use now – and he has gradually added to my army of lenses and other equipment. So, converting my fascination with photography into practical application owes a lot to Muppet, who recognised the latent interest that I had always kept under wraps since my childhood.

Muppet and I dated for three years before we made the decision to get married. I have always been cautious, and I would never have married anyone without having had this proper period of courtship. I believe the old Czech saying that in the first year of being in love, the romance obscures the partners from being able to see the real person that they are with. I think that you have to get past this state of having rose-tinted spectacles to see the reality of being married to this person for the rest of your life. So, I gave it three years, although to be honest even then I wasn't really expecting to get married, but Muppet had been my rock over a very difficult time and it was important to him to be settled, given that he was now into his 40s.

It wasn't a romantic proposal, and he certainly didn't get down on one knee. (I'm still waiting for that!). We just discussed it in a matter-of-fact way. I still wasn't sure, so I asked my mum for advice. She said that if I didn't marry Muppet perhaps I would lose him and I would then never get him back; but if I married him and it didn't work out then I could always get divorced. I had always been very open with my parents, especially Mum, about boyfriends and would be quick to introduce them. I think that my mum liked that – she preferred to know who her daughter was seeing. However, neither of my parents would ever really say anything about boyfriends, and they never pushed me towards or away from any of them. I think that my mum could see that Muppet was a good influence on me; she never said anything about our age difference (which might have bothered some mothers) and she could see that we were very comfortable together. These were not exactly the most romantic reasons for getting married but my mum, like me, is forever the pragmatist.

We didn't actually get engaged. There was nothing remotely formal about the whole affair. At that time, it was not usual for couples to get engaged in the Czech Republic in the formal sense of announcements and engagement rings, etc. So, although the lack of any formal engagement was just how we were, unwittingly we were following Czech tradition by not getting engaged.

We got married on 23 June 1999, which happened to also be my 28th birthday. I have to say that I deliberately chose my birthday as a good day for my wedding because it would be easier to remember the anniversary, although – like so many people – neither of us seem to have the time to celebrate wedding anniversaries anymore.

For anyone hoping to hear about a fairytale white wedding that would grace a ballet narrative, I'm afraid to say that it was more functional than memorable. We were married in Acton Town Registry Office, which was basically an office that couldn't have been any less romantic, but we didn't want a big event and I wasn't into the idea of a white wedding with all the trimmings. It just didn't suit either of us. We didn't even have a honeymoon because I was dancing in *Swan Lake* at the Royal Albert Hall and I just took the day off to get married. We invited just my mum and Muppet's mum, sister and brother-in-law (his father had also died by this time). The legacy of always fighting had created a situation where my brother, Radomír, and I were not at all close, so he wasn't invited.

I was given away by David Wall, with whom I had built up such a great level of trust as my ballet coach over the previous three years. The witness for me was one of my best friends from the Czech Republic, a well-known painter named Jan Kunovský, whom I met in my first year at the Czech National Ballet, when he came to paint the dancers. Since that time he has used me as a model in some of his most famous works. Muppet's best man was his friend, Paul. It may seem surprising but, with the single exception of David, no one from English National Ballet was invited to attend. I certainly wasn't going to invite Derek Deane since I just couldn't stand his bullying attitude.

We had a small party in Covent Garden after the wedding and everyone got very drunk. Jan was staying the night in our flat – as were several others, including my mum – and, unfortunately, he threw up in the taxi taking us all home! So, my wedding night was spent with a whole bunch of people all feeling ill, including Muppet. Although since Muppet doesn't drink alcohol, I can only assume that his sickness was caused by the stress of getting married to me!

There was never any thought of changing my name after I got married. Professionally, I had always been Daria Klimentová, and Muppet and I agreed that this had to continue, the idea of becoming Mrs Comer just never got off the ground. I have never even had a bank account or any papers in my married name – I like to feel independent and I was very happy to keep everything in my Czech name. I don't like to feel that I have become Mrs anyone.

I was always keen to have a child in my 20s and I suppose this had a lot to do with the decision to get married at the age of 28. Muppet was 42 when we married, so the idea of fatherhood so soon after marriage was fine with him, and my planning was fortuitous because I fell pregnant as soon as we started trying for a baby. I knew that I was pregnant before any test told me so. Suddenly I had a really strong irrational hunger, and I had to go and buy a whole pizza to eat all for myself! Any ballerina will know how unusual that is.

It was exactly what I wanted. Muppet left the timing up to me because I'm a dancer, and I had to somehow fit being pregnant and giving birth into my career. I thought that I had arranged it so that I was pregnant at exactly the right time. The season approaching did not contain a particularly exciting repertoire for me, so I decided that it was a good time to be on maternity leave and have a baby, since I didn't feel that I was going to be missing anything.

However, my great planning was to find a sting in the tail. On the very morning that I discovered that I was pregnant, I went to ENB and as soon as I arrived I was asked to go to Derek's office for a meeting. He told me that he was producing his own version of *The Sleeping Beauty* to be performed 'in the round' at the Royal Albert Hall in the summer and he wanted me to be the first cast Aurora. So, within two hours of discovering that I was pregnant, I was given the opportunity that every ballerina dreams of: having a major classical role being made on me by the choreographer. I hadn't yet been to see my doctor – all I had done was take a home pregnancy test – so I didn't say anything to Derek at that meeting, just in case. When he told me that he had chosen me to be his Aurora, I just nodded my head and said, 'That's wonderful,' while simultaneously thinking, 'Oh, no!'

One week later, my pregnancy was confirmed by the doctor, so I then had to go and tell Derek. His first reaction amazed me. I was happily married and approaching 30, and yet he asked me immediately, 'Are you going to keep it?' I suppose that I shouldn't have been so shocked. Derek had given his life to ballet. To him, this child was an inconvenience and he showed it. I did not feel any sentiment, caring or understanding; he was just irritated that I wouldn't be available to dance as Aurora in his new production. Funnily enough, his reaction didn't upset me, it just shocked me. But, from the moment that I had eaten that huge pizza, I was absolutely 100 per cent certain that this baby was now the most important thing in my life and, even though this new production was going to be choreographed on me, I also knew that I didn't need to be performing another round of *The Sleeping Beauty*. I wanted to have a baby, and I was so happy that it didn't bother me in the slightest that I was to miss out on being Derek's first-cast Aurora.

When I had been in the company in Prague, it left an indelible impact on me that I could see all these older ballerinas who had pursued their careers above all else but left it too late to have children. I had seen so many instances of dancers in their 40s trying to get pregnant for the first time but being unable to conceive. I was determined that this wasn't going to be my fate; I couldn't have lived without a child just for the sake of ballet, and it seemed to me that these other dancers had left it too late to start trying.

My simple logic was to start trying for a baby around the age of 29/30 and at least that would give me much longer to conceive; and then I could try for another baby perhaps when I stopped dancing. As it happened, Muppet and I struck lucky at the very first attempt. I wanted a baby before I was 30. Actually, I wanted my baby to be born in the year 2000 (as with my wedding anniversary, I thought it would always help me remember the child's age!). As it happened, I got married at 28, gave birth at 29, and my baby was born in November 2000. So, I achieved all my objectives. Everything just slotted into place. For someone who was never any good at mathematics, despite Mr Horvorka's best efforts, it will be immensely helpful that my daughter will always be the same age as the year, although she has to wait until the year is almost over before she catches up!

When I told Derek Deane that I was pregnant, I tried to argue initially that I could still dance as Aurora in the summer, even though I would be four to five months pregnant at the time. I had never been pregnant before, and I had no idea about what I would or wouldn't be capable of. Derek, of course, was having none of it and he immediately changed his plans for casting *The Sleeping Beauty*, and I was given the role of the Lilac Fairy but not in the first cast. You knew that when you said no to Derek Deane you would have to pay for it. I didn't mind because it was a lot less pressure and, although I didn't show too much as a pregnant Lilac Fairy, it was bliss not to have to perform in front of all the critics on the opening night. I certainly had to have a bigger costume made to cover my little bump and bigger boobs, which was certainly a bonus of being pregnant since I had never really had breasts before!

I managed to get through the performances as the Lilac Fairy without too many problems. Flexibility was fine, although there was one lift that had to be changed, where my partner was supposed to hoist me up and hold my stomach with his palms pressed into my abdomen, because it was too painful and may have harmed the baby. So, we arranged for the lift to be done in a different and less risky way, which was fine. The worst aspect of dancing while pregnant was learning to breathe differently.

Although these performances of the Lilac Fairy at the Royal Albert

Hall in the summer of 2000 were my last before giving birth, I carried on taking class every single day. My only concession was that in the last few weeks I stopped the jumping exercises, but I did *barre* and centre work all the way through until the last day before giving birth. When the autumn season began and the company went on tour, I carried on going into ENB headquarters in Jay Mews to take class on my own.

Being pregnant was not a great time for me since I felt nauseous 24/7 but I was not ever physically sick, so I guess that I didn't really have what people describe as morning sickness. However, I had a very peculiar experience about five months into my pregnancy, just after I had finished the performances as the Lilac Fairy, when I felt a sort of reverse claustrophobia: I just wanted to get the baby out of me. The whole pregnancy seemed to be suffocating me, and I was experiencing a very strange kind of panic attack about having this living thing inside of me, but, thankfully, even though it scared me a lot, it was a strange feeling that subsided as quickly as it had come.

Believe it or not, the main problem during my pregnancy was that I became too skinny. I had a bump in my tummy where the baby was and I had bigger boobs, for sure, but the rest of me was thin. Even though I ate a great deal more than I had done before I was pregnant, I stopped eating meat altogether and ate only salads. In particular, I craved tomatoes and anything that contained tomatoes and the doctors decided that I was anaemic so they prescribed special vitamins and iron because they interpreted this craving as indicating a particular vitamin deficiency.

Food has always been an issue in my life. In June 2012, I was interviewed by a journalist for a feature about my diet in the *Sunday Telegraph*. It was an annoying interview and a capsule example of what we ballerinas have to put up with. The journalist just kept repeating the same questions over and over again, and I'm sure that this was all designed to get me to admit to having an eating disorder, or to own up to a ridiculous faddy diet or something similar. I became more and more exasperated with the journalist and, eventually, I had to end the interview.

If you are a dancer and look like I do, many people think that you must be anorexic, even other dancers who should know better. It drives me mad. You tell everyone that you are fine and eat normally and naturally, but they just don't believe it and assume the worst must be true. There is also the jealousy of other dancers, who perhaps think that they want to be smaller and envy those dancers – like me – who are naturally thin. I eat what I want, whenever I want, and yes, it is probably not a lot compared to most people, but I'm certainly not anorexic. I am lucky to be blessed with a natural metabolism. I'm always with dancers who are often craving chocolate or doughnuts or something sweet, but I just don't desire those things and never have done.

My mum said that when I was little she always had a problem feeding me and some neighbours would say that she didn't feed me enough, like some stupid prying people do, but it wasn't my mum's fault: it was just me. I am an unusual ballerina in that I have suffered from being too thin, without it having been forced.

Halfway through my pregnancy we moved from my apartment to a family house, located in the very same road in Chiswick. I managed to swim on most days throughout my pregnancy but all of this was very hard since I felt tired the whole time and I just wanted to sleep. I would have loved to have been back in Grandma Ludmila's garden in Horni Počernice without a care in the world.

In 2000, towards the end of my pregnancy, Muppet took the decision to produce his own show. Working in partnership with the choreographer Christopher Hampson, they developed *A Christmas Carol*. Hampson (known to everyone as 'Hampy') had been a soloist with English National Ballet and had become an extremely successful choreographer in demand all over the world, from the USA to New Zealand. He choreographed *A Christmas Carol* and Muppet adapted the libretto from the Dickens' novel.

They created their own company in association with the entrepreneurial promoter Raymond Gubbay. They hired dancers and arranged for the show to be the 2000/01 Christmas/New Year production at the Royal Festival Hall. This was all happening at the end of my pregnancy. To tell the truth, at the time I was quite upset with Muppet because I wanted all the attention and he was working every hour on the new show. I suppose one could say that Muppet arranged both of his big new productions for the same time!

The other thing that happened in the last weeks of my pregnancy was that I tore the meniscus (cartilage tissue) in my right knee. The irony of this was that I had torn the meniscus in my left knee about a year before, through dancing, but it had healed and I had managed to get through the season up to and including the summer Royal Albert Hall performances of *The Sleeping Beauty* without missing any shows. I went to see the doctor and I was told that I needed an operation to fix the knee, but because I was pregnant it would have to wait. So we left it for the remaining four months of my pregnancy, by which time it had partially healed itself and was manageable by the time I went back to ballet. However, three years later I did have to have an operation to fix the left knee.

Having soldiered on through this problem, I then tore the meniscus in my right knee during the last few weeks of my pregnancy. I was working on some photographs on my computer at home and I knelt down, fully pregnant, to get some paper out of the printer and boom, the meniscus went as I stood up awkwardly. I should have known what I had done as soon as the terrible pain shot through my right knee, but I didn't. As a dancer you are used to living with pain, and I suppose I thought that it would somehow get better, or that it would just wear off.

That night I was supposed to be going to the Royal Opera House to see The Kirov Ballet perform *Romeo and Juliet* and I limped there. But at the end of Act I, I couldn't get up from my seat. The Russian ballet pedagogue, Michael ('Misha') Messerer – a cousin of the famous ballerina Maya Plisetskaya – was sitting near to me. Misha knew me well since he had taught me in the past. He saw that I was in pain and came over to me in the interval, and when he realised that I couldn't move or put any weight on my knee, he just said, 'You have to go to hospital.' Then, quite by chance, I saw Jackie Pelly, the physiotherapist from ENB, in the auditorium and she told me immediately that the meniscus was broken and arranged for me to get home. However, because I was in the later stages of pregnancy, I couldn't have an operation on either knee so I had to stay in bed for quite a lot of the time in those last few weeks, although I still limped along to ENB to take as much of a class as I could every morning.

Two days before my baby was born I had a strange exhilarating feeling of being very energetic. I came to do a class and felt exceptionally good, even though I was getting near to the full term of my pregnancy. I was at the *barre* and surprising myself about how high I was kicking my legs up! Later on, I was told that this sudden feeling of exhilaration and burst of energy is typical just before a woman gives birth. When I got home after the class, I started to clean the whole house! Later in the evening my waters broke and I didn't know what was happening. No one was home so I phoned Muppet, who was working on *A Christmas Carol* – the formal rehearsals were due to start the very next day – and he came and took me into the Queen Charlotte Hospital in Hammersmith (a building that, sad to say, doesn't exist anymore).

My labour lasted for 36 hours, during which time I didn't sleep at all.

At first I was scared, and then later the pain took over. Initially, the pain was worse because ballet dancers are generally advised not to have an epidural injection in their spine, since it can affect the way that they dance later in their careers. In particular, it can affect the height of their *arabesque*. I went into hospital with this advice in my head but, as soon as the labour pains intensified, I quickly opted for the injection – I think I screamed out something like, 'I WANT IT NOW AND I WANT IT QUICKLY!' To be honest, I don't know how women ever managed to give birth without it. I'm a dancer and dancers get used to dealing with pain throughout their careers – I had been dealing with torn menisci in both knees in the final weeks of my confinement – but nothing really prepares you for the indescribable pain of giving birth. I can remember everyone (even Muppet) screaming at me to push but, because of the epidural, I felt fantastic. I couldn't feel the muscles, and I didn't know whether I was pushing or not.

Eventually the birth had to be induced because nothing was happening and my lovely little Sabina was finally born at five minutes to midnight on 6 November 2000, weighing just under 3kg (6.5lb). She had arrived 12 days early.

I already knew the baby's gender from several weeks before, and I was so happy to have a baby girl. Everything was planned and we had chosen her name before she was born. I bought a book of names and Muppet wanted Georgina, but it sounded far too English to me – I really wanted a name that would work in Czech, English and in other languages. She has my family name as a second name and so in full, she is Sabina Klimentová Comer. We call her Sabinka as a Czech nickname (almost everyone in Eastern Europe has a designated nickname or a diminutive, so that, for example, Maria is always Masha, Mikhail is Misha and Dmitri is Dima).

When I returned to dancing after Sabina was born, I realised that everything I had been advised about the epidural was true and, in fact,

I don't think my *arabesque* has ever been quite the same, particularly on my left side where it has always been dodgy since that night in November 2000. Aesthetically, I hope that audiences aren't able to notice the difference because I have done a lot to try and compensate for it. When I returned to dancing, I had terrible pains in my back and hip, which I have learned to control over the years. So, to save my pain on one night of giving birth, I paid the price of suffering for several years thereafter!

On my first night as a mother I couldn't sleep at all. I was so worried about little baby Sabina in the cot next to me. It seemed that she was so still, quiet and lifeless that I just worried incessantly. So, on top of not sleeping for 36 hours before the birth, I then missed another night's sleep after she came. When I went home with her the next day, I looked so awful, having not slept for three consecutive nights.

The first few days were a continuing nightmare because, as I'm sure every new mother does, I continued to worry about her all the time. She was so quiet that I carried on thinking that she must not be breathing. I was so terrified that I still wouldn't sleep, and I was constantly checking that she was OK. On top of this, she didn't seem to be taking any milk. I tried to breastfeed her but it just didn't work and the nurses were really horrible to me. They put me in a room with a video film about how good it was to breastfeed your child because they seemed to assume that I didn't want to feed her myself in that way, but the truth of the matter was that Sabina just couldn't get any milk out of me. I felt really awful. I hadn't been sleeping and I was crying, and the nurses seemed to be blaming me for something that was not my fault. I wonder how many mothers are made to feel like that. Finally, after 24 hours of not taking any milk, the nurses relented – after some heated words from Muppet – and they brought some formula milk for the baby. I persevered with breastfeeding for six weeks on a sort of half-and-half basis.

I had been such a quiet baby but Sabina was quite the opposite. She was much more temperamental. On the first night that she spent at home, Sabina slept peacefully all through the night – with me, of course, wide awake checking that she was alright every five minutes. I should have taken the chance to sleep. Sabina may not have screamed at all on that first night, but then she screamed every night for the next three years!

My mum came one week after Sabina was born and helped with caring for the baby so that I could start dancing again as soon as possible. She was a great support but, because it had been 30 years since she had given birth, she was re-learning the ropes at the same time as me. Muppet took to fatherhood straightaway; he was very interested and hands-on. On the occasions that my mum wasn't with us, he would even sleep with Sabina in the living room to give me a rest. When my mum was there, we would all three take turns in looking after Sabina when she awoke screaming. Muppet's mum, Eileen (who has sadly since passed away) also came to stay in those first few weeks, and I remember sometimes thinking that it would be good to have some time on my own with my newborn baby. I am usually vulnerable to having lots of people around – I like my privacy – but the team support was really appreciated and it certainly helped me to catch up on my sleep!

A week after coming home with Sabina, I returned to English National Ballet to start taking class again, despite the problems with both knees. I knew that it was imperative to get back to the *barre* as soon as possible. It was only ten days since the last class I had taken before my waters broke. And four weeks after giving birth, I was back in hospital having the meniscus on my right knee fixed (the one that had torn when I knelt down to get some paper from the printer).

My first performance after having Sabina was back in Prague, in February 2001, about three months after giving birth (and two months after the knee operation), where I took part in a gala. For several months, I had this in mind as being my 'return' after pregnancy, so it was a major objective to be ready in time. However, I was careful and in the end I didn't perform any variations, just Aurora's *adage* from *The Sleeping Beauty*. Sabina came with me for her first trip to Prague, which was very special. I have many friends in Prague and, of course, they all came to see my new baby girl. My mum came with us and she very proudly took her new granddaughter all over Prague and Horní Počernice to show to her friends.

Derek Deane didn't really talk to me very much throughout this whole period. I didn't have any specific meetings with him and just bumped into him around ENB Headquarters. I certainly don't remember him making any kind of fuss about me having become a mum. Really, for him, it was just all about getting back to business as usual. But, to be fair to Derek, his attitude towards me as a dancer had not changed at all, and the first thing he did was to cast me as the opening night lead in *Giselle*. To be honest, once I had realised just how much I had let him down in having to refuse his offer of the opening night as Aurora in his new *The Sleeping Beauty*, I thought that this was it, that I was done at ENB but he bore no grudge towards me whatsoever and I seemed to go straight back in at the top of the pile with his immediate offer of the next opening night.

So, my first major full-length ballet, after coming back from having Sabina, was as *Giselle* in the spring of 2001, dancing with Dmitri ('Dima') Gruzdyev on the opening night in Southampton. I can remember vividly that the first moment of my entrance, stepping out of the door of Giselle's cottage, was awful because I had not been on stage like that for almost a year. So, for the first time in my life, I suffered a form of stage fright. I had a very uncomfortable dizzy feeling as I opened the door and the spotlight was upon me. It suddenly hits you and, although I had danced the role of Giselle so many times before, this was worse than the very first time. In a romantic role like Giselle everything has to come naturally. It has to flow with artistic feeling, but I was so conscious of the audience and the mechanics of my dancing that I knew it was a very artificial and poor performance. We had six more shows of *Giselle* together, in that spring of 2001, in Southampton, Manchester and Bristol, and although I tried so hard with Dima, we never managed to catch that feeling of absolute love between Giselle and Albrecht.

A lot of people have asked me how I find the time to be both a parent and a prima ballerina, dancing principal roles so regularly, and yet I have always found this dual life to work out very well. On an ordinary day, I will do class for an hour-and-a-half (usually from 10–11.30am) followed perhaps by two or three hours of rehearsals. This means that I'm invariably with Sabina in the early morning, and I can spend time with her on many afternoons. Although I perform regularly, it is now rarely more than once or twice per week, even at the height of the season. Throughout Sabina's early childhood, it was mostly me that was able to put her to bed. It was harder during the day, of course, but I was lucky to have my mum at home to look after Sabina whenever I was rehearsing or on tour.

I was once asked in an interview if I found it hard to switch from a very emotional performance such as Juliet to being a mum later the same evening. The answer, of course, is a resounding no! I'm an actress on the stage and a mum at home.

After my mum arrived to help me with Sabina, a week after she was born, she never really left! She has lived with Muppet and me for most of the time over the past 12 years. She goes back to Prague regularly, every few months, but it is really only for extended holidays, and then she comes back to look after me and my family. My mum knows exactly what she wants and things have to be done her way – my dad and I were always the quiet, obedient ones! But, strangely enough, it has worked very well, having her here in London looking after us all on a regular basis. She now has the second floor of our house in Chiswick.

Mum always needs to feel as if she is needed, so she cooks for us all the time. She is a great cook and since I don't enjoy it much, it's an arrangement that suits us all! To tell the truth, it is because my mum is such a great cook, and has insisted on always cooking, that I never really got around to doing much myself in the kitchen. Mum also looks after Sabina when I'm dancing and takes her to and from school. Obviously, we all really miss her when she goes back to Prague, but she always times her trips back home for when either Muppet or I are not working. The only problem is the cooking, and I suppose we all get hungrier when Mum is not there. We certainly buy in more takeaway food when she is not around!

If she gets too bossy then sometimes Muppet doesn't like it and, of course, I am the one caught in the middle of it all. But, by and large, we all get on very well. Actually, most of the time Muppet has no idea what is going on because when my mum wants to complain about something she does so by talking to me in Czech!

After a while, Mum found a new boyfriend here in London – perhaps a year or so after Sabina was born – so she started to be even happier. I helped to play cupid because – in typical Czech style – we met him together on the bus! There were no empty seats and, like a true gentleman, this nice man got up and offered Mum his place. Somehow there was a spark between them, which I saw immediately. My mum is a very charming and attractive woman, and Radek is a handsome man, a few years older than her. He originates from what was once Yugoslavia. Unfortunately, my mum didn't speak any English and neither could understand each other's language other than a few vaguely common words so I was called upon to help translate between them. It's a funny feeling acting as an interpreter-come-matchmaker for one's own mother! So, before we got off the bus, I made sure that I got his telephone number. All achieved within a couple of stops. Quick work!

After this I was pushing her to meet up with him, but Mum was reluctant because she was embarrassed that she couldn't speak any English. So, eventually, I called the number for her and set them up to meet. They have been together for around ten years now. Radek is still married but he hasn't lived with his wife for many years – they just haven't got around to getting a divorce. His wife has remained in Serbia, although Radek and his grown-up children are here in London. They are still good friends and his wife comes to visit once a year or so, and she seems to be very comfortable with the fact that her husband has settled into a relationship with another woman, who happens to be my mum.

Family holidays are fixed around Prague and ballet. Shortly after Sabina was born, Muppet and I started our Ballet Masterclasses in Prague, which have now been held every year for a decade. The original idea actually came from Muppet, who handles the administration of the events. They take up most of August and each year I bring over to Prague around 100 or so students and professional dancers from around the world (attendance is for dancers aged 16–30) to have professional masterclasses with teachers who are still active dancers. Part of my intention behind this is to bring great dancers to Prague, but also to make Prague the centre of attention for a short while in the world of ballet. These events have become remarkably successful and they are always over-subscribed. The Prague Ballet Masterclasses have also nurtured my own interest in ballet education and coaching.

Apart from this annual month in Prague, we have rarely had what may be described as ordinary family holidays. I can remember only once when Muppet, Sabina, Mum and I – together with my brother's daughter, Nikola – went to a beach holiday in Italy, when Sabina was still a toddler. I confess that I don't really like holidays where I just sit about on the beach in the sun: I don't sunbathe, so I am all covered up under an umbrella anyway. I much prefer spending my holidays teaching a masterclass in Prague!

Sabina is used to travelling because she came with me everywhere I danced before she started school, including Australia, Japan and China. Of course, Mum had to come, too, so that she could look after Sabina while I was performing. Mum loved this because she got to see a lot of places that she could never otherwise have visited. Looking back to my childhood in Horní Počernice, these are places that Mum could only have dreamed about when she was living in communist Czechoslovakia. I am so glad that I have been able to give her this renewed life and that she has remained young enough at heart to enjoy it all.

Unfortunately, many of the wonderful places that Sabina has been were trips that happened when she was far too young to be able to make any memories. But she has written about all of these trips in a book, and she already has very clear ideas about where she would like to go in the future. Right now, she is very keen for us to plan a trip to New York.

I am very keen for Sabina to grow up being multi-lingual, so Mum and I have kept to a routine of speaking only Czech to her. Her first word was actually *Babička*, which is the diminutive Czech name for grandmother, which just proves how much more time she has spent with my mum than me! Sabina had regular tuition in the Czech language from a young age and she now attends an International School, where she has four lessons in Czech each week. Muppet speaks English to her, and she loves writing stories in English and bringing them home for me to read. They are usually far too clever for me! Sabina has spent the first 12 years of her life growing up and learning both languages simultaneously. I know that lots of people try to do this when parents have different first languages but it doesn't always stick. However, we have persevered week-by-week over the years and it seems to have worked really well. Sabina has already told us that she wants to learn Chinese and Russian, in due course, as her next linguistic goals.

After having Sabina, I found that my dancing was very different. I was so happy to dance again, especially during the rehearsals, and I was also happy to go home and be with my beautiful little baby. In fact, I think that the first three years after Sabina was born was one of the happiest periods of my dancing career. It seemed as if my circle had been completed. The biggest plus of all was that I had achieved my goal of life being more than ballet: now, it was so much more. In an interview with Jeffery Taylor of the *Sunday Express*, just a few months after the birth, I said, 'I feel better since having the baby. I am fitter and have more stamina but my biggest improvement is up here [tapping my temple]. I'm not scared to do things like I was before Sabina... I'm more confident in general. Everything comes from the brain.'

Sabina was now the most important thing in my life; she was my future. Every day, I was worried about her and this meant that I worried less and less about *Giselle*, for example. It didn't mean that my performances were poorer – in fact, quite the opposite. The fact that I had Sabina somehow meant that I could come to the ballet studio and give absolutely 100 per cent concentration, more than I had ever been able to give before. I was never thinking about Sabina when I was dancing or rehearsing, but as soon as my sessions were finished, I would rush back to her at home. When I was with my little girl, I was never thinking about ballet. I had found a very balanced way of living and it made me so happy; life just seemed to be so beautiful.

However, this golden period didn't stay forever. It lasted for around three years and slowly I began to start worrying more and more about my ballet, even at home, thinking whether I could manage these *pirouettes* or some other piece of choreography. Gradually, these thoughts crept back and it stopped being possible to cut myself off from ballet as I had been able to do while Sabina was a baby.

In my bedroom at home, I have a plaque which says 'what is important in life?' just to keep me focussed on my true priorities. It helps to remind me of the fact that what is important in life are not those two *pirouettes*. I will always do my best, but I'm not going to stress about it.

I hear a lot from other ballerinas about how motherhood made them think differently and approach certain dance roles from a new angle, inspired by this new experience and responsibility. Our repertoire at ENB does not include that many dramatic roles, so I can't say that this has affected me that greatly although, earlier in my career, I performed Marguerite in *The Lady of the Camellias* when I was 20 and Anna Karenina when I was 22. I'm quite certain that I didn't fully understand those roles at that time. I would certainly approach them differently if I were to dance them again now as a mother of more mature years.

Chapter 9

Tantrums and Tears

*D*espite some reservations about the management style of Derek Deane and his acolytes and lack of dramatic, expressive roles in the company repertoire, my first few years at ENB were nonetheless happy, and the main reason for this was that I built up a wonderful relationship with David Wall, who was an amazing teacher and an incredibly supportive mentor.

In an interview in February 2000, I told Bruce Marriott of *Ballet.co magazine* that, 'We had built a relationship at work where he knows me so well. When he can push me and when not! It's amazing and frightening that he knows me more than I know myself. He doesn't give me any bullshit.'

I still felt, however, that I had not yet achieved enough in my dancing, and I really coveted dancing in opening nights and having a wider repertoire of choreography. Unfortunately, throughout my whole time with ENB, the company has generally had challenging financial issues and this means not being able to take risks with more neoclassical and expressive narrative works. In 2002, ENB announced that it had commissioned a new full-length version of *Les Liaisons Dangereuses* to be choreographed by Michael Corder to a score by Julian Philips, which was to be premiered in October 2004 at the Mayflower Theatre in Southampton, and I was told that I would have the lead on the opening night. But due to cuts in the budget, this new production didn't materialise.

However, three years later, I did get to have a title role of a full-length story ballet made on me by Michael Corder, when I became *The Snow Queen*. It is amazing in the economic climate that has prevailed throughout my dancing career to have such an opportunity because there are so few new full-length works being made. Corder took the fairytale by Hans Christian Andersen and cleverly reused the Prokofiev score for an old soviet ballet called *The Stone Flower*, which is unfamiliar to British audiences.

I worked very hard for six months prior to the first night in Liverpool (the opening performance of the 2007/08 season). With such a big project, the choreographer demanded that everyone was always in the studio for rehearsals, and he loved it when dancers gave 100 per cent. I loved that he really believed in me as his Snow Queen, and I enjoyed working with Corder since he is a choreographer who knows exactly what he wants: he comes to the studio with set ideas and he will go over the movements again and again until they are perfect. His choreography is what I would describe as very busy with a lot of high technical content, but we rehearsed so much that it eventually became second nature.

I didn't have a partner as such as the Snow Queen but I had two wolves – played by Esteban Berlanga and James Forbat – and they are both such lovely guys and solid partners that we had lots of fun during the rehearsals, even though we were working so hard. Unfortunately, as the opening show came closer, I twisted my ankle and since Michael had not yet choreographed my main solo, we all began to panic. I suggested that he choreographed it on the second cast but he insisted that the whole ballet should be made on me and – despite the fact that the premiere loomed near – he insisted on waiting until my foot was healed. He made me feel so special that it was an easy matter to go and give it my all in every rehearsal and every show. I loved the whole experience.

The Snow Queen was an oasis within an otherwise barren landscape of new work. There were always rumours of other new works or revivals of existing neoclassical pieces being set on the company over the years, which rarely came to fruition. Instead we were stuck doing countless performances of *Cinderella*, *Giselle* or *Swan Lake*. For me, this might mean up to 20 performances of the lead role during the season but for the *corps de ballet* it meant dancing the same steps over and over again, for weeks on end. It is an impossibly tough life.

My involvement with *Swan Lake* went back to my early days in Prague, where I first performed the *pas de trois* for one boy and two girls (a dance for three villagers in Act I) when I was just 18 and still in my final year at the Conservatoire in Prague. In fact, I performed the *pas de trois* 17 times in my brief career at the National Theatre with a variety of different partners. However, there are lots of roles in *Swan Lake* that I have never danced. I have never appeared as a swan in the *corps de ballet*; I was never a cygnet in Act II, one of the four 'little' swans who dance in perfect harmony with their arms crossed in front of one another, holding hands with the dancer next to them, performing the famous and much-parodied choreography by Lev Ivanov, including the 16 sideways *pas de chats*; and I have never been one of the princesses presented to Prince Siegfried in Act III for the purposes of choosing a potential bride.

I have to say that it was never my dream to dance the lead roles in

Swan Lake as a young dancer, as opposed to say dancing the role of Kitri in *Don Quixote*. I guess that this makes me very different to most other prima ballerinas, who will say that this was always the role that they desired the most. For me, as a young dancer, it always seemed to be far too serious a ballet!

In fact, I didn't perform the dual role of Odette and Odile in *Swan Lake* until I appeared in Galina Samsova's production for Scottish Ballet, which I danced in 1995, performing with Hans Nilsson, a guest artist from Royal Swedish Ballet, who was therefore my very first Prince Siegfried. He was around ten years older than me and an ideal first partner to help get me through this most difficult challenge. I gave 17 performances of the principal role/s in that 1995 Scottish Ballet tour (ten with Nilsson and another seven with the French dancer Laurent Novis). In the following season, I gave my first performances as Odette/Odile in the Czech Republic as a guest artist at the National Theatre in Prague.

After I joined English National Ballet, *Swan Lake* became a staple of my repertoire, being danced most years since I joined the company. ENB is, above all else, a touring company. Typically we will appear in ten to 12 UK cities each season and tour overseas at least once every year, so our audiences are continually changing. The repertoire choices have to be made according to what will sell at the box office. So, if *Swan Lake* sells tickets – as it does – then we need to perform it again and again. *Swan Lake* is certainly my favourite classical ballet, but I have to confess that I would rather have the opportunity to perform again in more expressive neoclassical ballets from my past such as *The Lady of the Camellias*, *Anna Karenina* or *Hamlet*.

We dance *Swan Lake* at ENB, both conventionally in a theatre with a proscenium arch but also 'in the round' at the Royal Albert Hall, surrounded on all sides by the audience. The normal staged version is obviously easier since you are only presenting one side of you to a conventional auditorium with the audience facing the stage. 'In the round' means having to be aware of the fact that the audience is seeing you from every angle.

When Derek Deane first proposed his 'in the round' *Swan Lake* for the Royal Albert Hall, to premiere in May 1997, towards the end of my first season with the company, I was scheduled to dance in the fourth cast (of four) with Laurentiu Guinea. But I did not perform, as planned. Deane's 'in the round' *Swan Lake* is an enormous production, which was a big risk for the company – costing some £1.8 million to produce and using 120 dancers instead of the normal 60 or so. Act II, by the lakeside, where Prince Siegfried first meets Odette (who has been transformed into a swan by the wicked sorcerer, Von Rothbart), will normally have a *corps de ballet* of 24 swans whereas the Deane production uses 60 dancers moving in unison, which is an awesome sight.

I have never admitted this before but I completely freaked out about the production and had terrible stage fright. I 'went off', meaning that I was indisposed and unable to perform. Already I had made myself ill – in Scotland – so that I didn't have to perform, but here I didn't have to make myself ill since the whole thought of presenting myself to the audience on every side made me ill. It was still not so long after my father had passed away and I was already in a raw emotional state. It caused such stress that I really couldn't have danced under any circumstances – I just lost control. I wasn't used to doing so many shows as I had performed with ENB in my first season and this had taken its toll by the end of the year. Derek didn't help either, with his demanding attitude as the choreographer in charge of the whole concept and under immense stress due to the financial risks of the enterprise.

The opening night was to be taken by the guest ballerina, Altynai Asylmuratova (a principal with The Kirov Ballet) – who danced with

Roberto Bolle of La Scala Ballet – and there were other guests in the principal roles from Dutch National Ballet in the brief season of just 12 performances. Only two of ENB's full-time ballerinas, Lisa Pavane and me, were entrusted by Derek to perform as Odette/Odile.

While preparing for the role, I had a back spasm because of the scoliosis on my spine, as a result of which I missed some part of the rehearsal process. I thought hard about my concerns, the fact that I had worked so intensely all year, the desperate need that I had to avoid any more of Derek's bullying and – perhaps, most of all – my fears about dancing such complex choreography 'in the round'. It was the easiest decision of my life to use the back spasms as an excuse to duck out of the performances. I could have gone on and risked the stage fright, but I decided that I wasn't going to dance. I remember being at home just before the performances began, now completely free of the back spasms, but happy that I was going to miss the next two weeks because it got me out of *Swan Lake* completely. I was only scheduled for two shows and Lisa Pavane took them over.

That was over 15 years ago and I have no regrets at all about my duplicity: it was necessary to retain my sanity. I feel no remorse, and in many respects I think that this shows the insecurity that has always been inherent in my dancing career. Over the years, I have learned how to control it, although it still flares up every now and again, and I think that overall my ambition to be a better dancer has helped me to conquer these insecurities, which sometimes earlier in my career had so completely taken me over to the point where I simply could not dance.

My first performance of *Swan Lake* for ENB was in Manchester at the beginning of my second season with the company in 1997/98. It was the conventional theatrical version, in which I danced Odette/Odile with Dmitri Gruzdyev as my Prince Siegfried. Our partnership had only just begun at the end of the previous season and

I remember that it was very hard. It was not my favourite ballet back then, although I have grown into *Swan Lake* over the years, and I had to work really hard at it.

To be honest, I didn't think that I was the swan. I hoped that, perhaps, in this country I could get away with it, but I knew that in Eastern Europe there were many dancers with much better physical attributes to portray the white swan, Odette. They were taller, had longer necks and more graceful, longer arms: in short, they looked more swan-like. This is just another manifestation of the insecurities I have as a ballerina. But I have grown to realise that I am not in competition with these other dancers. I'm not competing in the Prix de Lausanne, it is just me being watched in any performance. I am not being instantly compared to other ballerinas! Also, I have become aware that some of the greatest dancers in history didn't have these attributes. The most famous ballerina of all time, Anna Pavlova, was certainly not tall (she barely measured 5ft in height) and her delicate, wiry physique was probably more feline than avian, yet she will forever be associated with being a swan, so why should I be so worried?

The other critical aspect is that I need a partner as Prince Siegfried who brings out the best of me in both roles of Odette and Odile, and this didn't happen until much later in my career. I need to develop a special connection or friendship with my partners in order for our dance partnership to work; I also have to believe that they are the character that they are portraying to make me believe in what I am doing. This connection is fundamental to my ability to perform.

Once I had conquered my fears about performing *Swan Lake* 'in the round', dancing it in a conventional theatre became comparatively easy. The stage is smaller and you can rest briefly in between the variation and *coda* of Odile's big Act III *pas de deux*. Of course, no matter what age the dancer is, you have to start preparing for an upcoming season of *Swan Lake* as early as possible, particularly in terms of building up one's stamina for the 32 *fouettés*. As a young dancer, I found the 'white swan' (Odette) dancing of Act II much easier than the 'black swan' (Odile) dancing of Act III. I think that my body was looser as a younger dancer than it is now. But with the passage of years, I now find the 'black swan' much easier than the 'white swan' because my body is not so loose for all the hyper-flexible slow-bending that is required for Odette in the 'white swan' *pas de deux*. I now find that I have to push much more than I did as a younger dancer, whereas as Odile, I am stronger than I used to be technically and I find it easier, with the confidence of that strength, to just go for it more than I used to. When I was younger, I had the flexibility and looseness but I wasn't strong enough to hold positions that I can do much more confidently, now that I'm in my 40s.

I love Tchaikovsky's music so much now – much more than I did as a younger dancer – and it makes it so easy for me to switch automatically into that other fantasy world of a prince and a swan queen by the lakeside. I hear the music and I am just away with the swans! The good thing is that I get so lost in the music now that I don't even think about the steps anymore. I have come to love *Swan Lake* much more as the years have gone by, and my maturity both as a dancer and as a woman has grown.

Having missed my first opportunity to dance the Derek Deane *Swan Lake* 'in the round', I finally got to dance Odette/Odile at the Royal Albert Hall at the next time of asking, in the summer of 1999, although my first experience of this huge auditorium had been in Deane's *Romeo and Juliet* at the end of the 1997/98 season. My fears hadn't really subsided much, but I felt stronger and my ambition overcame the stage (or perhaps I should say 'arena') fright.

There are three reasons that are unique to the experience of dancing 'in the round'. The main problem is that dancers have trained all of their lives to dance to the audience, which is only on one side of the stage. I suppose it's a bit like a ballet equivalent of three-dimensional chess. I think it's easily the hardest thing that I have ever had to do. On a normal stage you start facing front and you finish facing front, but in one of Deane's 'in the round' productions, you start facing front and finish facing backwards. You have spent your whole career, from your earliest time at ballet school, thinking about how people will see you from the front, never from the side or from behind. In the Royal Albert Hall, you can hide nothing because people can see you from every conceivable angle, apart from below or directly above (and I'm sure that Derek is working on that)!

For me, the worst aspect is pointing my feet because on a conventional stage there are moments when you don't have to point your foot – you just have to make it look pretty from the front. But 'in the round' there is just no place where you can afford to be not pointing your foot correctly. So, you are extremely self-conscious all the time during a performance 'in the round' at the Royal Albert Hall.

The second problem is that the audience seems so much further away than we are used to, due to the size and configuration of the space, although paradoxically the first few rows are very close to the edge of the performance area and, of course, the 'in the round' concept means that you are literally enveloped by the audience.

The other issue that dancers don't have to confront anywhere but in these performances at the Royal Albert Hall is in having to enter and exit on the stairs of the auditorium, through the seated audience. For the 'black swan' variation, for example, Odile is running down the stairs and the music hasn't yet started. If it has started you wouldn't make it into position in time! It is always very tight and you are running, running to get into position and out of breath before you have even begun the variation. The dancer needs a lot of stamina for this role – even more than normal. And it does create some uniquely funny situations: I have had occasions where I have to go on, down the

stairs in my tutu – a short, stiff skirt that stretches out from my hips –
and I meet an audience member who has decided to take that moment
to leave to go to the loo! You just have to say 'excuse me' and try to
dodge around them without losing any time.

To make it worse, Derek is aware of how technically difficult a
performance 'in the round' has to be, and he is a very hard taskmaster
to ensure that everything looks good from every side. The
choreography is extremely precise so that the leading characters are
always looking in a particular direction, which has to change all the
time to avoid any perception that there is a 'front' and to allow every
part of the audience to feel as important as any other. It is very hard for
any dancer to put any of their particular flavour into the positioning –
it has to be precisely as Derek has set it. In this respect, one of the best
things to happen to the 'in the round' performances was ENB policy
of bringing in various guests from overseas to perform these ballets. It
was generally not possible to be so very precise with them because
there was often not enough time in rehearsals between their arrival
and the performance schedule to go through every nuance, and they
would therefore get away with slightly different positions. This opened
the door for the rest of us to do things slightly differently, which was a
very good thing.

At the beginning of Odile's variation in the Act III *pas de deux*, her
pirouettes have to be more than two; they are more like two-and-a-half
so that the turns face a different part of the audience. At first, Derek
wanted the ballerina in the Odile role to perform the famous 32
fouettés turning around, accomplishing them facing a different section
of the audience. The 32 *fouettés* are one of the hardest things a
ballerina has to do on stage and Derek wanted to make it even harder!
Normally, a dancer would get through these whipped turns and make
it into the wings just to have a hot flush and sometimes even to throw
up. Yes, I have seen some ballerinas vomit between the Odile variation

and coming back for the *coda*, although thankfully it has never happened to me; it wouldn't be possible to do this at the Royal Albert Hall because there is just no means of escape and you have to stay on the stage! There isn't even the opportunity for a sneaky cough. But I did come to a neat arrangement with the dancers playing Rothbart (Odile's sorcerer father) so that they would conceal a drink to bring out into the arena for me and then they would cover my legs with the long arms of their cape. This meant that I could relax and stretch my legs between the variation and the *coda*, without the audience seeing.

After Zoltan Solymosi and Laurentiu Guinea left ENB, my regular dancing partner for most of the next 12 years was Dmitri ('Dima') Gruzdyev. Dima – who, like me, was born in 1971 – had come to London from the famous Kirov Ballet, based at the Mariinsky Theatre in St Petersburg. He met his wife, Sarah Arnott, while she was a student at the Vaganova Ballet Academy and he followed her to London when she came to join the company in 1993. Actually, more to the point is the fact that he stayed in London after The Kirov's season at the London Coliseum that summer when Dima gave what one critic described as a 'dazzling performance' as the Golden Idol in *La Bayadère*. Given that the Kirov, which was its old Soviet title – it has now been reunited with its original name as the Mariinsky Ballet – has been one of the world's greatest ballet companies for over two centuries, it might be surprising that Dima left to join ENB. Of course, love had a lot to do with it but also I know that he didn't regret leaving The Kirov, aged 23, since he made much more rapid progress in terms of roles and promotion at ENB. Dima told an interviewer, Kevin Ng, in June 2000: 'I needed to have been taller in order to partner the tall girls in the Kirov.' An allusion to the then current breed of tall, thin Kirov ballerinas exemplified by Uliana Lopatkina and Yulia Makhalina, whom Ng described as being 'nicknamed "the basketball team".'

Although I had one 'scratch' pairing with Dima in *Coppélia* very early on in my first season at ENB (where one of us must have substituted for another dancer), my first planned partnership with him was in a short ballet called *Cut to the Chase* (choreographed by ENB dancer Paul Lewis). I had mostly been dancing with Laurentiu since Zoltan's abrupt departure at Christmas, but I had also danced with Giuseppe Picone in some of the ten performances I gave as *Alice in Wonderland* in Derek Deane's choreography during that first season.

At that time Dima was still a soloist in the company – he had joined three years before me – and I expect that Derek saw some similarities in our Russian Vaganova-school style and technique. Altogether, we did nine performances of *Cut to the Chase*, spread across venues as disparate as Bexhill-on-Sea, Scunthorpe, Barrow-in-Furness and Cambridge, to bring my first year with ENB to a close.

We actually did cut to the chase and our partnership started in earnest. I liked Dima and I particularly liked the way he looked. I thought that he was very handsome, with that particular balletic quality of strong nobility that the best male danseurs possess. It seemed to me that we could be a great ballet partnership in so many ways, not least because we shared so much in our Russian schooling and ballet heritage. At this point I began to see that perhaps we would be in a position to inherit the mantle of Tom and Agnes, as the public's favourite pair of principal dancers at ENB. I could also see the beckoning promise of opening nights and ballets being made on us. However, all of this initial thinking slowly changed as I became more and more aware of the problems that caused our inability to connect on stage.

With hindsight, I can now see that these issues stretched back to the very beginning of our partnership. I think that Dima was insecure with his partnering skills in relation to me: this is the way in which the

male danseur manipulates and secures the ballerina in a *pas de deux*.
But there was something about the Russian machismo in his character
that meant Dima would always blame the girl for all the problems. I
found that everything had to be my fault. Normally, dancers would
work out these problems together; it would be very much a
compromise of giving way and helping each other to complete the
most complex choreography that we are often expected to master. But
with Dima we could never seem to work it out. I would get very upset
and sessions would sometimes end in bouts of temper tantrums and
tears. I found it very difficult to have a conversation with Dima in an
ordinary way where our dancing was concerned, and I quickly became
fed up with always being deemed by him to be in the wrong.

I think that a major part of our problem was that we were both
comparatively young and insecure, and therefore inclined to become
overly defensive, and our immaturity didn't lead to a mutually
sympathetic relationship. In this sense, I blame myself as much as
Dima for a partnership that never reached the heights that it could
have done because there is no denying that he was – and is – a superb
classical dancer with impeccable technique. But, unfortunately, there
was virtually no sympathy on either side of our partnership. I tried to
talk to Derek about not dancing with Dima from early in my second
season, but he would have none of it. He was convinced that we were
a good pairing and he was not going to be deflected from this belief.

I wasn't enjoying the process with Dima in that second season,
where we danced together in no less than 14 shows of *The Nutcracker*
in Liverpool, Manchester, and at the London Coliseum, plus *The
Sleeping Beauty*, Glen Tetley's *Sphinx* and two performances of *Romeo
and Juliet* 'in the round' at the Royal Albert Hall to conclude the year.
However, it did get better for a while. I tried to find a way of making it
work and I realised that if my disposition was sunny, and I was smiling
at him all the time, it helped and then he would give back. But, if it was

not possible for me to be like this: for example, if I had my period and the usual pre-menstrual tension that comes before that, it was impossible for me to fake this warmth, so we would go back to square one and be unable to communicate effectively while we were rehearsing and dancing. At these times, I felt like I was always giving, giving and he would never give back.

A lot of Russian men are like this. They are not very forgiving to women or understanding of the problems of others. They are 'men's men' in every sense and Dima was very much in this mould. Although we didn't exactly hit it off, we still did a lot of guest appearances together in galas all over the world, simply because it was easier to make such arrangements with a dancer that I was partnering regularly, and knew the repertoire with, rather than having to learn it anew with someone else. Dima came with me to a lot of places, including Shanghai, Miami, Lithuania and especially to the Czech Republic, during the years in which we danced together.

Both of us were desperate to make our debuts as the leads (Nikiya the temple dancer and Solor the warrior) in the full version of the 19th-century classic ballet *La Bayadère*, and we were so ambitious that we arranged to dance the ballet together in Brno in the Czech Republic (where my great Uncle Josef had been a leader of the Resistance movement) because we knew that we would have no other opportunity to dance it. That performance in 2004 remains the only time I have ever performed the full ballet, and it is perhaps my best memory of dancing with Dima.

I remember that on that trip we managed for the first time to have a decent private conversation about our problems. Dima admitted to me that his burning desire was to be the best dancer possible and that he was insecure about some aspects of his dancing. Like me, he also wanted to make our partnership the top pairing in ENB, just as Tom and Agnes had been. In fact, we wanted to be better than they were. We rarely did opening nights because Tom and Agnes were always doing them for every production. Dima was really competitive – and so was I, albeit in a quieter way – and our aims and objectives were the same. It was just hard for us to work cooperatively towards achieving this mutual goal. We tend to see things only through our own eyes, and while I found it difficult to work productively with Dima, I'm sure that there are many things about me and my attitude that he would look back on and say, 'Well, she was the problem.'

Now that I have been in the fortunate position of being cast many, many times to take the opening nights of each major production, I must say that I have never really agreed with ENB's way of doing this. The company's policy has always been to reward the long-standing principal couple by being chosen for the opening night of every production. To be honest, I would never cast that way if I were the artistic director because each person suits different roles. It is also awful that many dancers have to wait their turn, and for so long, to get cast on opening nights.

When I was pregnant and couldn't perform as Derek Deane's first cast Aurora at the Royal Albert Hall, it was my friend, Erina Takahashi, who benefitted from my enforced withdrawal. In August 2012, I was unable to dance for the opening night of *Swan Lake* at the London Coliseum, and again Erina took my place. I was so very happy for her because she has been a principal ballerina at ENB for 12 years and has rarely had the opportunity to take opening nights in ballets that she really shines in. She works so hard and is so good as Aurora and Odette/Odile, but even still, she only gets to dance on the opening night when someone else (in this case me) goes 'off'.

Certainly Dima and I were very frustrated not to be dancing on opening nights for the first five years of our partnership, but always to be the second or third casts in the big ballets. But it has made me more understanding towards other dancers now who have the same frustrations as we had back then.

Although Dima and I certainly progressed in our partnership over the first few years – despite our personal issues in the studio – I think we eventually became stale. I certainly felt stuck in a dancing relationship that seemed unlikely to improve further. This was exacerbated by the fact that we were continually dancing the same repertoire year after year and so, both technically and emotionally, we were marooned in a ballet backwater. He must have been feeling the same because I was getting nothing back from him in our performances, and it is so hard to be emotional as a heroine in a classical ballet if there is nothing to respond to in the emotionless performance of your prince.

We argued a lot. I remember more than once Dima would suddenly walk out of the rehearsal studio yelling at me to 'fuck off' at the top of his voice. He would get upset, I would retaliate, there would be long silences and then eventually it would erupt into temper and tears. It happened so often. I would go home and cry about it all to Muppet and he would get angry with Dima, too! Poor Muppet, I think that I must have come home almost every day for many years complaining about the artistic friction with Dima.

But we put on a brave face. In the interview with Kevin Ng, which was given in June 2000, some three years after we first danced together, and just before his opening night of the 'in the round' *The Sleeping Beauty* (the one that I was supposed to have danced before announcing my pregnancy), Dima said, 'My favourite partner is Daria Klimentová. I dance a lot with her; we have a good partnership. We have good times and we have bad times!' I suppose it was as honest an assessment as could have been given back then, especially since at the time of the interview I was five months pregnant and it had been some while since we had rehearsed or performed together. Absence certainly makes the heart grow fonder, even for dancers!

In 2001, a scandal broke regarding Derek Deane, who was accused of harassing Daniel Jones, a good-looking dancer in the company. Fiona Barton wrote about it in the *Mail On Sunday* and the story was picked up elsewhere in the media, partly because Derek was allegedly a confidant of the late Princess Diana and he had also been a friend of Princess Margaret. So, it suddenly became a big story that this 'close friend of the Royals' should be accused of bullying a handsome junior soloist and 'bombarding him with mobile phone text messages'. Derek went on long-term sick leave in February prior to leaving the company altogether at the end of the season.

Incidentally, in her piece for the *Mail On Sunday*, Barton captures both sides of Derek very well. On the one hand, he was the 'saviour of ENB, having turned its fortunes around since joining in March 1993', but on the other, he 'offended dancers with his outspoken views'. Barton quotes him as describing homespun dancers thus: 'an English dancer with a stocky body can do the steps but the aesthetic look is not as pleasing as a French or Russian dancer. [English girls] can be too bummy, too titty, or too short in the neck. A true ballerina is much finer, much longer.' Re-reading this over a decade later, I find myself wondering into which category did he place this Czech ballerina.

When Deane left, he had to go quickly, and there was around half a year (between February and September 2001) when there was no artistic director in charge of the company. The ballet master and my good friend David Wall took on an interim role in charge of the artistic affairs. I don't think that anyone asked him to do this officially, but he just filled the void because someone had to. Nothing changed for me. In fact, it all worked out very well at that time since I was so close to David. He had, after all, been the only person in the whole of the ballet world to attend my wedding.

The company advertised for a new artistic director and Matz Skoog, previously the artistic director of Royal New Zealand Ballet, was appointed to take over the post from the beginning of the 2001/2 season. Born in Stockholm, Skoog's early dance career had been with Royal Swedish Ballet. His cool, Scandinavian outlook on life could not have been more different from Derek – it was like going from one extreme to another. Where Derek was loud and always irritable, Matz was quiet and reserved. I would say that he was equally tough but in a very understated and business-like way and he certainly didn't shout at people, as had been the custom during Derek's reign.

Matz would come to the studio very regularly and he would almost always take his shoes off and sit on the floor, just as the dancers do (we rarely sit on chairs in the studio). He would always be carrying paper and invariably writing notes. I remember in the early days of his directorship all of the dancers (including me) were intrigued about what he was writing. Derek would certainly never have sat on the floor, taken his shoes off or written notes!

Matz was so laid-back by comparison: I remember that he actually fell fast asleep on the floor during one early rehearsal! It was so funny. Matz and his wife, Amanda, had two young children and I'm sure that they were having nights of interrupted sleep. We were rehearsing Act II of *Swan Lake* and the slow music obviously got to him, and the next thing the dancers knew we had a sleeping director on the floor! We didn't mind since it showed us that here was a director with a human side.

Although I didn't know Matz before he was appointed as director, Muppet knew him well since he had been a principal dancer with ENB for many years before retiring from dance. There are many video films of ENB in performance from the time when Matz was in the company that show him dancing, and I have seen a lot of these on video and DVD because one of Muppet's roles in those days was to film the

Manon is just the kind of expressive, dramatic role that I had coveted ever since joining ENB, so I was very lucky when we got to perform it.

Above left: Rehearsing the role of Manon with Dame Antoinette Sibley.

Above right: *Manon* with German dancer Friedemann Vogel.

Below: Rehearsing the ballet on stage with Vadim Muntagirov.

Photos © Daria Klimentová

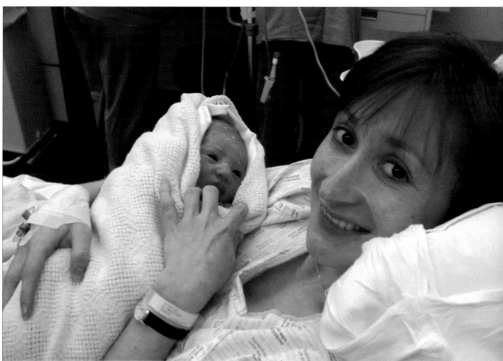

My family are the most important thing in my life.

Above left: Marrying Muppet (Ian) on 23 June 1999, which happened to also be my 28th birthday.

© *Daria Klimentová*

Above right: I was lucky enough to fall pregnant straight away.

© *Louise Bobb*

Below: My baby, Sabina, was born in November 2000. She means everything to me.

© *Daria Klimentová*

Above: Do you see a family resemblance? From left: Grandmother Ludmila in 1911, my mum, Ludmila, in 1945, me in 1972 and Sabina in 2001 – all aged one.

Centre: My grandmother, my mum, me and Sabina in 2001.

Below: Sabinka helping me rehearse!

Photos © Daria Klimentová

I have been lucky to work and dance with a number of amazing people.

Above left: With Zora Šemberová, the very first Juliet, in Sydney, 2001. *© Jeff Darmanin/Newspi*

Above right: With Glen Tetley after dancing *Sphinx* in Prague. *© Daria Klimentov*

Below: Dancing with Dima in *The Sleeping Beauty*. *© Daria Klimentov*

Above: *Double Concerto* choreographed by Christopher Hampson for me and Jan-Erik Wikström.

© *Daria Klimentová*

Centre: On stage performing *Giselle* with Vadim.

© *Patrick Bromilow-Downing*

Below: The Snow Queen was created on me by Michael Corder, and it was a privilege to dance.

© *Amber Hunt*

Above: Rehearsing *Apollo* with Carlos Acosta.

Below left: Dancing with Vadim Muntagirov in Christopher Hampson's *The Nutcracker*.

Below right: I am so glad to have found a dance partner like Vadim, and we get to travel all over the world together performing (but we never forget to take a photo as a memento).

Photos © Daria Klimentová

I've been lucky to meet a number of different performers, celebrities, politicians and royalty.

Above: This is a picture of Dima, photographer Mario Testino and me. © *Daria Klimentová*

Below left: Meeting Prince Andrew after performing *Romeo and Juliet* with Vadim.

© *Amber Hunt*

Below right: At a party with Tony Blair. © *Daria Klimentová*

I get photographed a lot in my profession, but I love to be the one behind the camera. The 14th exhibition of my photographs was held in St Petersburg during the autumn of 2012.

Above left: Simone Clarke and her partner, Yat-Sen Chang, readily agreed to pose naked for me.

Above right: A swan.

Below: English National Ballet's *Rite of Spring*.

Photos © Daria Klimentov

company. Matz was an excellent dancer with a wonderful physique, remarkable flexibility and a beautiful line – I particularly remember being impressed by him as Romeo on one of these tapes. He was perhaps a little small for the role, but technically and emotionally he was superb.

Matz was very observant. He came to the company with a blank sheet of paper, as I think every new artistic director should, without prejudice or preconceived ideas about the dancers, the ballet staff or the repertoire. From the beginning he arranged regular interviews with every principal dancer and he was always concerned about how we were and what support we needed. He went the extra mile beyond just getting to know us and it was very refreshing.

Derek had obviously seen something in my partnership with Dima that neither of us could see. Despite everything that I tried – and I think Dima, too – it was never possible to get Derek to agree to place us with other partners. I had no option but to accept the situation and carry on. After all, I was settled in London, The Royal Ballet was not an option and I was too young to retire from dancing.

Shortly after Matz arrived as the artistic director, I was supposed to be dancing with Dima in *Double Concerto*, a new one-act ballet for the company, made by Christopher Hampson, a choreographer with whom I have always had a special relationship. He was the man with whom Muppet had produced *A Christmas Carol* at the Royal Festival Hall for the Christmas spectacular, a year earlier. 'Hampy' had been a soloist at ENB not so many years before and was very well-known within the company. He has now made important works on major companies all over the world, and he was appointed as the new artistic director of Scottish Ballet in 2012.

During the rehearsals for *Double Concerto*, Dima started to have problems with Hampy. I don't remember any particular incident but it was just one of those situations of not really seeing eye-to-eye about the work, moaning and complaining about what he was being asked to do by the choreographer. It became a very unpleasant experience for us all.

The saving grace was that Dima got injured in one of these rehearsals and Skoog replaced him with Jan-Erik Wikström, a Swedish dancer who came to ENB at that time on a three-year sabbatical from Royal Swedish Ballet. In Sweden, the dancers have a contract for life with excellent pension arrangements, so it is foolish for any dancer to leave this secure arrangement and join the uncertain situation in most other companies (even some of the very best). However, the Swedish dancers were able to take up to three years' leave of absence without impacting on their job security or pension, and this is what Jan-Erik did so that he could join his countryman at ENB. Jan-Erik had been dancing professionally since 1987 and had performed all the major classical roles; in December 2000, the King of Sweden had conferred upon him the prestigious title of Royal Court Dancer.

Overnight, the whole process of creating *Double Concerto* suddenly became a dream, and the problems in the rehearsal studios were replaced with laughter all the way as everyone was giving to each other. With Jan-Erik everything was about the partner – the girl – and the choreographer's wishes. Nothing was too much for him, and suddenly we became a team, striving to help one another and working cooperatively towards creating this ballet together. A horrible time was changed into an amazing experience.

Helped by all of this, Matz switched me to dance with Jan-Erik on a more regular basis. Jan-Erik was an amazing and unselfish partner, although to be honest I think that any new partner would have made me feel that way. I could never quite understand why the relationship with Dima did not work out.

Nothing was too much of a problem for Jan-Erik and, more importantly, whenever something didn't work in the studio it was never my fault. He would always assume that the problems were down to him (even when they were not) and it was such a pleasure to form a partnership with a true gentleman. He made it work and he made me feel happy because I was treated nicely. Everything I asked of Jan-Erik, he would reply with, 'Of course, that's not a problem.' He was a ballet dancer who understood completely that what he was doing in a *pas de deux* was largely about presenting the ballerina in the best possible light.

All in all, Dima and I danced together for 12 years and it is the only part of my dancing career about which I have lasting regrets. It takes two to make a partnership and I'm sure that – in the later years especially – I had stopped trying to make it work. We just didn't seem capable of producing the same harmonious lines and emotions in our dancing. When his character was showing mine that he loved me, I found it very difficult to respond because I couldn't see it in his face. It was impossible. To be fair, I think that Dima was just as unhappy with me as I was with him and the reference to the 'bad times' in his June 2000 interview with Kevin Ng was no accident. A part of our problem was that we were both ambitious and we needed support from each other to be the best partnership possible, but we could both see that this was not working.

There is no doubt that Dima is a wonderful dancer and he has performed some fantastic roles for ENB since we split as a dancing partnership, particularly in forging new partnerships with Erina Takahashi and Fernanda Oliveira. When I discuss our problems together with people who saw us dance towards the latter part of our time together, when the partnership was at its most disastrous, they are always surprised and say that they saw us dance in such-and-such and we were lovely together; but the point is that we were both professionals and we had to try and make the performances work for those who had paid for their tickets. It is just that it rarely worked for us as artists after the first few years, and the partnership should have been dissolved a lot sooner than it was. I blame Derek for not doing that.

Dima and I didn't talk to each other for quite a long time after we separated (and, yes, it *is* like a marriage separation in so many ways). Even if we passed each other in the corridors at Jay Mews we would barely acknowledge the other for a time. I think that it took the best part of three years for us to forgive each other for the problems and begin to be civil again

I had three years to dance with Jan-Erik before he had to return to Sweden but the only problem, at this time, is that once I passed 30, I started to become injured more frequently. It is ironic, really, that Derek spent so much time at my interview asking me about my physical health and almost as soon as he left ENB, I started to get injured! So, having finally made the break with Dima, I couldn't really enjoy my dancing that much because I was 'off' for so much of the time.

The worst period was when I was 'off' for eight months because of my foot. The problems began at the time that I gave birth to Sabina in 2000 with the impact of the menisci tears in both knees. At the same time I had a bursitis in the area between my Achilles tendon and the bone in the heel of my left foot. A bursitis is essentially the inflammation of the small fluid-filled sacs (bursas) that lie between a tendon and either the skin or a bone.

To get back in shape after giving birth, I was doing an extra class at Pineapple Dance Studios in Covent Garden, instead of resting on my day off and wearing soft shoes. I felt something pinch in my heel as I was doing a *relevé*. This inflammation occurs regularly with dancers and normally we take a couple of days off and everything returns to normal, but I had a gala performance the very next day and so, of course, I didn't take the time off and I was rehearsing even though I couldn't stand on my foot. It is unbelievable what dancers can do to themselves and how professionalism takes over, and we dance while injured. The adrenalin of performance always overcomes the pain of the injury – or, at least it does while the performance and the curtain calls last!

I performed in the gala and somehow the injury improved over the next year, but the pain and the inflammation were always there. I would go to the doctor periodically and get cortisone injections to help. However, on one of these visits the doctor made a mistake and injected me in the wrong part of my heel and this damaged it even more. What made it worse is that we didn't know that it had happened straightaway, and it only became clear when the injury failed to improve: it just got worse and worse. However, I must take a lot of the blame personally because stupidly, I refused to stop. I carried on taking class every day, even if this was only sometimes at the *barre* because I was in too much pain to do any centre work. I did the classes because I didn't want to lose my technique, whereas in fact by carrying on with ballet exercises I was losing my technique by worsening the foot injury. It was a vicious circle. This happens to so many dancers who make injuries worse by obsessively trying to retain their technique. I still meet old teachers who insist that every dancer should take class every day regardless of their state of physical health.

The problems with my ankle led to a year when I hardly danced anything. In fact, I only did four shows in the whole of the 2002/3 season. I carried on doing *barre* and I visited so many doctors to try and treat the problem. I went to the best specialists in the UK and the Czech Republic. In Prague, I found some experts who tried to make me better with a machine that looked like a hammer and they would hurt my foot by whacking it with this machine, the idea being that this would promote and improve the circulation in my foot, which would enable the heel to heal more quickly. I discovered, worryingly, that this machine was used to enable tissue to be repaired that was almost beyond repair. So, once a week I had to submit myself to this torture, literally. The pain was indescribable and unbearable, every bit as bad as childbirth without an epidural. I had to scream and I didn't once have a session of this treatment without tears streaming down my face.

However, the torture was worthwhile in the end because my foot did get better. In fact, it improved enough for me to consider being fit enough to take the opening night in one of my favourite ballets: as Swanilda in *Coppélia* with Jan-Erik as Franz. I started on the first day with ten minutes of rehearsal, and on each subsequent day I managed to add a little bit more until eventually, just before opening night, I was able to do a full run-through in the stage dress rehearsal but the next day, I was unable to walk so I couldn't do the show.

One of the side-effects from all the cortisone injections was the tissue around the ankle of my left foot eroded. It was almost as if there was nothing but paper-thin skin and I could touch my fingers together when pressed on either side of my ankle. It was so thin that there was nothing left inside. I was so damaged that I just had to stop and have a very long time off to fully recover, and for the tissue to regenerate. It was decided that I needed an operation to repair the damage but the surgeons had to wait three months before they were of the view that my ankle was sufficiently robust to undergo the knife. It was only then that they were able to repair the damage, and it was another five months before I could perform again.

Several years later, I still have residual problems from this injury. Often the heel still hurts; I can't bend my foot properly and I have lost some of my *plié* and have had to learn how to dance with this deficiency. Interviewed by Donnachadh McCarthy for the magazine

Dance Europe just after I had returned to dancing following this injury, I said, 'It was much harder than giving birth.'

My ability to get back to dance so soon after the operation was due to the excellent recuperative care that I received from ENB's physiotherapist, Jackie Pelly, who was incredibly supportive. She came with me every day to the swimming pool and would work on my leg and foot. I also did daily Pilates routines. This is a body conditioning system of exercises – invented by Joseph Pilates in the early 20th century – that puts emphasis on spinal and pelvic alignment, and allowing oxygen flow to muscles. It develops core strength and stability (abdominals and back), builds flexibility, coordination and balance. Almost every dancer uses Pilates these days and many ballet dancers become Pilates' teachers after they retire. Needless to say, it is a remarkable tool for helping dancers to recover from injury and rebuild their strength.

I have a very small foot, only a UK size 3: it is very narrow and my toes are short. All of this helps me as a dancer. If you have long toes then they obviously have to bend more when the dancer is *en pointe* (standing on the tips of their toes in ballet shoes) and this is the main cause of the worst of all problems for ballerinas: the bunion, which is essentially an enlarged piece of bone or tissue around a joint on the foot, often but not always by the big toe. So, despite this terrible career-threatening injury to my ankle, I'm very fortunate that the physiology of my feet has mattered a lot over my career insofar as I have reached the age of 41 with no long-term damage to my feet and no bunions at all. The same applies to turn-out and a dancer's hips because a large hip socket enables natural turn-out, which will not only make life a lot easier as a ballet dancer but leads to a lot fewer hip problems (and even replacements) in later life.

David Wall was a great help in preparing me to get back on the stage with appropriate rehabilitation. He was coaching me every day, building exercises in small bite-sized chunks and gradually making me stronger. He was a godsend and I really appreciated his help and support. This is something that we are better at in the Western companies than in Russia and the Eastern Bloc, where there is so little attention given to the very particular needs of dancers coming back from injury. It is getting better, but in Russia and the Czech Republic, for example, the emphasis is often on the dancers themselves doing what they can to affect their own rehabilitation. In 2002/3, for a while I genuinely thought that I would not come back to dancing. It was only the second time in my life that I thought about giving it up (the first was when I was in my very early 20s, feeling homesick in Scotland, with my hormones all over the place).

When I came back from the foot injury I didn't go straight into principal roles. My first performance after returning was in Manchester, playing the Fairy Godmother in *Cinderella*, at the beginning of the 2003/4 season. This is a comparatively small role that enabled me to get back onto stage without testing my much depleted stamina after eight months off. The Fairy Godmother appears only in Act I and in the final scenes: in Act II she doesn't do anything at all. So, on the first show back I sat in the wings, took my pointe shoes off to rest my legs and put my feet up to watch Cinderella dancing. Unfortunately, my foot became swollen and I couldn't get my shoe back on for the final act. There was no other dancer standing by who was able to go on as the Fairy Godmother, so I was in utter panic trying to force the shoe back onto my swollen foot! Eventually, I managed to squeeze the shoe on after warming my foot up with plenty of *tendus*; laughing all the while because I felt like one of the ugly step-sisters trying to squash her oversized foot into Cinderella's slipper. It seemed a very appropriate tight squeeze.

I went the whole autumn of 2003 on tour around the UK, only doing the Fairy Godmother and the Summer Fairy (dancing with the lovely Gary Avis, who has been a major star of The Royal Ballet for many years and danced with Darcey Bussell in the ballet sequence, choreographed by Christopher Wheeldon, for the Closing Ceremony of the London Olympic Games). However, by the winter season I was back dancing the role of the Sugar Plum Fairy in *The Nutcracker* with Jan-Erik. This is a very hard *pas de deux* but again it is a comparatively short amount of time on stage; all of this was gradually helping my foot to strengthen and get back to how it had been before the injury.

The injury affected me greatly and I had to learn how to do lots of ballet steps all over again because I needed to do technical things differently due to the weakness in my ankle. Worst of all was that I lost my *plié*, which is a crucial part of every ballet dancer's technique, because I didn't have the strength to bend my foot as much as I had before. This impacted upon many aspects of technique that require the *plié* as the basis for beginning the movement. So, for example, in the *pirouette en dedans* you need to begin by squeezing from the *plié* before going up and turning *en dedans* (which means turning inwards towards the front leg) and after my injury I couldn't do this at all from the left because I no longer had the flexibility, and I was too stiff to get the position that I needed to make the *pirouette*. I have had to relearn how to do it without relying on the *plié* by applying a different set of principles to my movement; and also by padding my left foot to compensate. Over time it has improved but it is still far from being how it was before my foot injury and the subsequent lengthy absence from the stage.

The most frustrating thing about missing out so much due to injury was not just that I missed dancing with Jan-Erik but also because Tom and Agnes had left the company and this meant that I was being cast in the opening nights, but obviously I missed all of them in 2002/3 due to the foot injury.

When I eventually came back, I was cast to do the opening night

Sugar Plum Fairy in *The Nutcracker* at the Coliseum, but on the morning of the performance, I tore my meniscus yet again. This time on the right knee: so in the space of four years I had three operations on my knees – two on the right, and one on the left. It meant missing yet another opening performance with Jan-Erik. Regrettably our intended three years of dancing together were significantly reduced to around only 30 performances, but it was well worth it. After his three years' leave of absence was up, Jan-Erik had to return to Royal Swedish Ballet in order to keep his contract and pension arrangements secured. He is still there in Sweden and still dancing.

While I was off, other dancers benefitted from taking over my roles. Two of these were Sarah McIlroy and Simone Clarke, an English dancer from Yorkshire, both of whom were promoted by Matz Skoog from soloist to principal during this time. Simone was a good friend of mine and she was in a relationship with another company principal, Yat-Sen Chang, with whom she had a daughter.

Some years later, in December 2006, Simone gained notoriety when a membership list for the British National Party was leaked to the *Guardian* newspaper and she was 'outed' as a BNP member. Given Simone's relationship with a Cuban dancer of Chinese origin, and the fact that they had a daughter together, it seemed particularly incongruous that she should be a member of a party with such strong views on race and immigration.

The news of Simone's membership of the BNP broke just as the company was dancing a season of *Giselle* at the London Coliseum and there were suddenly hordes of demonstrators with placards condemning Simone out in front of the theatre. I was asked to standby to take over her role as Giselle on the evening of 12 January 2007, just in case the demonstrations got out of hand. Even though some protestors bought tickets and got into the show, and a few actually stood up and shouted at the stage when she was performing, Simone got through the ordeal without me having to deputise – even though I was in costume and made up, just in case!

I recall that Simone's father was at that particular show, as were some prominent members of the BNP, including a man called Richard Barnbrook who was then the BNP councillor for the London constituency of Barking. Who would have thought that a performance of *Giselle*, the most inoffensive of ballets, could have stirred up so much rancour? I thought that Simone and this BNP councillor seemed to be close and about a year later it was announced that they planned to marry (although I believe that the wedding never happened).

I have to say that Simone was always very friendly to me and to all the other ENB dancers and staff who came from overseas, so I can't say that there was ever any direct evidence of her discussing politics within the workplace. The company refused to get involved for some time but eventually, not much later, Simone left the company. She is now teaching ballet.

I had seen very little of my brother, Radomír, in the years since leaving the Czech Republic. I would occasionally see him in Horní Počernice, usually at our parents' appartment when we happened to visit. Otherwise, I only heard news of him from Mum. But in the summer of 2002, exactly ten years after I left Prague, the devastating weather that hit Central Europe was to change our lives forever.

Radomír and I had fought a great deal when we were growing up in Horní Počernice and, after I had left home, we did not remain close. He could be a very good man with an open heart, but I was never able to forgive him for all the teasing when we were growing up. I am very stubborn like that. If someone upsets me then I can hold that person responsible for years. It is one of my greatest regrets that I was never able to forgive him.

Actually, looking back at our childhoods together, I believe that I was jealous of Radomír. I was always so quiet and rarely, if ever, in any trouble. However, my brother was always in trouble of some kind or another and this, of course, meant that he was the centre of my parents' attention. They may have been angry with him most of the time but he consumed their attention in a way that I never could. I often thought that they didn't care about me.

In many respects this carried on into adulthood. I never needed money from my parents from a very early age. In fact, I had won prize money from competitions in my teenage years and had earned good money as a dancer straight from my graduation from the Conservatoire. On the other hand, my brother always needed financial help. My parents were constantly bailing him out of some difficulty or another and they even bought a flat for him as soon as he got married. I think that they both worked extra hard, doing extra jobs, partly because they needed to support Radomír.

All this extra attention bred the same feelings I held as a child that he somehow meant more to them because of this. Of course, it wasn't true. I didn't need their help but Radomír did: it was as simple as that. As well as causing me to become jealous about all this extra support that my brother received, I also felt that my parents were creating a rod for their own back in constantly bailing him out. I think that they should have said 'no' and he wouldn't have kept coming back for more. I can see now, very clearly, how much of a disappointment Radomír was to my father, but I couldn't see it clearly until after my father had passed away.

Radomír got married young, aged 21, to a girl named Vendula, who had been in his class at school in Horní Počernice. It was very normal in those days for Czech people to marry young. I knew her a little from my own childhood. My parents (Mum, in particular) didn't get on with Vendula but the flat that they bought them after Radomír and

Vendula married was so close to their own apartment that they could see it from their balcony.

I rarely saw Radomír or his wife whenever I went home to Horní Počernice. I didn't go out of my way to meet with him, but if I was staying with my mum and he came to visit her, then of course we would talk, but we had no kind of close brother/sister relationship. I was still angry with him because he was so unreliable.

I have recounted how he stole my savings as a teenager but that didn't stop when he grew up. I remember, for example, that the video machine I had bought with my competition winnings from the Prix de Lausanne was left at my parents' apartment. It was at a time when very few people had video machines in our neighbourhood. So, of course, Radomír asked to borrow it when I was not there and it was never seen again. I'm sure that he sold it because he needed the money – he did many things like that over the years.

Radomír was one of those people that would do these terrible things but he would also give a lot as well. If he had money then he would think nothing of sharing it with friends, which is probably why he never kept any for the longer term. My mum always thought that he was schizophrenic because his character would change so easily, and she often wanted to take him to the doctor as a teenager and a young man but Radomír would never go.

Once he tried to jump out of a window of a high building but he would never have done it: he just wanted the attention of making people think that he might do it. In that respect, he was an attention seeker. He was always in trouble somewhere, frequently mixing with dodgy people and often the centre of some drama or other. Radomír was actually shot once following a drunken argument with a 'friend'. This man owned a gun illegally and they got drunk and had a ridiculous argument, and the man got the gun and fired at him. The bullet grazed his face and he had a scar there for the rest of his life.

Radomír's erratic behaviour kept him permanently at the edge of trouble mainly because he was always mixing with bad people, who would manipulate him for their own ends. I am sure that it was because of my brother's exploits that my mum had to take medication for her nerves at a comparatively young age.

Unfortunately, Vendula was every bit as unstable as my brother and they were a terrible match in terms of saving money. She was invariably rude to my mum and there were so many problems with money concerning my brother and his wife. Vendula didn't work and after my mum was widowed, she would come and visit her regularly. This was at a time when my mum was doing knitting and sewing work from home, and she just could never get anything done.

Seven kilometres outside Prague is a village called Jirny, which is where my father's family came from. Radomír had a friend there, with whom he used to build cars from scratch and sell them. It started as a hobby but it grew into being Radomír's means of making a living. He really enjoyed it, and he was actually very good at making those cars.

It was at this time when there were heavy rains and floods all over central Europe in the summer of 2002 that the second tragedy befell the Kliment family in the space of just a few years. On 4 July, it had been raining around Prague for days and some workmen had been repairing a road between Horní Počernice and Jirny. It wasn't a main road, but a side road (we would probably call it something like a B road or a country lane here in the UK). The workmen left the site with a hole that was around 2m (6.5ft) deep and they didn't put signs up around it.

It rained torrentially through the evening and the hole filled up with water. Radomír drove to his friend's house in Jirny late that night on his motorbike and I guess that he thought it was just a puddle. He rode into the hole and I suppose that he was knocked unconscious by the impact; he drowned in that hole. The next day when the rainwater subsided, some children found his corpse at the bottom of the hole, still grotesquely seated on his motorbike. Mum was in Horní Počernice at the time. Coming just a few years after she lost her husband, aged just 53, this was another massive blow for her. My brother was just 35.

I was dancing in a gala in Spoletto (in fact this was the only time I have ever danced in Italy) when my mum called to tell me the news. It was awful to get this news by phone, as I had about my father, six years earlier. You feel that you are screaming out loud, but the scream is all caught up inside. It's a very strange, numbing feeling. I couldn't stop crying all day and I was due to dance in the evening at the gala, which I did because I had promised to dance and it would have been disappointing for everyone if I did not perform. Luckily, it was the Act II *pas de deux* from *Giselle*, where she has become one of the ghostly Wilis, the spirits of women who have died after being jilted before marriage, so it was somehow appropriate to dance this role after having had such terrible news. It was also a godsend that I was dancing in Italy with Stanislav Fečo, my first partner from the Czech National Ballet, and it was immensely supportive and comforting to be with another dancer from Prague at this terrible time. Lots of photographs were taken at the gala and, when seen in the cold light of day, I looked awful, although somehow I was still appropriate for the deathly pallor of the ghost of Giselle.

Of course, the Kliment family doesn't do funerals so there was no service for Radomír either: just the ritual collection of his ashes. There was, however, a big inquiry into the cause of his tragic accident and my brother's wife won a lot of money from the local council, but what is the money worth when a woman has lost her husband and a little girl has lost her father?

His daughter, Nikola – my only niece – was very angry with Radomír when he died. She didn't get on very well with her mother, and she just blamed him for leaving her as a young girl (she was 12 when it happened) in such terrible circumstances. It wasn't as if he died from an illness but from driving a motorbike down an unlit country road, late at night.

Nikola is now an adult and she is making a successful career as a potter. I am pleased to say that she and my mum (her grandma) are very close. She has also become very friendly with Sabina and they see each other whenever Sabina is in Horní Počernice, so even though Radomír and I didn't get on as brother and sister it is nice that the bond has jumped a generation and our daughters are now very close as cousins.

Later that year, my beloved grandma, Ludmila (my mother's mother and namesake) died peacefully, not far short of her 93rd birthday, on 4 December 2002. My father and brother had both also passed away on the fourth day of the month, so unsurprisingly it is not my favourite date.

Chapter 10

Saved By My Handsome Princes

I didn't plan to add professional photographer to my CV but after Muppet reawakened my interest in photography during our courting years, buying me a succession of better and better cameras and equipment, it quickly progressed from being a hobby into something much more serious. In fact, through the early years of this century I would regularly spend up to five hours a night on my photography, after Sabina had gone to sleep in the evening.

I didn't really plan for it to become that serious, but I suppose that it isn't surprising that my life as a ballet dancer became the inspiration for my photography. This keen interest in photography was captured in an interview with James Hickie for *Student Culture* magazine in 2003, when I explained to him, 'I'm a very visual person and being a dancer makes it easier to photograph ballet, to know what looks right.' My early attempts at professional photography were inspired by an inherent desire to capture the movement of dancers, and I was hugely supported by Matz Skoog, who readily gave me permission to take photos of the dancers. Unsurprisingly, ENB became my first client when the company started to buy pictures from me. Then a dancewear manufacturer called Wear-Moi commissioned me to take photographs for their first catalogue.

I started making annual calendars featuring dancers from ENB. The first year (2003) I funded the project myself, hoping that I might perhaps make the money back. Muppet and I would go around all of the ballet shops and sell a few copies to each one. It made me happy, and I just about recouped my outlay. And then, from the second year, I managed to persuade ENB to become involved and the company invested in the project and marketed the calendars, which is how it carried on for another five years. It took quite a bit of time, but it was fun to do and although no one really made any money out of the calendars, we didn't lose anything either.

As a dancer, I love photographing the human form in movement, so this means that I like photographing naked bodies. My most interesting project was a whole series of naked people jumping on beds. It was initially inspired by a simple picture of a young child jumping on a bed, and I extended the concept into different types of body: fat, thin, tall, etc. It then developed into the idea of showing ballet positions while a naked dancer jumped on the bed. I liked the way it displayed their musculature, and I thought that it was an interesting, unusual and yet quite a shocking concept. Although I am quiet and reserved, I do have a wicked, feisty side to me and I guess that it comes out in ideas such as this.

I am far too shy to have considered approaching strangers – even professional models – to pose for me, so my subjects were all friends or acquaintances. I had all kinds of people doing it, including pregnant dancers. It wasn't hard to persuade friends to do it – I just asked! Believe it or not, there were actually a lot of people who were willing to pose naked. Being a dancer helped a lot since although most people will understandably refuse to have their naked body photographed, many dancers pose willingly. Dancers are generally exhibitionists.

Usually, I would take lots of pictures before a subject would feel comfortable enough to disrobe and jump on the bed naked but some just plunged straight in! When Simone Clarke was pregnant, she and her partner, Yat-Sen Chang, readily agreed to pose naked bouncing on a bed, and it proved to be one of the very best photos from the collection. Photographing Simone in her pregnant condition led to a second series of photographs, just featuring pregnant dancers, mostly photographed naked. For a while I was keen to develop a new project, which would be a calendar of naked dancers (like a ballet version of the *Calendar Girls*) but it hasn't happened... yet!

Since 2007, I have had 15 exhibitions of my photographs given in Prague and elsewhere in the Czech Republic; two exhibitions have been held at the Royal Albert Hall in London, and there have also been exhibitions in Germany and Poland. Some of these exhibitions have been given jointly with the Czech photographer Petr Našic. His work has largely been photographs of me, while my work has been photographs of other dancers so, in these exhibitions, I have been both the artist and the model. In September 2012, an exhibition of my photographs of ballet dancers was held in St Petersburg alongside paintings of dancers by Jan Kunovský.

I met Jan when I was just 18. He was given permission by the authorities in the National Theatre to draw and paint the dancers in the studio, so he spent a great deal of time being inspired as we rehearsed for *The Sleeping Beauty*. He took a particular interest in me and I remember that he spent ages sketching my foot and my leg. Over the years he has become one of my best friends, and I suppose one could say that I have been his muse. As well as working with Jan in Prague, he has come to both Scotland and London to work with me. His art has developed into a unique style where Jan paints onto the model and then photographs the image created by the art on the dancers' bodies to create a series of projections. These projections of painted dancers are often then superimposed onto other dancers, performing live, to create a multiplicity of painted bodies in which it is hard to distinguish the art from the human form. His work, featuring me, was used in a pop video for a well-known Czech band. He is a prolific artist, who is very well known in the Czech Republic, and his exhibitions are more like entertainment shows, fusing art, dance and music.

I hope perhaps one day that I will produce books of my photographs. A particular project that I have in mind is a book of my photographs of Tamara Rojo. I first met her in my final season at Scottish Ballet in 1996, when she had arrived from Spain to dance as a guest in Galina Samsova's *Swan Lake*. In due course, she also came to ENB, arriving a season after me, in 1997. She was rapidly promoted to a principal dancer and Derek Deane created the role of Juliet on her for his production of *Romeo and Juliet*. Tamara joined The Royal Ballet in 2000 and, after a distinguished career with the company, she returned to ENB for the 2012/13 season both as artistic director and principal dancer.

Tamara and I have been friends over this whole period, and I have amassed a large collection of photos that I have taken of her, both in performances and rehearsal and also in her dressing room, applying make-up, or just in everyday circumstances. She is amazingly photogenic with a fantastic bone structure and a beautiful face and body. I like her very much, and I have immense respect for her talent as a dancer but also for her commitment and enthusiasm. Tamara is very opinionated but she has a huge knowledge of ballet and politics, and she is such an activist. She sits on the boards of organisations like Dance UK (a campaigning organisation for the dance industry) and if there is a cause to support in dance you can be sure that she will be there, fighting for it. When Dance UK launched the new National Institute of Dance Medicine and Science in 2012, I was not surprised to hear that Tamara was there to speak at the launch. When she was appointed as the new artistic director of ENB, the company held a press conference at a smart London hotel and Tamara spoke of her plans eloquently. I so admire her for that. For me, public speaking is a much more difficult skill than performing the Rose Adage!

Matz Skoog remained artistic director of ENB for just five seasons, before being succeeded by Wayne Eagling in 2006. There was no particular drama about this, as I recall, although there were always money worries in the company. Matz went back to New Zealand, where his wife, Amanda, is the Royal New Zealand Ballet's general manager and, for a while, in 2011 he took temporary charge of the company again as the acting artistic director, prior to the appointment of the ABT principal dancer, Ethan Stiefel, to become artistic director.

I was very sorry to see Matz leave ENB since he had understood the problems between Dima and myself, and had created a new partner-ship for me with Jan-Erik Wikström (even though my time out through injury had prevented this from developing as I would have hoped). So, to be honest, when I heard that Matz was leaving my first thought was, '*Oh my God, what's going to happen now?*'

I didn't know Wayne Eagling, who had been the artistic director of Dutch National Ballet since 1991. Born in Montreal, he had studied at The Royal Ballet School before joining The Royal Ballet in 1969, and he became a principal dancer in 1975. The most worrying thing was that he was almost an exact contemporary of Derek Deane, and I was sure that they would be friends with a foreboding that this might not augur well for me. I knew of Wayne's versatile and powerful dancing only through having seen him on video tapes. But his time at Dutch

National Ballet meant that he had to have worked hard to maintain a classical, neoclassical and modern repertoire, and he had a reputation for commissioning new work, all of which was promising.

There were two other impacts of this change of director. Firstly, that David Wall retired. This was a major blow to me since he had been the constant through my ten years with the company, and it was David's calmness and support that had often brought me through the bad times. For his retirement party, I made him a picture which was a collage of every ballet dancer in the company, with David at the centre of them all. On his final day, Jay Mews was full of dancers in tears, and it had nothing to do with acting the emotions of the ballet. The second change was that Wayne brought in Maina Gielgud (niece of the famous actor, Sir John Gielgud) as his right-hand person within the company. Maina had been interested in offering me a job when she was artistic director of The Australian Ballet in the early 1990s. Wayne also brought back Ros Whitten to the coaching staff, which was to be another reminder of the Deane regime.

My initial fears were soon realised, when very early in Eagling's tenure as director, I was surprisingly thrown back into partnering Dima again. I suspect that it was just a simple matter of when a work was to be revived, Wayne or Maina would look back at the lists of who had danced it before. Of course, having partnered Dima for so long, there were lots of roles that came back in Wayne's time that we had performed together in former years. So, Wayne would just cast us again because it was the easy option. Of course, I didn't like this – and I'm sure that Dima was none too keen either – since for both of us it was a question of going back and not forward. However, we are both professionals and when cast together by Wayne, we just accepted it and moved on.

This renewed tie-up with Dima was made more palatable because it was at the time that Friedemann Vogel came to guest with the company. He is a German dancer who trained at the Princess Grace Academy in Monte Carlo and won the Prix de Lausanne in 1997 (and the international competition in Jackson, USA, a year later). In 1998, he joined Stuttgart Ballet but has been a guest principal dancer all over the world, including with the Mariinsky in St Petersburg, La Scala in Milan and National Ballet of China.

In 2008, Friedemann came to ENB as a guest to help us make the new *Strictly Gershwin* ballet, for which Derek Deane returned as choreographer. This was his new ballet to be performed 'in the round' at the Royal Albert Hall, made entirely to the music of George Gershwin, as a celebration of the glitz and glamour of Broadway and Hollywood. Derek cast me to partner Friedemann in two duets within the programme, to 'Summertime' and 'The Man I Love' and also to dance with him in the *Rhapsody in Blue* ballet, which evoked the kind of mini-ballet that had featured in the Hollywood films of, say, Gene Kelly in the 1950s. The duet to 'Summertime' was created on us, and we spent two lovely months working on it with Derek, and preparing for the opening at the Royal Albert Hall. I loved working with Friedemann because he would always give emotionally, and it was therefore so easy for me to give back. I would dance with him in a way that allowed me to forget that people were watching me on stage, which was so crucial for me to be able to deal with my insecurities.

After all that had happened before, the process of making the 'Summertime' duet with Derek was remarkably smooth. We even laughed a lot during rehearsals, which was not something I remember ever having happened with Derek before. I think that it helped enormously that Derek liked Friedemann a lot, so there was a really good atmosphere in the studio. It also helped that, with Friedemann, I was in a world of absolute enjoyment with my dancing and my partner, and that was the crucial ingredient to boost my self-confidence.

Even though he was always a guest principal, I danced a lot with Friedemann in the 2008/9 season. However, our very first performance together was in the summer, in *Swan Lake*, at the end of the previous season. This was danced in the very unusual and beautiful circumstances of a platform sitting on an actual lake in front of the Palace of Versailles. The performance had been due to be given with Dima but he was injured at the last minute and Friedemann, who was already there to dance in another cast with Sofiane Sylve (another guest principal, then dancing with New York City Ballet, but now in San Francisco Ballet), became my late substitute as Prince Siegfried.

It was a very difficult performance because the mist from the real lake affected the stage and it became incredibly slippery. By Act III it was like an ice rink and we had to decide on the spot not to dance the variations to save us from injury, so we just did the *adage* and the *coda*, and this meant that the 32 *fouettés* were the best that I have ever done because I wasn't tired from Odile's variation, which always comes just before in the *pas de deux*. Act IV was impossible and Friedemann was just so brilliant, holding me and saving me from falling with certain and secure partnering. We only did one performance in Versailles but it was worth it, despite the slippery conditions. Though we may have been thrown together on an actual lakeside for our first *Swan Lake*, I was certain that this wasn't to be our last. The drama of this event is captured in the first of Martin Kubala's documentary films, made for Czech TV.

After the success of *Strictly Gershwin*, the next ballet I danced with Friedemann was *Manon*. I was so happy that ENB gained the rights to perform Kenneth MacMillan's masterpiece, which tells the tragic story of Manon, an ambitious courtesan who becomes trapped between avarice and her doomed love for a young student named Des Grieux. The original 18th-century novel by Abbé Prévost is perhaps now best-known for the operas it inspired (by Puccini and Massenet) but

MacMillan's ballet (which premiered at the Royal Opera House in 1974) is now a major classic performed around the world. *Manon* is just the kind of expressive, dramatic role that I had coveted ever since joining the company.

ENB didn't have enough men with the ability to dance the lead role of Des Grieux, so Friedemann was once again asked to come over and guest with the company. I was originally cast to dance with Dima but there were the same old tensions in the rehearsal studio and I was very upset by this. I'm afraid that I became hysterical and I went, in tears, to Wayne Eagling and said that I couldn't dance with Dima any longer, and that I would have to leave the company. I have no doubt that I would have gone; I really was at the end of my tether with this ongoing situation of being forced into dancing intensely emotional scenes with Dima. And, in my view, *Manon* would be the very worst ballet to dance without an emotional connection with your partner. After all, in this ballet you die in his arms.

Wayne agreed that he would sort the problem out and he must have seen that the ballet performances would suffer if there was no emotional bond between us. He agreed that I could dance with Friedemann and the casting was swapped around. However, Friedemann had commitments with his home company in Stuttgart, so he couldn't attend the opening stages of the rehearsals for *Manon* and – although I couldn't believe it – after all that had happened, when the schedule for the first rehearsals came out, I was once again down to dance with Dima! I erupted in uncontrollable hysteria. I thought that this was all a ploy: that Wayne had placated me by agreeing to change my partner but then used Friedemann's absence as a reason to put me back in the rehearsal studio with Dima. I was quite certain that the next simple step would be for the management to say, 'Well, you rehearsed with Dima, darling, you may as well dance with him.' This had been going on for years and I had to bring it to closure, or leave the company.

I stormed into the director's office, crying hysterically all over again, and insisted that I would not rehearse with Dima. Everyone in the company knew of our problems. One director had already split us apart and now after so many years, we were being thrown back together again. One of the other dancers, who was not even cast as Des Grieux, James Forbat, who had recently joined the company and was then still a first artist, came to my rescue by agreeing to rehearse with me until Friedemann arrived from Germany. James is a really lovely guy and I guess that he wanted to learn the role. But, anyway we had lots of fun and he filled in for Friedemann superbly and, in doing so, kept me dancing, since I am quite sure that I would have walked if my problem had not been quickly solved. When Friedemann arrived we had a blissful two months learning the roles and touring around the UK, performing *Manon* in Bristol, Manchester, London Coliseum and Oxford. I opened my 2009/10 season by performing the bedroom *pas de deux* with him in Taipei.

MacMillan's *Manon*, danced with Friedemann Vogel, is certainly one of my favourite ballets. Friedemann is sensitive and kind, and we worked on our partnering a great deal. He is big and strong, and I am a tiny dancer for him, so we could take risks. This almost backfired in our very first performance in Bristol because there are two sequences in the bedroom *pas de deux* at the end of Act I, where Manon slides across the floor as part of the duet, that we went for so energetically that I badly bruised my foot. It hurt like the blazes, especially when I had to do it again moments later, but there was no way that I was going to go 'off' and miss dancing with this wonderful partner, so I persevered through the pain.

I am from the Russian school of partnering, where the ballerina is taught to stand on her legs for her partner, to get into the positions and to make the work easier for him, and I think Friedemann enjoyed that because it meant that he had to do only the minimum and put less strength into the partnering than he had been used to giving. The other wonderful thing about Friedemann is that he always goes full out in acting the dramatic content of a narrative and integrating his amazing expressiveness within the ballet. This is what I love; working with him on *Manon* gave me no chance to remain as Daria in the ballet. He immersed himself completely in the role of Des Grieux and left me with no option but to be Manon with an equal certainty.

This feeling began in the studios with every single rehearsal. I left Daria at the door and immediately became Manon when we started working together. There was never a single second when I felt like Daria learning the role of Manon: Friedemann made me believe that we were our characters from the very first moment. This is what I loved about working with him. Friedemann made me feel so comfortable that any shyness about the role and any concerns about the technique or movement just melted away when I was dancing with him. I have only ever danced the whole show of *Manon* with Friedemann Vogel (although I have danced the bedroom *pas de deux* with others at galas around the world).

I liked dancing with Friedemann so much that I started to ask him to do guest performances with me. The feeling was sufficiently mutual, I believe, that he considered joining ENB and I think that the company almost got him. Wayne Eagling certainly wanted him – what director wouldn't want a tall, strong, handsome dancer who had already performed the whole classical repertoire? In the end, I think it was the company's inability to meet the money Friedemann was already earning in Stuttgart that became the showstopper. But little did I know that while all of this was going on, and I was so desperate for Friedemann to join the company and partner me, another young dancer destined for world-class stardom was already in Wayne's sights.

At that time, a very young man from Perm in Russia, by the name of Vadim Muntagirov, was completing his training at The Royal

Ballet School. His parents were both principal dancers at the Chelyabinsk Ballet Company, which is located to the east of the Urals, close to the border between Europe and Asia, and as a very young boy he was sent to train at the Perm Ballet School. At the end of his time completing his ballet studies in London, he had won numerous laureates and prizes at international ballet competitions. He had a fine reputation and was seen as a rising star but surprisingly on graduation The Royal Ballet didn't take him into their ranks. At the time, he had a contemporary who was another great virtuoso talent and it was this young man, Sergei Polunin – who came from Kiev in the Ukraine, who was preferred by the director of The Royal Ballet, Dame Monica Mason. And so it was Polunin who went into the company. It was rumoured throughout the dance world that she was influenced by the fiery handsomeness of the young Ukrainian dancer but fire brings with it the danger of being burnt and the tempestuous nature of this hugely talented dancer finally led him to walk out of The Royal Ballet in January 2012, after weeks of unhappiness when he was not attending class and posting strange late night messages about partying and drugs on his Twitter account.

I didn't meet Sergei until after he had left The Royal Ballet, when I danced at a series of shows promoted in Japan during the spring of 2012 by The Royal Ballet's principal ballerina, Alina Cojocaru. At that time he was contemplating giving up dancing altogether, and I couldn't understand why when he had such incredible talent. At those Japanese shows, I encountered a young man with energy and dedication but perhaps lacking guidance and direction. I liked him very much and I hoped that someone would provide the mentoring that this young man needed. At the time that I write this, it seems that his talents may be saved for ballet since he has come under the wing of the great Russian dancer, Igor Zelensky, who is now the director of

Moscow Stanislavsky Ballet in Russia, where Polunin is now based as a principal dancer.

Discovering that his counterpart at The Royal Ballet was not taking Vadim, Wayne Eagling was in like a shot and offered him a great deal to join ENB. Knowing the company, and having come to know Vadim, I doubt if the attraction of this arrangement would have been so much about money because the main temptation would certainly have been the prospect of being offered the major classical roles to dance early in his career, which is every dancer's dream. To whet his appetite even more, Wayne offered Vadim the chance to dance the role of Albrecht (the lead male role in *Giselle*) before Christmas in his very first season, which meant that within six months of leaving ballet school, he would be headlining in a major ballet in a major company. This was completely unheard of, but Wayne clearly had every confidence in the young Russian boy.

Despite his reputation, I didn't even know this young man had joined the company. Rushing home after class and rehearsals to be with Sabina often meant that I was a bit behind on the company gossip! I'm certainly not a diva, but I don't really mix with the younger dancers who are in their early years in the company. I guess that it is a generational thing more than anything else, and it is probably the same in any other working environment: I mix with the older dancers who have been in the company for awhile and, of course, they tend to be the more established dancers. Many of them are now also parents and share the same issues of managing a dance career and a family.

The first time that I noticed this new boy was one day in class. Not because he was doing exercises any better than anyone else but because I could see that he was very shy. I noticed that he was new and also that he was sitting on the floor, completely on his own, so I went over to say 'hello'. We had the briefest of chats and when I came away – and for some time afterwards – I hadn't even realised that he was Russian.

I had no idea that Wayne had earmarked him for swift elevation through the company ranks, I just thought that he was a new young boy in the *corps de ballet.*

At that time we were rehearsing for *Giselle* and, because Friedemann had gone back to Stuttgart, I was scheduled to dance with yet another new partner, Esteban Berlanga, a Spanish dancer who had joined the company in 2006. I liked Esteban and I was very happy to dance with him. At some point later, I discovered that the young man I had met sitting on the floor was also going to dance the lead role of Albrecht. I was very surprised, but I certainly had no idea that it would have any relevance to me.

I did, however, immediately realise why this meant that he was a bit of a loner. There is always an element of jealousy within any ballet company – it goes with the territory. Here was a talented young man, joining ENB at 19 years of age and immediately getting set for leading roles. Naturally he was leapfrogging over other men who had been waiting for years to get such a chance. I recognised this problem because I had suffered similar jealousies from the older ballerinas when I graduated into the Czech National Ballet and was cast in soloist roles during my first season, but I had enjoyed the twin safeguards of at least being from the country that I was dancing in and coming up from the school with several friends who also joined the company at the same time. Vadim, on the other hand, had trained at the school of a rival company and there were no contemporaries of his that had joined ENB, which meant that he had no pre-existing friends in the company. He was to all intents and purposes completely alone, and suffering from the envy of others.

We went on tour to Barcelona at the beginning of the 2009/10 season, where we danced *Les Sylphides*, a one-act plot-less ballet in which a young man (perhaps a poet) dances with a group of sylphs (mythological, ethereal beings usually associated with woodland).

With choreography by Mikhail Fokine and music by Chopin, it was the first classical ballet to be about form rather than a story. It remains a staple ideal of the romantic 'white' ballet. I was cast to dance with Anton Lukovkin, a young Russian dancer who had recently joined the company from Mariinsky Ballet in St Petersburg, and Vadim was due to dance with Anaïs Chalendard, a French dancer who had joined the company in 2008. They were a very good match in terms of physicality and proportion, and I imagine that many of us assumed that this was going to be his intended partnership.

I only noticed Vadim's dancing for the first time in the rehearsal studio in Barcelona as we prepared for *Les Sylphides*. Neither of our partners had yet arrived in Barcelona and another couple were rehearsing the *pas de deux* that we were also going to perform, albeit with other partners, so I went over to Vadim and asked if he would rehearse the duet with me. His initial response really shocked me since he replied that he didn't want to. I interpreted this as youthful arrogance but I wasn't taking 'no' for an answer, so I effectively pulled rank to make him rehearse with me. It was awful. Dancers have to be pretty intimate with each other from the very beginning. If a man is rehearsing a *pas de deux* with a ballerina and has to lift her then it is very likely that he is going to have to grip her high up on the thigh and touch her more or less anywhere on her body! There is certainly no scope for being prudish in any way. On this first rehearsal, Vadim hardly dared to touch me at all and he kept missing me at important moments because he was especially nervous in those vital aspects of holding me. After a few minutes he managed to find an excuse not to carry on with the rehearsal and dashed off.

Apart from being shocked at how awful his partnering was, I wondered why he so obviously hadn't wanted to dance with me. It crossed my mind that as a Russian, Vadim may have heard that I was difficult to get on with in the rehearsal room, since it was natural that he would have talked to another Russian dancer in the company, namely Dima. Anyway, I gave up asking him to rehearse with me again in Barcelona since I didn't see the sense in flogging a dead horse, and I more or less forgot about him. To tell the truth, I even forgot his name.

The tour of *Giselle* began in Liverpool and I did a couple of shows with Esteban, as planned. Vadim wasn't yet dancing in *Giselle* with Anaïs. It may have been that they were being held back for later casts in other towns, or Anaïs was injured. However, at that time, I wouldn't have been able to confirm that he was even dancing the lead role of Albrecht because I was in my own little world, beginning to establish a new partnership dancing with Esteban. Then, one day I got a message that Wayne wanted to see me in his office and my first thought was, *'Oh no, what I have done wrong?'* as it usually is when the director wants to see any dancer!

Wayne told me that he wanted me to dance with Vadim in *Giselle* and, when I picked my jaw back up from off the floor, he went on to explain that Anaïs was injured and he needed a reliable, experienced partner for his new young prodigy. I had what I guess might be described as a panic attack and started to cry. I couldn't understand why Wayne wanted me, a woman approaching 40 and the company's senior ballerina, to dance with a boy fresh out of ballet school, who was nearly 20 years younger than me: literally half my age. I pleaded with the director to change his mind, but he was adamant that it had to happen since he had no one else available and capable of performing the role in the place of Anaïs.

It was completely unheard of that anyone should come from school straight into dancing a principal role within a matter of a few months. I now thought that Wayne must be mad. My initial panic was exacerbated by the awful experience of briefly working with Vadim in the studio in Barcelona. I couldn't understand how anyone so inexperienced could carry off such a key acting role, which requires an immense emotional maturity.

I also thought that I would be humiliated in public. How could I be a realistic young village girl (Giselle) falling in love when I must look like my paramour's mother? I honestly thought that audiences would laugh at me because of the difference in our ages, although I was by this time well used to dancing with younger men. Esteban was at least ten years younger than me but somehow this didn't seem to be as bad. I guess that the worst aspect of my concern was that Vadim had recently come from school.

I also felt, albeit irrationally, that this must be some kind of a delayed punishment for me asking to leave the company if they forced me to dance with Dima. I saw it as a kind of rough, poetic justice: I refused to dance with one Russian principal, so they paired me with a Russian boy just out of school. I know now that such feelings were ridiculous but at the time I was so upset that anything seemed to be part of a general conspiracy against me.

After being given this ultimatum by Wayne, I went home and cried to my mum, telling her that I couldn't dance with someone that much younger than me. I remember telling her that I would look like a grandmother compared to this boy. Not for the first time in my life, Mum had a unique way of putting these matters into perspective. She laughed at me and said, 'You must be mad! You are going to be living every older woman's dream to have such a good-looking, virile younger man falling in love with you.' With the sense of irony that only a mum can have towards her only daughter, she told me, 'You will just have to bear the pain and humiliation of having this young, handsome boy telling you that he loves you!' She then added that I could instead be asked to dance with a 'miserable, grumpy man who is closer to your own age' before finishing with, 'and which would you enjoy the most?' This advice hit the spot like a guided missile. My mum always knows how to make me feel good and telling me to go and enjoy myself was exactly the right thing to say to overcome my fears.

In the cold light of day and looking back with the benefit of hindsight, I can now see that Wayne had no alternative. He had brought Vadim to the company with the promise of dancing the role of Albrecht before Christmas and his intended partner had gone 'off' injured, so the director was stuck in a hole. I'm certain that he didn't intend to make a partnership out of Daria and Vadim; it was just that I was the only viable option to enable Wayne to fulfil his promise to this new young recruit. He just needed a partner for Vadim, and I was the only person available that could dance in that show.

I had no choice but to agree to dance with Vadim and Mum had made me realise that it wasn't the end of the world, but I didn't attend every rehearsal with him. Already I had danced the role of *Giselle* more than 20 times (with three different partners) at ENB, and my one condition was to tell Wayne that I wasn't going to spend hours waiting around while this young boy learned his role for the first time. I wasn't going to work on every step, over and over again, because I had already passed through all of this 20 years before. Wayne understood and he agreed that this wasn't necessary, so poor Vadim rehearsed his first big role almost entirely on his own. I only worked with him to prepare the *pas de deux* that we did together.

Our first rehearsal was in a tiny little studio in Liverpool, where we ran through the important sequence of when Giselle and Albrecht (who is a nobleman masquerading as a villager called Loys) meet outside her mother's cottage early in the first scene. When I came into the studio, Vadim was already there lying on the floor, playing some computer game, as he always did (and still does)! Our ballet coach, Maina Gielgud, wasn't there yet so we waited in complete silence while he carried on playing his game, ignoring me. It really didn't augur well for the emotional connection that we needed to forge in the scene where Albrecht declares his undying love for Giselle.

After several minutes of silence, I thought, '*Well, if I'm going to have to dance with this boy, I'm going to have to make the effort.*' I was conscious that we were about to embark on rehearsing scenes of love and devotion, yet here we were and I barely knew his name let alone the slightest thing about him. I interrupted his game by asking him questions. It was just small talk, really – trying to get to know him in an attempt to break the ice between us.

One of the first questions I asked him was whether he had a girlfriend because I thought that he was a young man and they like to talk about these things. He told me that he did have a girlfriend and then a few moments later he changed his mind and said, 'No, actually I don't have a girlfriend!' It seemed pretty odd to lose your girlfriend in the space of a few sentences. Dancers have a very well attuned antennae for other dancers' sexuality, so I was absolutely certain that he wasn't gay (I would say that at least 50 per cent of male ballet dancers are gay), but apparently he couldn't remember whether he had a girlfriend or not. It was a completely uncomfortable situation and my attempts to break the ice totally backfired!

When Maina eventually turned up and our first rehearsal got underway, horrible is an understatement to describe how appalling it was. He couldn't even look at me, let alone do a step properly. My very worst fears had come to fruition. But this time, something almost maternal took over within me. Instead of running off, hysterical and not wanting to go through with what I thought was going to be the most humiliating experience of my career, I just knew that I had to persevere. I accepted that this was going to be very hard work but – on that day in Liverpool – I suddenly had a striking and overwhelming sense of responsibility. I was older and had over 20 seasons of experience, and here was a boy being asked to do a principal role straight from school. He hadn't asked to do it, any more than I had asked to dance with him, so I went back to my tactic of trying to coax the best out of him rather than thinking what the potential downsides were for me.

For the rehearsals that followed, I would always make an effort to interrupt his gaming to speak to him before we began. I have always been interested in psychology and I knew that if you make people feel good about themselves then you get the best out of them. I had done this with all my partners, including Dima, and it had helped some of the time.

With Vadim, I particularly tried to make him laugh because I thought that this might help to reduce the age difference between us, which I had come to see as the key problem from his perception as well as my own. I came to realise that my interpretation of his deficiencies in the studio was actually all down to his shyness, and nothing whatsoever to do with arrogance. His lack of confidence came back to the fact that I had been a senior principal with the company for many years. In fact, I had joined ENB as a principal before he had even gone to junior ballet school. This, I realised, was the root of the problem. So I set out on a deliberate campaign to make Vadim feel good about himself as a dancer, and to do that I had to make him feel that he was my equal in the studio.

The other problems I could do nothing about. To play a love scene, I think that you have to know about love, and I'm sure that Vadim had not experienced anything like this at that time, so he was faking an imagined emotion rather than drawing on his own experience of life. I knew that it was going to make it very difficult for us to make the emotional connection that is vital to an effective reading of this most romantic of ballets.

An even bigger problem was that he had so very little experience of a full-length narrative ballet. Vadim had grown up, all his life, in a ballet environment. His mother and father were both dancers. He was sent, on his own as a nine-year-old, halfway across Russia to start his ballet training and then came to England aged 16, not speaking the language or knowing anything about the culture, and he has been on his own in that sense ever since. No wonder he sought solace in computer games – it was a comfort blanket in every sense.

Vadim's training and the competitions he entered meant that he had danced extracts of ballets and he may have had some minor involvement in full-length ballets as a student, but he had never had to carry the whole of a story in a major expressive role. This was his very first experience of that pressure and I came to realise that it was the main cause of his discomfort: he had never played a lover or acted out a major character through a whole show. Not only this, but instead of having a low-key debut in the 5th or 6th cast on a Wednesday matinee, he was to make his debut with the most senior ballerina in the company. No wonder he was nervous. Actually, I could feel his tension and that made me very uncomfortable, too.

Unsurprisingly our first show at the Mayflower Theatre in Southampton didn't go that well and neither of us enjoyed it. Act I was particularly difficult with the pair of us appearing to be uncomfortable strangers while we are going through the business of a very romantic courtship. In our first scene together, the character of Albrecht pulls petals from a flower in the traditional 'He Loves Me, He Loves Me Not' rhyme and, counting down the petals, Giselle sees that it will end with 'he loves me not', so secretly Albrecht removes an extra petal so that the right result will ensue. I think that the people watching that first show in Southampton would have been surprised about the 'he loves me' ending since we must have looked as if we had just met awkwardly for the first time and couldn't bear each other's company! However, we had got through the choreography unscathed (which I hadn't initially thought was possible) and Act II was much better.

One major eye-opener for me during Act II in Southampton was that I had never previously seen Vadim dance his variation as Albrecht because I had not been attending his rehearsals due to my deal with Wayne. I watched from the wings in awe because his solo was exceptionally good, and I was both surprised and very impressed by the strength of his technique and his incredible talent. In that few minutes, I came to see why Vadim was being fast-tracked into principal roles at such a young age.

After the first show in Southampton, I assumed that I would be going back to dancing *Giselle* with Esteban, especially since the performance with Vadim had been so uncomfortable. However, Wayne saw our performance through different eyes, so we performed *Giselle* again in Southampton and then in Oxford (although I did the second Oxford show with Esteban) and, although I could not say that we achieved the connection that is necessary between these doomed lovers, gradually we began to feel more comfortable together. The main impetus was that we were able to communicate more freely with one another and, crucially, Vadim would start to ask me how to do things. We also came to realise that we share the same sense of humour, both coming from Eastern Europe, and we used to converse mostly in Russian. There came a point when I could feel the thaw quicken from rehearsal to rehearsal and our partnership was beginning to blossom.

Much later when we had become friends, Vadim told me that the problem was solely that he was too shy to dance with me and had been trying to think of all kinds of excuses to get away. However, my efforts to evaporate our age difference by speaking to him as an equal and to make him laugh had worked, and this had boosted his confidence to communicate – and therefore to dance – with me. Even though I readily admit that my primary motivation was to make an effort for the sake of the show, he decided that I was doing it just because it was natural for me to be so nice. I started off being motivated by very selfish reasons, because I wanted to be able to get through (and perhaps even enjoy) the show, but in some ways, I think that he also helped me to become a nicer person to work with in the studio. Everything began to click into place. He became more confident and that meant that he was more giving to me as his partner; in turn, I responded by giving back and this virtuous circle kept growing in the emotional connection between us.

It is also important to say that I came to recognise that I had been very selfish about doubting his abilities, since hadn't I myself gone through exactly the same immediate elevation when I left the Conservatoire in Prague? I was dancing principal roles within a few months of becoming a professional dancer and I had always been carefully groomed towards that end. If it was OK for me, albeit 20 years earlier, then how could I begrudge Vadim the same early success and, once I saw his full potential as a remarkable dancer, when I watched from the wings in Southampton and Oxford, I knew that he deserved it and I appreciated that Wayne Eagling's talent-spotting had been brilliant.

By the time we got to the London Coliseum for our traditional winter season in the capital, everything between us had got better; we both realised that we were on the same wavelength and that we wanted to achieve the same ideals with our dancing. We were ready for the expert London audiences. The opportunities for London balletomanes to see classical ballet are many and frequent, and there are those in the audience who come to every show that The Royal Ballet, ENB and all of the many visiting international ballet companies make in a year. They can be seeing first-class ballet five or six times every week and many of them do.

The first night of the *Giselle* run at the Coliseum was taken by Dima, dancing with his new partner, Fernanda Oliveira, a Brazilian ballerina who had been with the company since 2000, but at least one critic still got in to see our only performance. Writing on the *ballet.co* website, the Hong Kong-based critic Kevin Ng said, 'Muntagirov was a revelation. He had a formidable technique with high powerful jumps. His classical dancing was stylish and elegant. His legs had a fresh delicacy which showed off perfectly his youth and human vulnerability. His acting was heartfelt, and his partnering of Klimentová was pretty strong'. Even more interesting, given the circumstances of how Vadim came to be at ENB, the reviewer had seen a performance of *The Sleeping Beauty* at The Royal Ballet on the same day with Sergei Polunin as the prince. Ng said he found Muntagirov 'a better danseur noble and technically even more exciting'. He concluded his review by saying that 'Muntagirov is definitely a potential future star to watch out for,' and added how lucky for Daria Klimentová to have this new partner. If only he had been in that studio in Liverpool a few weeks before!

In the summer of 2009, I achieved my dream of dancing with the great Cuban virtuoso, Carlos Acosta, when I partnered him in *Apollo* in Manchester and then again, early in 2010, at Sadler's Wells in London. Carlos is rightly regarded as one of the world's greatest male dancers and he had been a principal at ENB, briefly before my time, in 1991/92. Since the late 1990s, he has been involved as a principal and guest principal artist at The Royal Ballet and as an international guest star in huge demand all over the world. Often he organises his own shows, usually having at least one season per year at Sadler's Wells or the Coliseum for himself and some friends, and on this occasion he asked me to be Terpsichore (the dancing muse) to his Apollo. For me, it was a dream come true: Carlos is an amazing partner and a dancing phenomenon. Unfortunately, however, as with many such dreams it ended up as a disappointment because we were not able to make the connection I always hope for. It is difficult when you are thrown together like that for a one-off series of shows (in Manchester it was just three performances on successive days, and at Sadler's Wells a further five shows over a week). We had only three rehearsals and we didn't have a chance to stamp our mark on this dance, or even get to know each other very well. We both respected each other but we just didn't have time to arrive at any special connection. Having said that, the performances went well and the audiences certainly appreciated them: he is an unbelievable partner and it really was a dream come true!

At the time that I started dancing with Vadim, I was planning a gala in Prague to celebrate my 1,000th stage performance. For the whole of my career, I have recorded every performance in which I have danced in a little exercise book – which is now badly tattered and falling apart – and idly counting them up one day in 2009, I realised that I was getting close to performing a thousand times. At this time, I was 38 and preparing myself mentally to quit dancing. I had been thinking that perhaps it might be that season or the next when I would stop. I was especially concerned that the forthcoming ENB repertoire in 2010 was the same as I had been dancing for a while and there seemed to be nothing to look forward to.

When I found out about this special milestone it seemed to me that my target for retiring might be a special gala to celebrate my career at the 1,000th performance. A kind of 1,000 and out event! So, I set out to design the gala with this prospect in mind. My heart has always been in Prague and it seemed appropriate to arrange the gala to be held in my home city. However, after a while – and perhaps Vadim had something to do with this – I decided that it was premature to stop dancing and I turned the gala into a celebration of ten centuries of my dancing days and nights on stage.

After performing *Giselle* with Vadim I invited him to perform at this gala, which was held in the spring of 2010, not because I particularly wanted to dance with him since I had planned the event around dancing with my two favourite partners, Friedemann Vogel and Jan-Erik Wikström: the plan being to dance the *Manon pas de deux* with Friedemann and Balanchine's Tchaikovsky *pas de deux* (or *Tchaipa*) with Jan-Erik. Vadim came with Erina Takahashi to dance two *pas de deux* from *Giselle* and *Le Corsaire*. By this time, I knew beyond all doubt that he was a rising star of ballet, and I just wanted him to be a part of my gala, even if not partnering me.

I organised the whole gala by myself. I had booked the dancers, arranged their travel and accommodation, agreed what they were going to dance and ensured that the music was sorted. I had made all the arrangements with the National Theatre: in fact, everything a promoter and producer of a performance would have to do. What made all of this more complicated was that neither Friedemann nor Jan-Erik were able to perform because they both got injured only days before the event, so I had to rush around even more arranging for substitutes.

As it happened, I danced at the gala with three partners: the *Manon pas de deux* with Esteban Berlanga; the Tchaikovsky *pas de deux* with Yoel Carreño, the Cuban dancer who is the brother of the former ABT star dancer, José Manuel Carreño, and now dances with his wife, Yolanda Correa Frias, at the Norwegian Ballet; and the Mashkovsky Waltz with Tamás Solymosi (the brother of Zoltan, my first partner at ENB). Tamás had actually retired from dancing at this point but this waltz is a dance where the man mostly throws the girl into the air and he could do that without much rehearsal. In addition, I danced a solo by my old friend, Christopher Hampson.

At this time, I still thought that *Giselle* was just a makeshift pairing with Vadim as a sort of water-treading exercise while Anaïs Chalendard recovered from injury, but after the excellent reaction to our London Coliseum performances, we then moved on to be paired in Christopher Hampson's interpretation of *The Nutcracker*, which I had danced so many times previously with Dima. By this time, even though we still had some work to do on improving our partnering skills together, I had accepted that the partnership was working, and I was looking forward to dancing the role of the Sugar Plum Fairy with Vadim in a way that I hadn't felt for a long time.

One of the vital ingredients in my partnership with Vadim has been sharing and developing a mutual sense of humour. We can now see situations almost simultaneously that will make us both laugh out loud. The impetus comes from him because at first I was self-conscious about doing silly things in front of a much younger man. I would make some jokes to help our communication but he would often do such silly things to make me laugh. He is exceptionally good at imitating people, especially other dancers but also actors and singers. An outstanding mimic, he can capture both the vocal and physical eccentricities of a wide range of people in a very funny way. He has a brilliant catalogue of impersonations of a whole galaxy of Old Russian dancers, which pick up and exaggerate their particular idiosyncrasies and characteristics. And, although this is always funny, he does it in a very reverential and respectful way. It is caricature but he is not making fun of them. One of the motivations for this is that Vadim knows that these previous generations of dancers had a richer variety of ballet movement than we do today, where the emphasis has become like the Olympic motto 'faster, higher, stronger'. Now it is all about multiple *pirouettes* and higher elevation in the jumps but then it was about artistry, and both Vadim and I feel that much has been lost in this increasingly acrobatic/gymnastic age. He feels it even though he can do so many *pirouettes* astonishingly well and jumps higher than anyone I've ever danced with.

Vadim is a very cerebral dancer and, of course, ballet has been in his blood since he was born. I doubt that there was ever a chance that he was going to be anything other than a ballet dancer. He may play a lot of computer games, as every young man probably does these days, but he also watches every ballet film that is available on YouTube, as well as having a huge collection of his own ballet DVDs. Also, he can describe in detail just about any dancer's technique with their strengths and weaknesses, but the key to this is that he will never tell just anyone this. It is intensely secret knowledge that he shares only with his closest friends and family, and the same is true of his private imitations.

Vadim is a remarkably caring partner and we both give each other as many corrections as we can in a mutually supportive way. When we are dancing together but one of us is offstage, we will always be watching the other from the wings. There is never any thought of just going to get a drink or have a rest. I love this depth of involvement, and I am so glad to have found a dance partner like Vadim, even if it has come in my twilight years as a principal ballerina.

My favourite ballet is now *Romeo and Juliet*, but only ENB's version choreographed by Rudolf Nureyev, and only when danced with Vadim, which is made all the more special because for most of my career I thoroughly disliked dancing the role of Juliet. Vadim was the first partner to make me feel like I am 16, even though I was approaching 40 when we first danced together. When Vadim dances, you can see that he is Romeo in every possible way. The ironic thing is that, at first, I really didn't want to dance as Juliet next to him: I had big issues with our age difference, and I couldn't see how it would be at all believable for the audience. I honestly thought that it would destroy the show for the people watching.

Since Vadim made me feel as if I really were this teenage girl and the same roles had been a major success story for Margot Fonteyn and another young Russian dancer, Rudolf Nureyev, who had exactly the same age gap, I thought why not, and I was so glad that I took that particular plunge. Somehow it wasn't hard because when I see Vadim jumping these high jumps, just for me, then what have I to worry about? I just throw myself into the role, buoyed by this incredible connection between us.

I had danced *Romeo and Juliet* with other dancers before Vadim, notably with Laurentiu Guinea, Jan-Erik Wikström and Dima. I think that those early performances with Laurentiu and Jan-Erik were fine, although both dancers were of the unselfish type that cared too much for how the ballerina looked and did not put enough into their own performances. I remember having to tell Jan-Erik after one performance that he had to look after himself as well as me. I have to say that I felt like an old woman whenever I danced Juliet with Dima. There was just no connection as there should have been. I was not Juliet, he was not Romeo: we were Daria and Dima trying to be these characters and failing miserably. We managed to make some people believe, somehow, because we must be good actors but my own enjoyment was just not there.

I love the romantic notion that has evolved that somehow Vadim and I were designed to be the new first couple of ENB with all the emotional associations linking us to the pairing of Fonteyn and Nureyev, some 45 years earlier, at The Royal Ballet. By coincidence the 19-year age difference between Vadim and I is identical to the age difference between Fonteyn and Nureyev (she was born – as Peggy Hookham – in 1919; and he was born – on a train journey in Siberia – in 1938). But, the truth is much more prosaic. We were not created by plan or design but through the necessity of being thrown together as a result of an injury to another dancer. It is an age-old story of the ballet. Wayne certainly deserves the credit for seeing that the partnership worked and then persevering with it. I'm very glad that he did.

One particular ritual we now have is that wherever we go in the world, we find a local landmark and Vadim will put me into a high lift for a souvenir photograph! After one performance in Hong Kong, I suggested that he lifted me for a photo and the concept stuck. The photographer in me is always interested in the idea of a series of similar visual images, like my naked people jumping on beds or the pregnant dancers. Now a new series is that we have photos of Vadim lifting me high, taken all over the world. One day, I will create an album of all these photographs put together. Perhaps it can illustrate another book?

In the summer of 2012 we were performing together in Denmark and due to some strange arrangements we had to take class in a gym beside a swimming pool. We both saw the potential for a funny film that showed me fighting to perform a series of multiple *fouettés* before coming off balance and falling into the pool! Vadim filmed this and we put it on both YouTube and Facebook, and these few seconds of film got thousands of views! Although I am a good swimmer, I hate my head going underwater but it was worth conquering that fear to make such a funny film. It was especially funny because, like all ballerinas, I have spent my career fighting with the *fouettés* and I have fallen more than once.

I remember once falling over during the *fouettés* in *Swan Lake* on a tour of Australia, early in my career at ENB. All of a sudden, I was sitting on my bum looking decidedly inelegant in my beautiful black tutu. Instead of crying, I just started to laugh nervously and the audience loved it. From that point onwards, I had them on my side.

Much more recently, I fell over in front of Vadim in Serge Lifar's difficult ballet *Suite en Blanc*, attempting a double at the end of the *fouettés* at the London Coliseum, ending up on my back with my legs in the air. It was an important debut for me in a very important ballet, and I had lots of fans there to see me. When I was younger and fell on the stage I would get very upset, but it happens and you get used to accepting it as part of the deal as a ballet dancer. I guess it's similar to a gymnast like Beth Tweddle falling off the beam or a diver like Tom Daley over-rotating on a dive. It's just one of the hazards of the profession. If I fall now, my reaction would probably depend on what kind of a mood I'm in, but when it happened during *Suite en Blanc* I was very pre-menstrual and I took it so seriously, like the end of the world, and I started to cry. Vadim came to see me backstage because he knew that I was going to be upset and I hit him because I was furious! He just laughed about it and the next day, after my period had started, I was able to see the funny side, too, and I apologised.

My life as a dancer has been seriously affected by my menstrual cycle. When I was a gymnast in the Czechoslovakian Olympic Squad, I had been too young for anyone to mess around with my periods, as happened with some of the older girls, but I was to find out that I didn't need anything to mess up my menstruation. It messed me up plenty! I have always just put up with it but the pre-menstrual tension makes me especially moody and it leads to lots of tears and arguments; and it has got worse as the years go by. It has led to a few missed performances over the years.

Unfortunately, I have had a life-long aversion to taking pills, so I have never taken any contraceptive pills that might have helped to regulate my periods and lessen the PMT, the stomach cramps and everything that goes with it. I would take medication if I felt it was absolutely necessary (and by this, I mean potentially life-saving or to recover from an injury), but I am against regularly 'popping' pills just to control a little bit of pain or discomfort. Even in my 40s, I will take a lot of pain before resorting to any painkilling drugs. When the doctors prescribe pills for me, I tend to read the leaflets and get worried about all of the side effects listed; often they just sit in the kitchen and I never take them.

Having been dragged almost kicking and screaming to dance with

Vadim in the first place, there eventually came a time when we were both cast to dance with somebody else, but this time I went and said that I just didn't want to change my partner again. A 19-year age difference means that I won't be the only established partner that Vadim has, but I certainly now intend that he will be my final dance partner, and I will carry on partnering him for as long as I can do so to the level that satisfies us both. I am clear that had I not been thrown together with Vadim in 2009, I would not still be dancing in 2013. I would have retired by now, that's for sure.

So when they tried to split us up not long after we had become comfortable with one another, we both made it clear in separate interviews with Wayne Eagling that we did not want to be separated, and we fought together to remain as a partnership.

Chapter 11

Agony and Ecstasy

*B*BC cameras came into ENB in 2010 to film three fly-on-the wall documentaries under the series title *Agony & Ecstasy: A Year with English National Ballet*. The first episode featured preparations for the opening night of Derek Deane's 'in the round' *Swan Lake* at the Royal Albert Hall. This was to be Vadim's very first performance in the greatest classical ballet of them all. He had just celebrated his 20th birthday and here he was, rehearsing for one of the toughest ballets. Just to make it worse, it was to be the unforgiving 'in the round' version from which there is no escape from the audience's scrutiny (although I had managed to flee from it the first time around, back in the 1990s). It was to be supervised by the choreographer himself – a man very hard to please, as I knew to my cost – and it wasn't to be a low-key debut on a wet afternoon in Southampton but at the Royal Albert Hall, not to mention one filmed to be seen by millions on the BBC!

As the cameras rolled on towards the opening night in June, a new drama emerged as it became evident that Polina Semionova, a glamorous guest ballerina from Russia, now a principal with the Berlin State Opera, was in danger of being prevented by visa problems from arriving in time to dance with Vadim, and this 'will she/won't she?' issue meant that I had to step in to rehearse with Vadim before his debut.

Eventually, we discovered that Semionova wouldn't arrive in time to dance on the opening night, so the main thrust of the film changes to focus on another ballerina being catapulted into the limelight to save the show. That would be me! So, some long while after I had convinced myself that I would never dance the difficult dual role of Odette and Odile again (and certainly not in the circumstances of being seen from every angle at the Royal Albert Hall), there I was, not only being expected to dance in that arena again but being thrown to 'the lion' at the same time! Because the sub-text to the whole documentary became the battering that I received from Deane as I was flung into dancing a role that I never expected to perform again. And it soon transpired that he wanted me no more than I wanted it. Having described Semionova as one of the three best ballerinas in the world and the 'Cindy Crawford' lookalike of dance, he tells the camera that 'all the buzz' left him when he discovered that Polina was unable to perform.

I was 39, considering retirement, and genuinely feeling too old to be dancing with a 20-year-old boy prince in *Swan Lake*, especially since I was to be a late replacement for a famous young ballerina, whose fans would be flying in from all over Europe to see her perform. They had bought their flights and tickets, and they were still coming but now to see me instead of the ballerina they really wanted. I was dreading it and Deane made me feel less like a swan and more like a dead turkey, ready to be plucked for Christmas dinner. It made for some really great and melodramatic TV.

The film crew came to make a documentary about dancers but it was to be Derek's bullying that stole the show. I'm sure that Derek knew from the outset that playing the villain would make great television and put him at the epicentre of the documentary, so he really played up to being the bad guy. The opening credits of the film headline his chosen role when he is seen, seated, saying to no one in particular, 'Do this. Derek says, "This is what it is." Do it!' A few minutes later, he adds, with admirable understatement, 'I have this reputation for being tough,' before concluding the sequence by saying that the difficulty for him is getting, 'Absolute 100 per cent commitment from the dancers – emotionally and physically – so that they will almost bleed for me.' In my experience, it rarely stops at 'almost' with Derek!

'I hate the word "bully" but I do bully them, but I bully them in a constructive way,' Deane says to camera, before telling the *corps de ballet* that they look like 'turtles'. He agrees reluctantly not to make an injured dancer do something that will damage her further before adding a loudly-audible aside that if the cameras were not there he would have made her do it! He doesn't know the dancer's name (Adeline Kaiser), so he calls her 'operation girl'. As the choreographer, Derek had the power and he was intent on showing the TV audience that this was the case. It reminded me of how he would shout at dancers when he had been the artistic director of ENB.

But, for those who haven't seen the film, I'm going to leave it for others to describe how bad Deane really was. Writing on *theartsdesk.com* in March 2011, the respected dance critic, Ismene Brown, compared *Agony & Ecstasy* with *Black Swan*, Darren Aronofsky's film that had been released a couple of months earlier, which had just won Natalie Portman the Oscar for Best Actress. Brown wrote, 'You thought *Black Swan* was a nightmare depiction of the ballet world? Now watch *Agony & Ecstasy* and squirm. Compare

Natalie Portman's tormenting ballet master with ENB's Derek Deane, as each of them stages *Swan Lake*. One tells his ballerina she'll need to masturbate to discover her inner black swan; the other contemptuously dismisses his ballerina as too old, too knackered, past hope.'

Well, Deane didn't ask me to masturbate but being 'too old, too knackered, past hope' is precisely how he had made me feel. But I clearly didn't let it show as Brown goes on to say, 'Then compare the ballerina characters: Portman miserable, wrung out, almost incapable, mentally unstable; ENB's Daria Klimentová smiling again and again, as Deane kicks her again and again.'

I had put up with so much from Derek during my early years with the company that it seemed appropriate for his bullying to be so brutally exposed in the full glare of this BBC film (directed by Rob Farquhar, produced by Alice Mayhall and superbly narrated by David Morrissey). As I watched while the film was being screened at the Žofín Palace in October 2012 – opening Czech TV's tribute to me during the Golden Prague Festival – I thought how odd it was that Derek knew full well he was being filmed and yet he seemed not to care about the villainous role that he was ascribing for himself. On two occasions, Farquhar cleverly shows him, accompanied by ominous background music, hurtling through the London streets in a black cab as if for all the world he is Rothbart, the evil sorcerer in *Swan Lake*, coming to torment his captive swan queen. It seems funny now but, looking back, I know that the person being tormented was me!

Deane is filmed saying these words, 'You have to look at it psychologically, because you can damage the person rather than build them if you're not careful with them.' Quoting him in her fascinating article, Brown expertly sharpens the critic's withering pen by adding, 'Psychological care to you and me is a howitzer to the balls to Deane, a man who makes even the most ferocious of dance critics seem like amateurs. He bludgeons and criticises his doughty ballerina (me!) – pays her the worst insult after the general rehearsal of saying he isn't going to bother to give her any corrections (because) there are so many he doesn't know where to start.' Brown described Deane's frankness as 'recklessness', adding that his casualness implies that this behaviour 'is a norm of some kind'. These observations describe with forensic accuracy the behaviour that I had endured for so many years.

And Brown was not alone. Writing in the *Guardian*, another major dance critic, Judith Mackrell, said that the BBC cameras had, 'Found, in the choreographer Derek Deane a bully to match Aronofsky's gothically sadistic ballet master.' She added, 'Principal ballerina Daria Klimentová was the prime victim, as Deane – unable to work with his first-choice dancer – petulantly lambasted her technical flaws, her lack of personality, even her age. It was humbling to watch the ballerina's stoicism as she smiled sweetly through every onslaught.'

The *Daily Mail* also carried a piece about *Agony & Ecstasy*, written by Mary Greene, which was not published until June 2011 (a whole year after the events portrayed in the film). She starts the feature by focusing on the scene where I am fighting back tears while nursing a throbbing ankle. I say to camera, 'Old ballerina crying', while drawing attention to my belief that I was rehearsing for the final demanding *Swan Lake* of my career. Greene describes this as, 'More shocking by far than the physical pain was seeing sweet-natured Daria a victim of domineering choreographer Derek Deane, reacting with graceful dignity to his barrage of destructive criticism.' One blast from Derek was, 'God almighty, look at her! Absolutely dreadful! It wastes my time talking to her.' Of course, I knew Derek was blunt – I had endured five years of his bullying on a regular basis – but even I was shocked when I saw the documentary for the first time, since many of his most withering comments about me were made out of my hearing, and I didn't know about them until I viewed the film.

Greene also drew the parallel with the *Black Swan* movie, making it clear that while that was fiction, this was life; a real ballet company and dancers preparing for a major show. She concluded that this first part of *Agony & Ecstasy* was 'made for compelling viewing, but it left a nasty taste' – a verdict that seems to be shared by many others who have seen the film.

Brown focused her review on the emergency partnership of Vadim and me, and the role of Deane in between us. 'He so clearly favours the young lad,' she said, 'Looking him up and down like a prize bullock that the sheer heroism of the old heifer deserves medals from every country she's danced in.' In fact, Vadim was not immune from Deane's unpleasantness (although less of this featured in the final edit of the film) but since his Russian training involved a lot of being screamed at, even hit, Vadim was able to brush it off as normal. As Brown notes in a throwaway comment, 'Deane is something he's used to.'

I had only recently seen the film for the first time when I was interviewed by Greene for the *Daily Mail*, and this rawness shows in my long response to her question about Deane's attack on me. 'You know what?' I said, 'He will never speak to me like that ever again. Some days it doesn't upset you. But some days, if you're feeling more fragile, many times I end up crying. He achieves results because we are all scared but he makes a scar on people for the rest of their lives. I'm not less than he is: he's a choreographer, I'm a prima ballerina. I'd like to see how he'd react if I said, "This is shit choreography and I have to dance it."'

Looking back at this emotional response, I feel that I was casting my net over many years of baggage accrued from the abusive treatment that I, and many other dancers, had endured from Derek. I was certainly not just referring to a few weeks of rehearsals in the early summer of 2010.

The great thing is that this scratch performance cemented my partnership with Vadim and the critics loved our interpretation of *Swan Lake* – even if the choreographer didn't – giving us especially strong notices. It changed my life, and it changed the way I danced.

Writing in the *Guardian*, Judith Mackrell described my performance as, 'Heroic in her confident command of the auditorium,' while she wrote that Vadim's debut performance as Prince Siegfried was, 'Remarkable: he sings through his first act solo with sweetly melancholic lyricism, and etches his third-act fireworks with the glitter of steel.' Meanwhile in the *Independent*, Zoë Anderson said that Vadim was, '[A] surprisingly steady and tender partner,' while I was, 'An assured Swan Queen, making her dramatic moments stand out against the hurly-burly of Deane's production.' In the *Sunday Express*, Jeffery Taylor remarked that I was, 'Flashing thrilling dancing all over the place.'

Best of all was the review by Luke Jennings in the *Observer*, who declared that I had delivered, 'A nuanced interpretation with great subtlety and tact, Klimentová sublimated her performance to her partner's, positioning herself with especial care for the lifts, aligning herself to his rhythm, and buoying him up with her steady, serene gaze.' The description of Vadim's Act III variation and *coda* brings back the memories as if Jennings' words conjure the images on film, 'High, precisely drawn turns in the air that seemed to snap from the music's surface like wave-caps, a bravura series of *grandes pirouettes* to compliment Klimentová's *fouettés*, and a beautiful, soaring *manège* of *split jetés* that had the audience shouting its applause.'

But it was in Jennings' post-show description that the inner truth can be found, 'And at the curtain call, with touching self-deprecation, Klimentová muted her presence so that Muntagirov could take the cheers. There is, at times, an elusive resonance between an older ballerina and a younger male dancer that performers of similar age cannot access. That was the case on Wednesday; not so much in the tale of the Swan Queen and her prince, but in the human story of two performers, and it was enthralling.' So, the critics loved this performance, so hurriedly and brutally put together, but on that particular night, we received more than just good notices. A partnership was born and, as David Morrissey says at the very end of the BBC film, 'Since *Swan Lake*, Daria and Vadim have become English National Ballet's number one partnership, with their performances winning rave reviews, comparing them to Nureyev and Fonteyn.' This resonance with the greatest ballet partnership of them all (at least, the greatest here in Britain) came to be a regular allusion from critics and balletomanes alike over the next two years. Though we are nothing like them as dancers – and certainly not as people – we seemed to have become, overnight, the next Fonteyn and Nureyev. We never saw ourselves this way: we were just the first Klimentová and Muntagirov. We loved that the website *Londondance.com* conjured up the unique name of 'Klimentagirov' to describe us! Our stage partnership is so strong that it seemed right to give it a single name.

But, even after the performance – with such great reviews – we still see, in the final minutes of *Agony & Ecstasy*, Derek coming to my dressing room to complain that I had not been 'going over the top' in the final act and I didn't look as if I was suffering enough. As he leaves, I say to the camera, with heartfelt emotion, 'It is very hard to please Derek. It's very, very hard to please Derek, but if you please him, it means something but – you know what – I'm happy!'

Thinking about the potential end of my career, as I had done when planning my 1,000th performance in Prague, a few weeks earlier, gave me such a renewed love of ballet that suddenly I wanted to dance as much as I could, and after our nerve-wracking but exhilarating performance of *Swan Lake* in front of an audience of 5,000 in the Royal Albert Hall, I convinced myself that dancing with

Vadim would prolong my career. Suddenly, I couldn't care less about the age difference between us: all I could do was agree with my mum's early observation that I should enjoy this wonderful experience and make the most of it while it lasted. When you are not sure whether you will still be performing in a year's time, it makes every moment very special.

I had been thinking about stopping dancing but now, in the summer of 2010, I decided that I had to continue dancing, and I wanted to carry on performing with Vadim for as long as I possibly could. I started the film by saying that perhaps I had another year to dance but I ended it hoping for much more. Everything had changed on that one night and to continue dancing was suddenly a great priority for me.

The second of the documentaries in the BBC *Agony & Ecstasy* series featured preparations for *Romeo and Juliet*, with the spotlight on other dancers; but the third programme focused on the difficulties of the creative process as Wayne Eagling tries to choreograph his version of *The Nutcracker* in time for its opening at the London Coliseum as the Christmas show for 2010. The film shows him working on aspects of the ballet right up until the last minute, bedevilled by choreographers' block and not helped by the early onset of winter, which marooned the sets in the snowbound ENB warehouses in Kent. Dancers are seen learning their choreography from a mobile phone and many of the cast were unable to have a proper run-through before the opening night. One of my fellow senior principal ballerinas, Elena Glurdjidze, is shown being unable to continue rehearsing on the Coliseum stage due to a technicians' break and she says plaintively, 'But I'm the one who has to be on stage and I don't know the steps!'

Vadim and I were cast to take the opening night. With more than a week to go, I was smiling in the Jay Mews studio, saying to the camera: 'I'm laughing now but we'll see in a week's time.' And sure enough, one week later at the dress rehearsal I'm filmed in tears – head in hands –

having failed to make a crucial lift in the final *pas de deux* and then messing up my variation. Hardly surprising given that the *pas de deux* was such fiendishly complex choreography and we'd had so little time to absorb it. It all seemed very ominous for the opening night on the following evening, especially since Wayne had not yet settled all the choreography. Still having six minutes of dance to complete on that last couple of days, he jokingly says to the camera that he was contemplating just freezing the action – having the dancers stay still on the stage – to cover the missing bits! It may not have been a joke at the time.

Well, needless to say it was alright on the night! In fact, more than alright for Vadim and I, since we received great reviews from the London-based dance critics. Judith Mackrell wrote in the *Guardian*, 'Daria Klimentová and Vadim Muntagirov excelled themselves. Muntagirov was that prize combination of generous partner and audacious virtuoso, while Klimentová, in the music-box choreography of the grand *pas de deux*, surely danced the performance of her career.' Writing in the *Daily Telegraph*, Sarah Crompton noted, 'Klimentová and Muntagirov perform with finesse,' while over in the *Sunday Telegraph*, Louise Levene was even more detailed in her praise, saying, 'Klimentová has been an ENB principal since 1996 but she has never looked better. Her long legs and jump-jet elevation give her a girlish leap that sails through space like a paper plane. In the exquisite Sugar Plum Fairy solo her tiptoeing *pas de bourrée* seemed wired to Tchaikovsky's twinkling celesta.' She added, 'Muntagirov shares Klimentová's brilliant-cut technique and innate musicality.' It was wonderful to get such positive reviews for a ballet in which we didn't know all the steps the day before. Thank heavens the critics weren't there for the dress rehearsal!

I am often asked which ballet I have danced the most, and the answer is *The Nutcracker*. The main reason is that while every classic ballet is danced by every classical ballet company, few are danced every single year, apart from *The Nutcracker*, which is performed by most companies in their Christmas season. Ironically, I didn't dance *The Nutcracker* in the National Ballet in Prague, although I had danced in a *pas de trois* in the ballet, aged just 13, when I was in my fourth year at the Conservatoire. But I have certainly made up for it ever since leaving the Czech Republic, having danced over 110 performances of six different productions in South Africa, Scotland and at English National Ballet.

There are hundreds, perhaps even thousands, of different versions of *The Nutcracker* around the world, created for different productions in each ballet company, where the choreography and set/costume designs are different. Although, of course, the staple ingredients that never change are the essential narrative of *The Nutcracker and the Mouse King* by E.T.A Hoffmann, Tchaikovsky's lavish, romantic score and some iconic choreographic sequences (by Lev Ivanov) that go right back to the initial production, which was first danced in the Mariinsky Theatre in St Petersburg on Sunday, 18 December 1892. Companies will often change their production of *The Nutcracker* over time. ENB has had ten different versions since the company was formed in 1950, and the third film in the *Agony & Ecstasy* documentary series for the BBC concerned the final rehearsals for Wayne Eagling's choreography for that tenth ENB version.

There are two principal roles for a ballerina in *The Nutcracker*. One is for the young girl Clara (or Masha in Russia) – the daughter of the Stahlbaum family, in whose house the opening Christmas Eve party is set – and the other is as the famous Sugar Plum Fairy for the grand *pas de deux* that comes at the very end of the ballet in the kingdom of the sweets (to where Clara dreams that she and the nutcracker prince have travelled). In a few productions, the two roles are combined so that Clara becomes the Sugar Plum Fairy in her dreams. I have never danced this dual role, although in Eagling's production the set revolves so that the little girl playing Clara suddenly grows up to be me! I was used to this sudden onset of adulthood since the same process occurred to me in Derek Deane's *Alice in Wonderland*.

My very first performance in a lead role in *The Nutcracker* was as the Sugar Plum Fairy, and I only appeared for the *pas de deux* in the final act. This happened in 1991 when I was invited to go to Cape Town Ballet as a guest – dancing with Johan Jooste – for four performances of the version of *The Nutcracker* choreographed by the Cape Town Ballet's artistic director, Veronica Paeper. Years later, in 2003, Johan was shot and critically injured in an attempted car-jacking. His life hung in the balance but thankfully he survived, although a bullet is still lodged in his back and in August 2011, he helped me to select two young dancers from Cape Town to be awarded scholarships from the Keith Mackintosh Scholarship Fund to attend my International Masterclasses in Prague.

When I came to Scottish Ballet, I danced in the version of *The Nutcracker*, choreographed by Paul Darrell with Paul Chalmer, a guest principal who came from the National Ballet in Canada, before joining Stuttgart Ballet and Les Ballets de Monte Carlo. There have been only three of the 17 seasons that I have danced at ENB in which I have not danced in *The Nutcracker*. In the *Agony & Ecstasy* film the (then) chief executive of ENB, Craig Hassall, says that this ballet traditionally brings in 30 per cent of the company's income from ticket sales every year. Over my time with ENB, I have danced four different productions: first by Ben Stevenson, then Derek Deane, Christopher Hampson (with designs by Gerald Scarfe) and finally, the recent production by ENB artistic director, Wayne Eagling. So, I have managed to learn no less than six productions of *The Nutcracker* in my career to date.

Although I have danced the *pas de deux* for the Sugar Plum Fairy and her prince so many times, I could never get bored with it since I absolutely love Tchaikovsky's wonderful music, especially for the *adage* (the slow section). It really gets into your heart and helps the ballerina to forget everything apart from the music and the duet.

I'm often asked about the people who go to see multiple performances of the same ballet, sometimes several times in the same week. It's an obsession that exists with ballet (and perhaps also with opera) but not so much with other branches of the theatre. The term 'balletomane' was invented by the eminent dance writer and historian, Arnold Haskell, to describe these audience members. I can understand why people want to see so many performances, even by the same dancers, since ballet dancers live by the feedback that they receive from ballet masters, répétiteurs and colleagues, and we change things very subtly from performance to performance. If we didn't do this, dancing the Sugar Plum Fairy would become very boring after the fiftieth time!

Of course, we don't change the steps but we do play with the emotions and, to some extent, even the timings. As I told the dance writer, Bruce Marriott, in an interview at the turn of the Millennium, 'That's what's enjoyable – it's you who is on the stage and you can do anything you want. I love that.' However, in that same interview, I also described the downside of live performance, 'Some nights it's difficult. The audience is just sitting there – you have to first feel it yourself and the audience can feel it. If you don't feel it, they don't feel anything – it could wait forever.'

I love *The Nutcracker* and I count myself very lucky to have been able to dance so many different versions by great choreographers. If I had to choose just one then I would opt for Christopher Hampson's version for the very selfish reason that the *pas de deux* was mostly choreographed on me as the Sugar Plum Fairy, dancing with Jan-Erik Wikström, even though it was Tom (Edur) and Agnes (Oaks) who performed on the first night as guest principals. But since they were not at ENB for the period in which the ballet was being made, it was Jan-Erik and I that worked in the studios, with Chris Hampson creating the choreography, which is a very important aspect of dance for ballet dancers and the reason why 'Hampy's' ballet will always have a very special place in my heart.

It is so much more exhilarating to be making dance for the first time than merely learning steps that have already been choreographed on other dancers, perhaps many, many years before. Dancers often talk about 'having work made on them' and being a crucial part of that creative process is vital to every ballet dancer. Making dance with Chris Hampson was especially rewarding because it was always so comfortable between us in the rehearsal studio. He would sometimes leave Jan-Erik and I to improvise an element of the movement, and then say, 'Yes, I really like that, let's leave it in,' or he might just tweak what we had done a little to suit his overall schematic.

I also feel strangely comfortable in the version choreographed by Wayne Eagling, which will probably be the last *Nutcracker* that I shall dance. Eagling's interpretation has very complex choreography for 'grown-up' Clara (in the *grand pas de deux* usually danced by the Sugar Plum Fairy) and, although extremely difficult to dance, I love it! I am thrown around in high lifts and passionate clinches, but I have such an unbelievable partner in Vadim that I am so comfortable with the choreography, however difficult it is.

In November 2009, I almost got my wish to dance with The Royal Ballet, although I had danced at the Royal Opera House when ENB performed there in 2002, during Matz Skoog's time as artistic director, performing Christopher Hampson's *Double Concerto* with Jan-Erik.

I had always enjoyed dancing in a neoclassical ballet by the late Glen

Tetley, a revered American choreographer, entitled *Sphinx*, which follows the line of Jean Cocteau's play *The Infernal Machine* and concerns the myth of Oedipus's encounter with the Sphinx. It is danced to intensely difficult neoclassical music by Bohuslav Martinů, a Czech composer. Because of this link to my homeland, earlier in my career, I had been very fortunate to work directly with Tetley himself when performing as a guest in the Czech Republic. Years later, I was again lucky to be able to dance as the Sphinx with Thomas Edur, although it was a little nerve-wracking because his wife and usual partner, Agnes Oaks, wasn't cast with him and she watched us from the wings at every show so there was a lot of pressure.

I was invited by The Royal Ballet's director, Dame Monica Mason, to dance as a guest principal at The Royal Ballet in *Sphinx*, because Marianela Nuñez had been injured and had to go off. Although this would have made another dream come true for me (having already achieved my other ambitions of dancing with both Irek Mukhamedov – I had danced with him twice in 2001 – and Carlos Acosta), I was only given two days' notice due to Marianela's late injury, and I hadn't danced in *Sphinx* for seven years. I could have agreed just to dance at The Royal Ballet and hopefully get some good notices, but I would have killed myself for it. I wanted to go to The Royal Ballet when I was much younger, but this opportunity came when I was 38, and by then my ego wasn't big enough to accept the challenge.

When I was offered the chance of dancing *Sphinx* at Covent Garden, I had reached the age where I questioned the real value of everything, and I realised that nothing would actually change in my life if I was finally to guest as a principal at The Royal Ballet (and in any event I had already danced on the stage of the Royal Opera House). I had reached the stage in my career where I didn't need to say that I had danced for The Royal Ballet. I'm not really that type anyway, and sometimes it is also liberating to be able to say no! They weren't going to give me a job on the strength of it. It was too much of a risk and so I had made the pragmatic decision to turn it down.

Chapter 12

I'm Still Dancing

$\mathcal{A}$ s a young dancer, you assume that you will stay dancing until you are at least 35, but as you get older it is not hard for a ballerina to think, '*This is going to be my last season*'. It all goes so fast that it's crazy. I have been preparing myself for the end for a long time, telling people since I turned 30, especially whenever I was upset, that I was going to give up dancing. The next day, I would always be back! But, when I was 30, I'm certain that I didn't see myself still dancing in my 40s.

Just after my 33rd birthday, in 2004, I told the Czech journalist Martina Kubáňová emphatically, 'I'll hold out till I'm 35, that's two years from now and I don't really feel like it. Time flies. Physically, I feel fine but in two years' time I may have had enough.' At that time I hadn't danced with Friedemann or Vadim, and I couldn't have foreseen the impact on my desire to continue dancing that they were to have. Scarily, as I gave that interview, Vadim was just 14 and still two years away from starting out at The Royal Ballet School! Well, thanks to him, here I am eight years later, in much the same situation: hoping that I'll hold out for another couple of years.

It's nothing unusual. Ballerinas often continue to dance well into their 40s. I was 41 in June 2012. Margot Fonteyn was 42 when she first danced with Rudolf Nureyev in 1961, and she was approaching 46 when she premiered in Kenneth MacMillan's *Romeo and Juliet*. The partnership with Nureyev came at a time when she was considering retirement, but it gave her a new lease of life, extending her dancing career – in one way or another – for 15 more years.

Today, there are ballerinas still treading the boards as they approach their 50th birthday. The great former Bolshoi ballerina, Nina Ananiashvili, directs the national ballet company in her homeland of Georgia, and she still dances as the prima ballerina at the age of 49. And she still looks amazing! In the Philippines, Lisa Macuja runs Ballet Manila and still dances the principal roles, and she was born 18 months after Nina in 1964. And, at The Royal Ballet in London, Australian dancer Leanne Benjamin is still considered to be at the very top of her game, also at the age of 48. She was voted as the best female dancer in the UK National Dance Awards of 2009 – for the second time in her career – when she was 45. The condition that sets Ananiashvili, Macuja and Benjamin apart is that they are all tiny! And they have obviously looked after their bodies very carefully.

Now that I have rid myself of the habit of prematurely saying I'm going to retire whenever I feel down, I plan to dance on with Vadim for a few more years, provided my body can take it. If I emulate Ananiashvili, I could keep going for another eight seasons. Oh, what a terrible thought!

The mind is important to any dancer's ability to keep going, but the body is the most important thing. Having survived one major injury, I am all too conscious of how fragile our bodies are. I hurt after every show. I have three inflamed vertebrae, which plague me so that I can no longer sit still in one place for more than a few seconds. I rarely sit in a chair and I am most comfortable sitting on the floor, with my back stretched out against a wall, but even this respite will only last for a short while. So, I would certainly be lying if I was to say that I still feel like a 20-year-old. But, with Vadim, I am enjoying my dancing more than ever and that can keep me going for as long as my body can stand up to it. The biggest question for me right now is how do you know when it's the right time to call it a day? For me, I'm sure it isn't yet, but I still worry if I will recognise when it is the right time. The truth is that the body will always tell a dancer when it is time to quit, and we must never stop listening to our bodies, no matter how our heart or our head might try to convince us otherwise.

English National Ballet has entered the 2012/13 season with a new artistic director. Ironically, she is someone who once danced with the company before – and also danced with me at Scottish Ballet before that – moving on to create an even bigger name for herself as a principal dancer at The Royal Ballet. Tamara Rojo is three years younger than me, and she plans to continue dancing while directing the company (just like Ananiashvili and Macuja). It will be a difficult juggling act for her to manage but she is still dancing as well as ever, with an irrepressible passion and energy. If anyone has the appetite to be a 'player-manager' (if I can borrow the football expression for the same juggling act) then it is Tamara.

I have been friends with Tamara for many years, ever since she came to the UK when she was just 20, and I admire her enormously. I used to photograph her all the time because she is so photogenic with those big, gorgeous eyes. She is a very sexy and beautiful woman, and an incredibly expressive dancer. I love watching her perform since she is unquestionably a unique star of the ballet. Tamara has achieved so much in her career, and she is so determined and very political. Over the years that I have known her, she has often confided in me about her ambitions and – to date – she has always achieved everything that she has desired. I am a driven woman but I could never match her energy, and I could never have achieved all that she has done: she is an amazing woman, who meets all the goals that she sets herself. She was unafraid to make it clear that she wanted to be the artistic director of English National Ballet – and now she is, and she has made the transition to director while she is still able to dance.

Tamara danced with Vadim in the gala, held in Athens, to celebrate the 85th birthday of the famous Russian ballerina, Maya Plisetskaya, in May 2011. They performed the virtuoso *pas de deux* from *Le Corsaire* to great acclaim on the day after Vadim's 21st birthday. She also danced with Vadim in Milton Keynes on the opening night of her tenure as artistic director of ENB, performing as Aurora in *The Sleeping Beauty* while I danced as the Lilac Fairy. Tamara has always been a beautiful interpreter of Aurora, with her stunning long *balances* in the Rose Adage.

Reviewing this opening show on *artsdesk.com*, Ismene Brown drew attention to the problems of her new dual role, 'Has the great ballerina Tamara Rojo ever done a more nerve-racking performance than she did last night in Milton Keynes? She had to inhabit the skin of a dewy 16-year-old discovering the world – all the while watching the stage with the steel gaze of a boss to see if her employees were doing their job to standard.'

I had already decided not to dance the role of Aurora – I hadn't been enjoying the pretence of being 16 for some time – and so I was happy for Tamara to borrow my partner for her opening performance. Also, instead of dancing Aurora, I get to continue dancing the vitally important role of the Lilac Fairy, which I hope to continue performing for a few years to come. It seemed to work in Milton Keynes, where

Brown referred to my portrayal as, 'Klimentová's sweet and irresistibly poignant Lilac Fairy.'

Vadim and I have had to fight to stay together over the past three years, including both of us missing some shows to make the point that we wish to do so. On one occasion I was dancing in *The Nutcracker* with Vadim when he got ill and Wayne asked me to partner Dima again. The next day I got impossible back spasms, which meant that I had to go off as well. The spasms were genuine but I confess that they came at the most opportune time.

At some time, I will have to get used to the fact that Vadim will move on to dance with others. I am 19 years older than him and I cannot possibly dance long enough to fill his career. In any event, I'm certain that he will move away from ENB to become the next major world star in ballet. He knows exactly what he wants to achieve, and he has already made guest appearances during 2012 with American Ballet Theatre in both Washington's The John F. Kennedy Center and New York's Metropolitan Opera House, dancing the roles of Solor in *La Bayadère* (with ABT's new young Korean principal Hee Seo) and Siegfried in *Swan Lake* (with 39-year-old Irina Dvorovenko). He has also guested with the Mikhailovsky Ballet in St Petersburg and the Bayerisches Staatsballet in Munich. Already there is intense interest in Vadim from around the world, and he has been invited to dance as a guest with both the Mariinsky Ballet in St Petersburg and the Bolshoi Ballet in Moscow. There is such a dearth of brilliant young male dancers around the world that if (or, more likely, when) Vadim becomes available, there will be no shortage of major companies queuing up to sign him.

Having started my partnership with Vadim feeling that I was the experienced ballerina that had to work hard to get the best out of him, we have almost come full circle and he now advises me. He is remarkably intelligent and has exactly the right sense of judgement, regularly surprising me that such a young man can help in so many ways. We are now great friends and I trust him completely.

I expect that this will be the pattern of things to come. I plan to continue dancing those roles that I feel will challenge me and for which I remain technically and emotionally strong. We have danced all over the world together in 2012: in Europe but also in Japan, Singapore, Mexico City and Cape Town; and we already have many invitations for guest appearances in 2013, so I hope that we can keep going for a while yet. The one thing I can now say with absolute certainty is that my dancing days will end when I stop dancing with him.

People often ask me whether Sabina will be a ballet dancer. Like all parents, Muppet and I will support our daughter in anything that she wants to do, but I'm quite certain that it won't involve ballet. When she was a toddler, Sabina loved to dress up in princess dresses and tutus, practise her *pliés* and *arabesques* and she adored the *Swan Lake* CD, but I think that all this made her just like any other little girl! If she had shown interest in following in my footsteps, I would certainly have warned her that it is such a tough life. To be honest, I'm not even sure that I would put myself through it if I had my life over again. I may have stuck to gymnastics until I was in my early 20s and then opted for a much more normal life as a professional photographer, a graphic designer, something in computers or perhaps even a teacher or a lawyer! The only things I'm sure that I would never have been are a mathematician or an accountant.

I have always considered myself to be Czech and I am immensely proud of my nationality, my culture and my homeland. Although I have been dancing around the world since I was a young woman, I can see myself going back to live in Prague in due course. I have lived in London for many years; I have married an Englishman and I love the

British people, but I will never feel English or British: I am Czech through and through.

As I sit in the Žofín Palace in Prague, listening to many eminent people talking about my career, I realise that although my dancing in the Czech Republic was limited to just three seasons at the beginning of my career and regular guest appearances and gala performances since then – and I have now danced in the UK for 20 years – I am still much better known in the Czech Republic. This is, of course, partly because it is a much smaller country. I feel part of the cultural elite in my homeland, which is lovely and means that I can count many of the nation's greatest people as my acquaintances and friends. This is especially surprising since I am very shy and don't like parties or social occasions, so I turn down many, many invitations when I am in London and Prague. I almost didn't turn up to collect my award when the UK dance critics voted me as best female dancer of the year in 2011! I'm not a great social animal– I'd rather go to the park with Sabina. I suppose that I haven't changed much since that quiet girl who would rather sleep in her grandma's garden than go to parties.

The Czech people are very proud of their countrymen and women who succeed in the arts elsewhere in the world, and there have always been many opportunities for me to go back to the Czech Republic and perform alongside other successful Czech dancers. Each year for the past six years, the National Theatre has held a special event inviting Czech dancers performing with companies elsewhere in the world to come back to their homeland. The cream of Czech society would come and watch these performances and the late President, Václav Havel, and his wife, Dagmar, were regular attendees.

One woman, Olga Ambruzová, wrote a book that was a reference work about Czech dancers who were performing as principals in Prague and around the world. A well-known Czech photographer (Petr Našic) began to take photos of me regularly, and he would come to London to photograph me for publications back in Prague. He also made an exhibition of his photographs of me, which caught a lot of attention in Prague. Everything in Prague is much smaller in terms of social circles and, although I didn't necessarily know the right people Olga and Petr did, I came to much greater attention even though I was rarely to be found dancing in Prague. In a way, it is comparatively straightforward for the Czech Diaspora to become well-known in the Czech Republic. Artists who leave the Czech Republic and make a name for themselves in another country are well respected at home. And achieving success in the USA or the UK is about as good as it gets.

Petr wanted to make a documentary film about me but he couldn't raise the finance. At this point, Czech TV had already made a 20-minute programme about me dancing in England (ironically, the director was married to a girl that I had been to ballet school with). A Czech film director, Martin Kubala, heard that Petr wanted to do a film about me and he sort of took the project over. He involved Czech television and the first full-length documentary film about me was born. Martin followed me all over the world (to London, Paris and Taipei) for two years of filming before the work was complete. The film was so popular that it led to a second commission for a film by the same director, which has taken six years to make. It is now almost complete, but I suspect that Martin is waiting for me to finish dancing to give his documentary the ending that he wants!

His first film led to a huge number of projects being proposed in the Czech Republic, and I found myself getting invites to appear on chat shows and panel discussions on Czech TV. There are a lot of very silly shows on Czech TV and I had to say a resounding 'no' to a lot of things but I also agreed to accept many invitations, particularly if I liked the interviewer or chat show host! I have never sought to be famous, and I certainly don't enjoy all of the trappings that go with it, so it is a lot easier to say 'no' when I want to.

I was nominated for awards in the Czech Republic many times, particularly when I danced in Glen Tetley's *Sphinx* in Prague, but it seems to be impossible for a dancer whose career is based overseas to win dance awards in the Czech Republic. However, when I won two awards in successive years (2011 and 2012) in the UK National Dance Awards – voted upon by the dance members of the UK Critics' Circle – it garnered a great deal of attention in the Czech press and on television.

To tell the truth, I'm not a great fan of awards for dance. Ballet is not an Olympic sport and it is impossible to say whether one dancer here is better than another dancer over there. One dancer may have a better series of *pirouettes*; one may jump higher; while another might be considered to have more elegant *port de bras* – but what about dramatic expression? It seems to me to be an unenviable and difficult task to decide upon the best dancer but having said that, it's also nice when you win!

I was shocked when I won the Critics' Circle Best Female Dancer Award in January 2012. In the previous year, I had been given the Patron's Award by Dame Beryl Grey, a famous ballerina in the same generation as Margot Fonteyn. Beryl danced the Odette/Odile combination *in Swan Lake* at Sadler's Wells Royal Ballet (which later became The Royal Ballet) on her 15th birthday! She also pioneered Western cultural inroads into communist China when she danced in Peking and Shanghai in 1964, and she was the artistic director of London Festival Ballet (the company that became ENB) from 1968 to 1979. As the patron of the National Dance Awards, Dame Beryl was entitled to choose the recipient for her own award, and in 2011 she decided to give it to me, after seeing me dance with Vadim in Wayne Eagling's *The Nutcracker* at Christmas in 2010. I was surprised and honoured, but since it was an award in the gift of the patron, I assumed that it was a sort of 'lifetime achievement' award.

I hate being fussed over and was disappointed to learn that the critics wanted Dame Beryl to present her award to me at a special lunch held in a quiet but exclusive hotel in Kensington. They hired a well-known dance photographer (Elliott Franks), and Wayne Eagling and I were invited to join the chairman and secretary of the Critics' Circle. To be honest, I almost didn't attend and probably wouldn't have turned up but for a last-minute intervention by Graham Watts (the secretary), which enabled Vadim to come with me. The whole event was rather muddled; I remember that the preamble took so long that Dame Beryl was unable to stay for the lunch! Nevertheless, it was the thought that counted, and I was so pleased to have been given the recognition.

If I am really honest, however, I did feel that I might have been given this award out of some sympathy because the critics themselves had never voted for me to win an award. So it was a very big surprise, a year later, to be told that I was nominated in the best female dancer of the year category, especially since I was nominated alongside three wonderful dancers. I was thrown off the scent even more by the fact that the dance critics asked me along to a small event at The Place (the home of the London School for Contemporary Dance and the Robin Howard Dance Theatre), where the names of those nominated for the various dance awards were to be announced. When my name was read out, I remember giving a little surprised scream of 'yes'! The other nominees were all principals from The Royal Ballet: the Argentinean ballerina, Marianela Nuñez; the British dancer, Lauren Cuthbertson (who had recently been the lead in the new *Alice's Adventures in Wonderland*, The Royal Ballet's first new full-length ballet for 18 years); and my old friend, Tamara Rojo (who just a few weeks later was to be announced as my new boss at ENB).

I was convinced that I couldn't win. I know that I can dance really well and that I had enjoyed a resurgence of my career in my new partnership with Vadim, but I had never seen myself as a spectacular dancer like Tamara. Her star quality begins with such a wonderful face; with those enormous beautiful eyes. I can maybe jump a little higher but so what? To be a star, you need to have something really special, and I felt that both Tamara and Marianela have that 'x factor', much more than I do. Lauren is also a beautiful dancer and I felt that her performance in The Royal Ballet's first new major production for a generation might just give her the edge.

Graham Watts – now chairman of the awards committee – persuaded me to come to the presentation ceremony but I arrived late, after it started, and both Wayne Eagling and Graham were trying to contact me by text and phone, both certain that I had decided to stay away. The award for the Best Female Dancer was one of the last to be announced. Ironically, it was sponsored by Grishko, the Russian company that makes my pointe shoes, and it was the head of Grishko in the UK, Amanda Hill, who was making the presentation on behalf of the owner, Nikolay Grishko. By the time that Amanda read my name out as the winner, I had crept into the back of the auditorium and I just gave out a huge cry of relief! I remember bounding down the stairs with glee to accept the award and saying that it had taken me over 20 years to win it in my (unprepared) acceptance speech. I remember paying special tribute to Vadim as the man who had made me love my dancing again and to Wayne for having the foresight to bring us to dance together (and persevering against my own opposition). At the end of this memorable day, I stayed with Graham in the empty auditorium and we agreed to write this book together.

In 2012, I had the pleasure of working with another world-class Royal Ballet principal, Alina Cojocaru, in both Japan and Denmark. I watched her carefully while working with her, and it is clear that she doesn't enjoy a lot of advantages that other ballerinas have, but she has something indefinably special that makes her a unique dancer, loved all over the world. I see this quality of greatness in all other world elite ballerinas, but when I watch DVDs and videos of my own performances, I never see myself as others do. I am – like so many dancers – my own worst critic.

I do believe, however, that every dancer comes to peak at a different time. For some it will be in their 20s or 30s but I think that others – and I include myself in this cohort – develop a stronger technique as they grow older. I know my current limitations as a dancer, and there are some roles (Aurora in *The Sleeping Beauty* and Kitri in *Don Quixote*, for example) that I will no longer attempt to dance. However, there are others (Odette/Odile in *Swan Lake*, *Manon*, *Giselle*, for example) where I feel that I am stronger today than ever before. I still look forward to the exploration of new roles but for me the biggest problem remains that ENB is not a company that creates new story ballets with the sort of dramatic content that I would like to get my teeth into. I was very lucky that we got to do *Manon*. I would love to dance with Vadim in *Marguerite and Armand*, the ballet created upon Fonteyn and Nureyev by Frederick Ashton, which seems likely to be Tamara's last role at The Royal Ballet, since she is to return as a guest to perform in this ballet with Sergei Polunin in the spring of 2013. And I regret the fact that I got to dance as Marguerite Gautier in *The Lady of the Camellias* and as Anna Karenina when I was just a young girl. How much more could I make of those roles if I were to dance them now?

But I am a dancer with English National Ballet, and I have had an amazing 20-year career in London, which has just got better and better over the last few years. As a dancer under contract to ENB, I will always dance whatever I'm asked to perform and I see exciting times ahead under Tamara Rojo's leadership, but I doubt if the finances will extend to bringing in or creating new expressive story ballets.

Summarising my career is easy since I have always written every performance that I have ever given in a little grey exercise book, purchased when I was still a child in Czechoslovakia. It begins in 1982, in my second year as a student at the Conservatoire, and proudly records that I danced in two concerts that year; the next year I danced for the first time in *The Sleeping Beauty*; and in 1984/5 (my fourth year in the Conservatoire), I danced the *pas de trois* in *The Nutcracker*. The little book is now tattered and the pages are falling apart. I filled it up halfway through the 2004/5 season, and there is now an addendum of stapled sheets. I guess that I thought I would never need another book.

Now, here's the geeky bit! By the end of the 2011/12 season – my 23rd year as a professional dancer – I had danced in 1,237 works contained in 1,080 separate shows (some shows included more than one work); not including 44 performances while I was still a student but incorporating 67 galas (in which I danced a total of 118 *pas de deux* or variations). All this means that – having once decided to retire on the occasion of my 1,000th performance, I am now very close to clocking up 1,300 separate performances ranging from a three-minute variation to a three-hour ballet. The most number of performances I did in a season was 94 (in 1999/2000) and the least was four in 2002/3 (the year of my terrible ankle injury). I'm not slowing down because I gave 82 performances in the last season (my second-highest total across my career and the highest annual tally for 12 years – since before I became a mum). All-in-all, I was busiest at Scottish Ballet, where I averaged 62 shows a year – my annual average at ENB is 45.

I have danced in 32 countries. All over Europe, of course, but also in South Africa, USA, Australia, Japan, China, Hong Kong, Taipei, Vietnam and Mexico. Apart from the countries where I have been based my largest number of touring performances have been in Spain (where, to date, I have danced 26 times).

My performance history shows how ENB has changed over the

years as a touring company. In each of my first six years with the company, I performed around England many more times than in London. Collectively over the period, I danced in London 87 times and 178 times elsewhere around the country but this balance has reversed in the past five years, in each of which I have danced more in London than everywhere else added together (in total, 93 performances in London against 55 elsewhere around England). It shows a distinct shift in policy.

I have danced in some wonderful and obscure places, including Westminster Abbey, Prague Castle and the Foreign Office in Whitehall. Although I hated it to begin with, I have managed to perform 45 times 'in the round' at the Royal Albert Hall. Another big difference is that I have danced much more overseas in the latter part of my career and have been invited to perform in many more galas. I danced in just 12 galas in the first decade of my dancing career, but I have danced in 48 over the last ten years.

I have learned and performed 140 roles in 102 different choreographies of 70 separate works, with music written by 52 separate composers and choreographed by 57 different choreographers, although I have danced around 100 of these roles less than ten times each. At the other end of the scale, I have already given away the fact that I have danced more times in *The Nutcracker* than any other ballet (114 times, 83 as the Sugar Plum Fairy, plus seven performances of the grand *pas de deux* on its own, and 44 as the Ice Queen – on 13 occasions I danced both the roles of the Ice Queen and Sugar Plum Fairy in the same performance). Perhaps unsurprisingly, the Tchaikovsky/Petipa ballets dominate my repertoire. After *The Nutcracker*, it is *Swan Lake* that appears next (danced 89 times, 72 as Odette/Odile, plus 35 separate performances of the White Swan *pas de deux* and ten more of the Black Swan *pas de deux*); and then *The Sleeping Beauty* (performed 84 times, 45 as

Princess Aurora, although I have danced the grand *pas de deux* 32 times – and Aurora's variation a further three times – on its own for galas and other programmes).

My top ten ballets continue with *Cinderella* (63, 29 as Cinders herself); *Romeo and Juliet* (51, 42 as Juliet); *Giselle* (48, 34 in the title role); *Strictly Gershwin* and *Alice in Wonderland* (both 42); La Sylphide (21, 14 as Effie); and *Coppélia* (19, all as Swanilda). I have been very lucky with my roles, and I cannot complain since I have danced the full spectrum of the classical ballet repertoire, but there are three ballets that I have performed so few times that I wish I could have danced more often. I have only portrayed the temple dancer, Nikiya, in the full-length *La Bayadère* once (although I have danced the Kingdom of the Shades Act on its own a few more times); and I wish I could have had more opportunities to dance the full role of Kitri in *Don Quixote* (performed just five times early in my career in Prague) and the title role in *Manon* (danced only seven times, in 2008/9).

Perhaps the most surprising fact of all is that I have been lifted by 75 dance partners across the 23 seasons. More than one partner for every separate work that I have danced in! 54 of those men partnered me in less than ten performances each. Surely I can't be that difficult! It will hardly be surprising that the longest-lasting was Dima Gruzdyev, who danced with me in a total of 273 performances. In terms of quantity, my next most prolific partners have been Vladislav Bubnov at Scottish Ballet (103), Vadim Muntagirov (92, but still counting), Stanislav Fečo (54), Laurentiu Guinea (39), Jan-Erik Wikström (36) and Friedemann Vogel (33). The list of 75 includes some of the most wonderful and charismatic dancers of the modern era, not least among whom are Carlos Acosta, Thomas Edur and Irek Mukhamedov.

The 14th exhibition of my photographs was held in St Petersburg during the autumn of 2012, and I am hoping that my future will continue to involve photography. My dance career has always come first and in recent years, the demand to perform all over the world has meant photography becoming the main casualty, and I didn't take any photographs in an organised way for nearly two years. I would snap away, here and there, as always, but I would forget about them and I could never remember what I had photographed or where the images were stored. When I eventually retire from dancing, cataloguing my photos is the first job to be done.

We have now completed ten years of my Ballet Masterclasses in Prague. Through my contacts at the National Theatre, we have been fortunate to be able to use the company's ballet studios and I have had some wonderful teachers working with me over the years, most of whom are still dancers so that the students have the unique opportunity of working with those at the very top of their profession. Past teachers have included Julio Bocca, Nicolas Le Riche, Viviana Durante, Herman Cornejo, Tamara Rojo, Irek Mukhamedov, Tamás Solymosi, Cynthia Harvey, Sofiane Sylve, Isabelle Ciaravola and Daria Pavlenko. I have scored a big coup for 2013 in recruiting Darcey Bussell to be on my faculty of teachers, fresh from her first year as a judge on the BBC's *Strictly Come Dancing*. I'm so pleased that she is coming to teach in Prague.

Whatever happens to my own dancing career, I am sure that the Ballet Masterclasses will continue. I love teaching people who already know how to dance ballet to an advanced level. My strategy is always to make the dancers feel good about themselves as a first priority and then, having given them this confidence, I will readily apply whatever corrections are required to improve their technique. I believe that they are more open to correction once the teacher has established a mutual level of confidence with the dancer. I don't feel that anything is to be gained from a dancer who feels bad about themselves or the way they dance, so I do everything I can to prevent this from happening. Of course, it is impossible to apply this teaching technique to dancers who are not already at an advanced level.

The biggest legacy of having turned 40 is that I often feel tired and lethargic. I used to be able to do a lot more than I can do today. I could dance all day, come home and play with Sabina and then work on my photographs until the early hours of the morning before starting all over again the next day. Now, I just can't do that and I hardly ever feel like working on my photographs in the evening. I have to push myself to find the time (but having an exhibition just around the corner is always a big incentive) but when I do commit myself, I still really enjoy it.

Muppet and I bought a house in Horní Počernice in 2002, just three streets away from the apartment where I grew up and where my mum returns when she is not with us in London. There is a famous circus family in the Czech Republic called Berousek and they were having financial difficulties keeping and feeding all of their circus animals. They owned lots of properties, including this house in Horní Počernice, which is just one street away from my uncle and aunt (Antonín and Libuše). So they told me that the Berousek family wanted to sell this house before it came onto the market properly, and I managed to contact them privately and get the house for a very good price. It is a big house with four bedrooms and a large open-plan living space; actually much larger in terms of area than our house in Chiswick. I saw it as a good investment for the future and also, more importantly, it enabled me to buy a stake in my parents' village: in the place where I had grown up. Who knows, maybe I thought subliminally that I might even find some elderly snails in the back garden, with numbers painted on their shells!

Muppet converted the double garage in the basement of our house into a good-sized ballet studio for me, with a *barre*, mirrors and lots of photos and posters of me in various ballets, which I use whenever we are there. I call it my museum. The people who run Harlequin dance floors in the Czech Republic were kind enough to donate the dance floor for me.

At the moment, we spend much of the summer in our house in Horní Počernice (especially in August when I am doing the Ballet Masterclasses in Prague), and I return there as many times as possible, particularly for long weekends whenever I can get a break from dancing.

When I finally retire from dancing, I will have so many interests to follow. My photography deserves more time and attention. I have loved my Ballet Masterclasses, and I know that I have a strong aptitude to teach ballet, not at a regular ballet school but as a coach to professional dancers. I could always open my own conservatoire by continuing and perhaps expanding my Ballet Masterclasses. I suppose that the one thing of which I am sure is that I would prefer not to have a boss in whatever I do!

But for the moment, I am happy living life from day to day: being Daria, being Mum to my little Sabinka and dancing for as long as I can. I know that it cannot last forever but there are more performances to come, a lot more teaching and perhaps, I hope, one day the chance to direct my own company.

Sitting in the Žofín Palace towards the end of the *Tribute to Daria Klimentová*, I agree to answer some questions from the audience. Inevitably, I am asked what I will do next in my career. The simple answer – and the one I gave – is that I am still committed to dance for ENB and I don't know what is just around the corner. But, as I was being driven home to Horní Počernice that evening, I knew that the perfect next step in my career would be to return to Prague as artistic director of the Czech National Ballet. It may take a while to achieve, but it is now the perfect dream for me to have.

My Life in Dance:

A Danceography

*T*he following is a précis of my life as a professional dancer with a list of my debuts, performances and partners.

The number of my performances and shows is given in the table below, season-by-season. A dance season starts in the autumn and concludes in the summer of the following year. The number of performances is more than the number of shows because there may be more than one performance in a show (a triple bill, for example). If I danced more than one role in the same production, then this only counts as one performance (for example, early in my career at the Czech National Ballet, I often danced both as a friend of Aurora and in the Bluebird *pas de deux* in the same performance of *The Sleeping Beauty*).

YEAR	PERFORMANCES	SHOWS

Czech National Ballet (Soloist)

1989/90	78	76
1990/91	59	57
1991/92	54	51
	(191)	(184)

CAPAB Ballet, Cape Town, South Africa (Principal)

1992/93	42	38
	(42)	(38)

Scottish Ballet (Principal)

1993/94	61	61
1994/95	70	63
1995/96	73	62
	(204)	(186)

English National Ballet (Principal/Senior Principal)

1996/97	71	59
1997/98	43	43
1998/99	81	68
1999/2000	94	77
2000/01	34	26
2001/02	63	48
2002/03	4	4
2003/04	35	33
2004/05	25	24
2005/06	25	25
2006/07	60	48
2007/08	50	41

2008/09	36	36
2009/10	51	40
2010/11	46	40
2011/12	82	60
	(800)	(672)
Grand total	(1,237)	(1,080)

My Ballets

The following is a list of all the ballets that I have danced in since joining the Czech National Ballet as a soloist in 1989. It does not include any of the ballets that I danced as a student. It does include all of the divertissements and *pas de deux* that I have danced in galas since 1989.

I have always given the English title for the ballet unless the ballet is more generally known by a name in a different language. Where the work was only performed in the Czech Republic then I have stated the Czech name. I have always given the name of the ballet as I first performed it: thus, the ballet commonly known as *Les Sylphides* in the West is referenced here as *Chopiniana* because that is what it was called when I first performed it in Prague.

The names of the partners I danced with in each ballet are given against each season. The order in which they are listed is not alphabetical but corresponds to the frequency of performances (i.e. the partner with whom I danced the most is listed first). In a very few instances, where I have forgotten the name of a partner, none is specified.

The role is specified only where there is a given part. If I simply danced in an ensemble, then no role is given.

If a ballet was only performed in the debut season and not again during my career, then the number of performances given is just in that debut season and the year is not repeated.

Where I have danced in several productions of the same ballet (i.e. *The Sleeping Beauty, Swan Lake* etc.) then these are listed in the order in which I danced them.

Alice in Wonderland
Choreographer: Derek Deane
Composer: Pyotr Tchaikovsky (arr: Carl Davis)
Role: 'grown-up' Alice
Debut: 1996/7 – English National Ballet
Performances: 42 – 12 (1996/7 Laurentiu Guinea, Giuseppe Picone, Zoltan Solymosi); 14 (1999/2000 Filip Diaz, Nathan Coppen); 16 (2006/7 Dmitri Gruzdyev)
Role: Alice 'Dream' *pas de deux*
Performances: 5 (1999/2000 Filip Diaz)

Anna Karenina
Choreographer: André Prokovsky
Composer: Pyotr Tchaikovsky (arr: Guy Woolfenden)
Debuts: 1993/4 Scottish Ballet
Role: Anna
Performances: 9 (Roddie Patriczio)
Role: Kitty
Performances: 9 (Roddie Patriczio)

Apollo
Choreographer: George Balanchine
Composer: Igor Stravinsky
Role: Polyhymnia
Debut: 2008/9 – English National Ballet
Performances: 4 - 2 (2008/9 Thomas Edur); 2 (2011/12 Vadim Muntagirov)

Role: Terpsichore
Debut: 2008/9 – Carlos Acosta & Friends
Performances: 14 - 3 (2008/9 Carlos Acosta); 5 (2009/10 Carlos Acosta); 6 (2011/12 Vadim Muntagirov, Zdenek Konvalina)
Role: *Pas de deux*
Performances: 1 (2009/10 Dmitri Gruzdyev)

La Bayadère
Choreographer: Marius Petipa
Composer: Léon Minkus
Role: Nikiya
Debut: 2004/5 – Brno
Performances: 1 (Dmitri Gruzdyev)

La Bayadère (Act II 'Kingdom of the Shades')
Choreographer: Natalia Makarova after Petipa
Composer: Léon Minkus
Debuts: 1999/2000 – English National Ballet
Role: Nikiya
Performances: 7 (Dmitri Gruzdyev)
Role: Solo Shade
Performances: 4
Role: *Pas de deux*
Performances: 2 (Dmitri Gruzdyev)

Belong (*pas de deux*)
Choreographer: Norbert Vesak
Composer: Syrinx
Debut: 1995/6 – Scottish Ballet
Performances: 9 (Vladislav Bubnov)

Bruch Violin Concerto
Choreographer: Clark Tippett
Composer: Max Bruch
Debut: 1993/4 – Scottish Ballet
Performances: 6 (Robert Hampton, Wim Broexs)

Chéri
Choreographer: Peter Darrell
Composer: David Earl
Role: Fiancée
Debut: 1994/5 – Scottish Ballet
Performances: 9 (Campbell McKenzie)

Chopiniana (Les Sylphides)
Choreographer: Mikhail Fokine
Composer: Frédéric Chopin
Role: Mazurka
Debut: 1989/90 – Czech National Ballet
Performances: 12 – 6 (1989/90); 4 (1996/7 Laurentiu Guinea); 2 (2009/10 Anton Lukovkin)

A Christmas Carol
Choreographer: Veronica Paeper
Composer: Balfe, Benedict, Wallace (arr: David Tidboald)
Debuts: 1992/3 – CAPAB Ballet, Cape Town
Role: Ghost of Christmas Past
Performances: 3 (Nicholas van der Merwe)
Role: Fiancée
Performances: 3 (Nicholas van der Merwe)

Cinderella

Choreographer: Peter Darrell
Composer: Gioachino Rossini (arr: Tovey)
Debuts: 1994/5 – Scottish Ballet
Role: Cinderella
Performances: 13 (Vladislav Bubnov)
Role: Summer Fairy
Performances: 7
Role: *Pas de deux*
Performances: 1 (Daniel de Andrante)

Cinderella

Choreographer: Michael Corder
Composer: Sergei Prokofiev
Role: Summer Fairy
Debut: 1998/9 – English National Ballet
Performances: 20 - 11 (1998/9 Robert Marshall, John Cavali, Christian Duncan); 1 (2001/2 Alexis Oliviera); 8 (2003/4 Gary Avis)
Role: Cinderella
Debut: 1998/9 – English National Ballet
Performances: 16 – 6 (1998/9 Laurentiu Guinea, Robert Tewsley); 4 (2001/2 Jan-Erik Wikström, Vladislav Bubnov, Dmitri Gruzdyev); 4 (2009/10 Esteban Berlanga, Vadim Muntagirov); 2 (2010/11 Vadim Muntagirov)
Role: Fairy Godmother
Debut: 2003/4 – English National Ballet
Performances: 7

Concerto Grosso

Choreographer: Christopher Hampson
Composer: Alfred Schnittke

Debut: 1998/9 – English National Ballet
Performances: 11

Coppélia
Choreographer: Marius Petipa
Composer: Léo Delibes
Role: Swanilda's variation and *pas de deux*
Debut: 1990/91 – Czech National Ballet
Performances: 14 – (9 – variation only) 3 (1990/91 Pavel Plecháček); 2 (1991/2 Mario Radačovský); 3 (1992/3 – variation only); 6 (2011/12 – variation only)

Coppélia
Choreographer: Peter Wright after Petipa/Cecchetti
Composer: Léo Delibes
Role: Swanilda
Debut: 1995/6 –Scottish Ballet
Performances: 7 (Vladislav Bubnov)

Coppélia
Choreographer: Ronald Hynd after Petipa
Composer: Léo Delibes
Role: Swanilda
Debut: 1996/7 – English National Ballet
Performances: 12 – 6 (1996/7 Greg Horsman, Laurentiu Guinea, Dmitri Gruzdyev); 6 (1999/2000 Dmitri Gruzdyev)

Le Corsaire
Choreographer: Alexander Gorsky after Petipa
Composer: Riccardo Drigo
Role: *Pas de deux*

Debut: 1991/2 – Czech National Ballet
Performances: 4 – 2 (1991/2 Mario Radačovský); 1 (1993/4 Vladislav Bubnov); 1 (1994/5 Campbell McKenzie)

Cut to the Chase
Choreographer: Paul Lewis
Composer: Unknown
Debut: 1996/7 – English National Ballet
Performances: 9 (Dmitri Gruzdyev)

Don Quixote
Choreographer: Alexander Gorsky after Petipa
Composer: Ludwig Minkus
Role: Dryad
Debut: 1989/90 – Czech National Ballet
Performances: 4
Role: Grand *pas de deux*
Debut: 1991/2 – Czech National Ballet
Performances: 8 – 3 (1991/2 Mario Radačovský, Luboš Hajn); 2 (2000/1 Dmitri Gruzdyev); 3 (2011/12 Vadim Muntagirov)
Role: Kitri
Debut: 1991/2 – Czech National Ballet
Performances: 5 (Jiří Horák, Stanislav Fečo, Jan Němec)

Double Concerto
Choreographer: Christopher Hampson
Composer: Francis Poulenc
Debut: 2001/2 – English National Ballet
Performances: 14 (plus 6 *pas de deux* only) – 7 (2001/2 Jan-Erik Wikström); 4 (2002/3 Jan-Erik Wikström); 3 (2003/4 Jan-Erik Wikström); 6 (2006/7 Arionel Vargas – *pas de deux* only)

Duet
Choreographer: Wayne Eagling
Composer: Richard Wagner (arr: Franz Liszt)
Debut: 2008/9 – Bratislava
Performances: 2 (Tamás Solymosi)

Études
Choreographer: Harald Lander
Composer: Carl Czerny (arr: Knudåge Riisager)
Debut: 1996/7 – English National Ballet
Performances: 6 – 5 (1996/7 Nathan Coppen, Greg Horsman, Laurentiu Guinea, Dmitri Gruzdyev); 1 (2007/8 Thomas Edur, César Morales)

Extáze ducha (*Ecstasy of spirit*)
Choreographer: Robert Balogh
Composer: Wolfgang Amadeus Mozart
Role: Žena
Debut: 1989/90 – Czech National Ballet
Performances: 5
Note: This was part of a triple bill entitled *Z nejlepšiho (From the best)*. The other two parts *Život a smrt (Life and death)* and *Stmíváníčko (Little nightfall)* were choreographed by Libor Vaculík.

A Fond Kiss
Choreographer: Mark Baldwin
Composer: Igor Stravinsky
Debut: 1995/6 – Scottish Ballet
Performances: 10 (Vladislav Bubnov)

Four Horsemen
Choreographer: Irek Mukhamedov
Composer: Traditional Argentine Tango
Debut: 2001/2 – London Coliseum Gala
Performances: 1 (Irek Mukhamedov)

Four Last Songs
Choreographer: Rudi van Danzig
Composer: Richard Strauss
Debut: 1992/3 – CAPAB Ballet, Cape Town
Performances: 3 (Jeremy Hodges)

Giselle
Choreographer: Jean Coralli/ Jules Joseph Perrot
Composer: Adolphe Adam
Role: Peasant *pas de deux*
Debut: 1989/90 – Czech National Ballet
Performances: 14 - 3 (1989/90 Jiří Scudlik, Luboš Hajn); 7 (1990/1 Stanislav Fečo); 3 (1991/2 Stanislav Fečo); 1 (1992/3 Eugene Vrublevskyj)
Role: *Pas de deux* (Act II)
Debut: 2001/2 – Spoletto Gala
Performances: 3 – 2 (2001/2 Stanislav Fečo); 1 (2004/5 Dmitri Gruzdyev)
Role: Giselle
Debut: 2010/11 – Czech National Ballet
Performances: 7 – 2 (2010/11 Vadim Muntagirov); 5 (2011/12 Vadim Muntagirov)

Giselle
Choreographer: Derek Deane after Coralli and Perrot
Composer: Adolphe Adam
Role: Giselle
Debut: 1996/7 – English National Ballet
Performances: 9 – 3 (1996/7 Laurentiu Guinea); 6 (2000/1 Dmitri Gruzdyev)

Giselle
Choreographer: Mary Skeaping after Coralli and Perrot
Composer: Adolphe Adam
Role: Giselle
Debut: 2004/5 – English National Ballet
Performances: 18 – 4 (2004/5 Dmitri Gruzdyev); 3 (2006/7 Dmitri Gruzdyev); 11 (2009/10 Esteban Berlanga, Vadim Muntagirov, Fabian Reimair)

Hamlet
Choreographer: Veronica Paeper
Composer: Peter Klatzow
Role: Ophelia
Debut: 1992/3 – CAPAB Ballet, Cape Town
Performances: 6 (Johan Jooste, Hubert Essakow)

Haydn Pieces
Choreographer: Mark Baldwin
Composer: Joseph Haydn
Debut: 1994/5 – Scottish Ballet
Performances: 6 (Vladislav Bubnov)

The Lady of the Camellias
Choreographer: Robert Balogh
Composer: Giuseppe Verdi/ Ladislav Simon
Role: Marguerite
Debut: 1990/91 – Czech National Ballet
Performances: 10 – 2 (1990/91 Stanislav Fečo); 8 (1991/2 Jiří Horák, Stanislav Fečo, Jan Němec)

Loutky (Doll)
Choreographer: Unknown (could be Nikolai & Sergei Legat)
Composer: Unknown (could be Riccardo Drigo)
Role: Doll
Debut: 1990/91 – Czech National Ballet
Performances: 1 (Jiří Horák)

Love Lessons
Choreographer: David Slobašpycký
Composer: Unknown
Debut: 1995/6 – Portugal
Performances: 7 (Vladislav Bubnov, Karel Litera)

Macbeth
Choreographer: Daniel Wiesner
Composer: Václav Riedlbauch
Role: *Corps de ballet* – birds
Debut: 1989/90 – Czech National Ballet
Performances: 9 – 8 (1989/90); 1 (1990/1)

Manon
Choreographer: Kenneth MacMillan
Composer: Jules Massenet (arr: Leighton Lucas)

Role: 'Bedroom' *pas de deux*
Debut: 2007/08 – English National Ballet
Performances: 10 – 2 (2007/8 Dmitri Gruzdyev); 5 (2009/10 Friedemann Vogel, Esteban Berlanga); 3 (2011/12 Vadim Muntagirov)
Role: Manon
Debut: 2008/09 – English National Ballet
Performances: 7 (Friedemann Vogel)

Mashkovsky Waltz
Choreographer: Vasili Vainonen
Composer: Moritz Moszkowski ('Mashkovsky')
Debut: 2000/1 – Červený kříž Gala
Performances: 6 – 1 (2000/1 Irek Mukhamedov); 5 (2009/10 David Makhateli, Tamás Solymosi)

Melody on the Move
Choreographer: Michael Corder
Composer: Trevor Duncan
Role: The Girl from Corsica
Debut: 2003/4 – English National Ballet
Performances: 3 (plus 8 as a gala divertissement) – 3 (2003/4 Jan-Erik Wikström); 9 (2006/7 Arionel Vargas – all as divertissements); 1 (2007/8 Arionel Vargas – divertissement); 1 (2008/9 Arionel Vargas – divertissement)

A Midsummer Night's Dream
Choreographer: Veronica Paeper
Composer: Felix Mendelssohn
Role: Titania
Debut: 1992/3 – CAPAB Ballet, Cape Town
Performances: 5 (Nicholas van der Merwe)

A Midsummer Night's Dream
Choreographer: Robert Cohan
Composer: Felix Mendelssohn
Debuts: 1995/6 – Scottish Ballet
Role: Titania
Performances: 6 (Robert Hampton)
Role: 'Dream'*pas de deux*
Performances: 1 (Vladislav Bubnov)

A Million Kisses to my Skin
Choreographer: David Dawson
Composer: Johann Sebastian Bach
Debut: 2006/7 – English National Ballet
Performances: 16 – 8 (2006/7); 5 (2007/8 Thomas Edur, Anton Lukovkin, Fernando Bufala); 3 (2008/9)

The Nutcracker
Choreographer: Veronica Paeper after Ivanov
Composer: Pyotr Tchaikovsky
Role: Sugar Plum Fairy
Debut: 1991/2 – CAPAB Ballet, Cape Town (guest)
Performances: 4 (Johan Jooste)

The Nutcracker
Choreographer: Peter Darrell after Ivanov
Composer: Pyotr Tchaikovsky
Debuts: 1994/5 – Scottish Ballet
Role: Sugar Plum Fairy
Performances: 12 (Paul Chalmer, Daniel de Andrante)
Role: Ice Queen
Performances: 3 (Paul Chalmer)

The Nutcracker

Choreographer: Ben Stevenson after Ivanov
Composer: Pyotr Tchaikovsky
Debuts: 1996/7 – English National Ballet
Role: Sugar Plum Fairy
Performances: 9 (Laurentiu Guinea, Zoltan Solymosi, Greg Horsman)
Role: Ice Queen
Performances: 8 (Greg Horsman)

The Nutcracker

Choreographer: Derek Deane after Ivanov
Composer: Pyotr Tchaikovsky
Debuts: 1997/8 – English National Ballet
Role: Sugar Plum Fairy
Performances: 29 – 15 (1997/8 Dmitri Gruzdyev, Alexander Antonievich); 7 (1998/9 Robert Tewsley, Dmitri Gruzdyev); 7 (1999/2000 Dmitri Gruzdyev)
Role: Grand *pas de deux*
Performances: 4 – 1 (1997/8 Dmitri Gruzdyev); 3 (2000/1 Nathan Coppen)
Role: Ice Queen
Performances: 33 – 13 (1997/8); 11 (1998/99); 8 (1999/2000); 1 (2001/2)

The Nutcracker

Choreographer: Christopher Hampson after Ivanov
Composer: Pyotr Tchaikovsky
Role: Sugar Plum Fairy
Debut: 2003/4 – English National Ballet
Performances: 22 – 3 (2003/4 Jan-Erik Wikström); 5 (2004/5 Dmitri Gruzdyev); 4 (2005/6 Dmitri Gruzdyev); 5 (2006/7 Dmitri Gruzdyev); 2 (2008/9 Zdenek Konvalina); 3 (2009/10 Vadim Muntagirov)

The Nutcracker
Choreographer: Wayne Eagling after Ivanov
Composer: Pyotr Tchaikovsky
Role: Grown-up Clara (including grand *pas de deux*)
Debut: 2010/11 – English National Ballet
Performances: 7 – 3 (2010/11 Vadim Muntagirov, Junor Souza, Esteban Berlanga); 4 (2011/12 Vadim Muntagirov, Junor Souza, James Forbat, Max Westwell)
Role: Grand *pas de deux*
Performances: 3 (2011/12 Vadim Muntagirov)

Onegin pas de deux
Choreographer: Vasilij Medvedev
Composer: Pyotr Tchaikovsky
Role: Tatiana
Debut: 2001/2 –Donéck Ukraine
Performances: 4 (Stanislav Fečo)

Pa Papageno
Choreographer: Robert Balogh
Composer: unknown
Role: *Pas de deux*
Debut: 1990/91 – Czech National Ballet
Performances: 1 (Jiří Horák)

Paquita
Choreographer: Marius Petipa
Composer: Eduouard Deldevez/ Ludwig Minkus
Role: Solo girl variation
Debut: 1989/90 – Czech National Ballet
Performances: 2

Role: *Pas de deux*
Debut: 1990/1 – Czech National Ballet
Performances: 2 (Jiří Horák, Pavel Plecháček)

Paquita
Choreographer: Derek Deane after Petipa
Composer: Eduouard Deldevez/ Ludwig Minkus
Role: Grand *pas de deux*
Debut: 1996/7 – English National Ballet
Performances: 11 – 3 (1996/7 Laurentiu Guinea); 4 (1998/9 Nathan Coppen, Dmitri Gruzdyev); 4 (1999/2000 Nathan Coppen, Dmitri Gruzdyev)

Perpetuum Mobile
Choreographer: Christopher Hampson
Composer: Johann Sebastian Bach
Debut: 2005/6 – English National Ballet
Performances: 2 (Arionel Vargas)

Peter Pan
Choreographer: Graham Lustig
Composer: Edward McGuire
Role: Wendy
Debut: 1993/4 – Scottish Ballet
Performances: 8 (Roddie Patriczio)

Petrushka
Choreographer: Mikhail Fokine
Composer: Igor Stravinsky
Role: Solo girl
Debut: 1989/90 – Czech National Ballet
Performances: 7 – 6 (1989/90); 1 (1990/1)

Princ Bajaja
Choreographer: Daniel Wiesner
Composer: Václav Trojan/ Jan Klusák
Role: Princess Zdoběna
Debut: 1989/90 – Czech National Ballet
Performances: 9 – 6 (1989/90); 3 (1990/1)

Raymonda
Choreographer: Norman Furber after Petipa
Composer: Alexander Glazunov
Debuts: 1992/93 – CAPAB Ballet, Cape Town
Role: Raymonda
Performances: 2 (Francisco Joubert)
Role: Raymonda's variation
Performances: 1
Role: Pas de deux
Performances: 1 (Nicholas van der Merwe)

Raymonda (Act III)
Choreographer: Derek Deane after Petipa
Composer: Alexander Glazunov
Role: Raymonda
Debut: 1999/2000 – English National Ballet
Performances: 5 (Filip Diaz)

Raymonda
Choreographer: Marius Petipa
Composer: Alexander Glazunov
Debut: 2007/8 – Andorra
Role: Raymonda
Performances: 2 (Dmitri Gruzdyev)

Return to the Strange Land (*Návraty do neznámé země*)
Choreographer: Jiří Kylían
Composer: Leos Janácek
Role: *Pas de trois*
Debut: 1991/2 – Czech National Ballet
Performances: 4 (David Pospíšil, Ivan Matouš)

Romeo and Juliet
Choreographer: Miroslav Kůra
Composer: Sergei Prokofiev
Roles: Capulet waltz, *Corps de ballet*
Debut: 1989/90 – Czech National Ballet
Performances: 9

Romeo and Juliet ('In the round')
Choreographer: Derek Deane
Composer: Sergei Prokofiev
Role: Juliet
Debut: 1997/8 – English National Ballet
Performances: 8 – 2 (1997/8 Dmitri Gruzdyev); 3 (2000/1 Dmitri Gruzdyev); 3 (2004/5 Dmitri Gruzdyev)

Romeo and Juliet ('Proscenium')
Choreographer: Derek Deane
Composer: Sergei Prokofiev
Debuts: 1998/9 – English National Ballet
Role: Juliet
Performances: 11 - 9 (1998/9 Dmitri Gruzdyev); 2 (2000/1 Dmitri Gruzdyev)
Role: 'Balcony' *pas de deux*
Performances: 9 – 4 (1998/9 Dmitri Gruzdyev); 2 (1999/2000 Dmitri

Gruzdyev); 3 (2000/1 Vladislav Bubnov)
Role: 'Bedroom' *pas de deux*
Performances: 1 (2006/7 Jan-Erik Wikström)

Romeo and Juliet
Choreographer: Rudolf Nureyev
Composer: Sergei Prokofiev
Role: Juliet
Debut: 2001/2 – English National Ballet
Performances: 23 – 10 (2001/2 Jan-Erik Wikström); 8 (2004/5 Dmitri
Gruzdyev); 5 (2010/11 Vadim Muntagirov)
Role: 'Balcony' *pas de deux*
Performances: 5 – 1 (2004/5 Dmitri Gruzdyev); 4 (2010/11 Vadim
Muntagirov)

Satanella pas de deux
Choreographer: Vasilij Medvedev
Composer: Cesare Pugni
Debut: 1991/92 – Moravian National Ballet (Guest)
Performances: 1 (Vasilij Medvedev)

Scotch Symphony
Choreographer: George Balanchine
Composer: Felix Mendelssohn
Debut: 1993/4 – Scottish Ballet
Performances: 5 (Vladislav Bubnov)

Silent Sentences
Choreographer: David Slobašpycký
Composer: None
Debut: 1995/6 – Portugal
Performances: 3 (Pavel Knole)

The Sleeping Beauty

Choreographer: Miroslav Kůra after Petipa
Composer: Pyotr Tchaikovsky
Debuts: 1989/90 – Czech National Ballet
Role: Friend of Aurora
Performances: 11 – 8 (1989/90); 3 (1990/1)
Role: Bluebird *pas de deux* (Princess Florine)
Performances: 21 – 11 (1989/90 Jan Kadlec, Petr Šimek, Jiří Horák); 9 (1990/1 Stanislav Fečo); 1 (1991/2 Stanislav Fečo)
Role: Fairy variation #5
Performances: 2
Role: Grand *pas de deux*
Performances: 4 – 2 (1989/90 Jiří Horák); 1 (1991/2 Jiří Horák); 1 (2000/1 Jiří Kodym)
Role: Aurora Variation
Performances: 2
Role: Aurora
Performances: 7 – 1 (1989/90 Jan Nečas); 6 (1990/1 Jan Nečas, Jiří Horák)

The Sleeping Beauty

Choreographer: David Poole after Petipa
Composer: Pyotr Tchaikovsky
Debuts: 1992/93 – CAPAB Ballet, Cape Town
Role: Aurora
Performances: 3 (Kiril Melnikov, Francisco Joubert)
Role: Bluebird *pas de deux* (Princess Florine)
Performances: 1 (Stanislav Cašov)
Role: Grand *pas de deux*
Performances: 1 (Nicholas van der Merwe)

The Sleeping Beauty
Choreographer: Galina Samsova after Petipa
Composer: Pyotr Tchaikovsky
Debuts: 1993/4 –Scottish Ballet
Role: Aurora
Performances: 16 (Vladislav Bubnov, Daniel de Andrante)
Role: Lilac Fairy
Performances: 5
Role: Grand *pas de deux*
Performances: 1 (Daniel de Andrante)

The Sleeping Beauty
Choreographer: Marius Petipa
Composer: Pyotr Tchaikovsky
Role: Grand *pas de deux*
Debut: 1996/7 – English National Ballet
Performances: 26 – 2 (1996/7 Laurentiu Guinea); 7 (2000/1 Nathan Coppen); 12 (2001/2 Dmitri Gruzdyev); 2 (2005/6 Dmitri Gruzdyev, Jan-Erik Wikström); 3 (2009/10 David Makhateli)
Role: Aurora's variation
Debut: 2008/9 – Brussels
Performances: 1

The Sleeping Beauty
Choreographer: Ronald Hynd after Petipa
Composer: Pyotr Tchaikovsky
Debuts: 1997/8 – English National Ballet
Role: Aurora
Performances: 4 (Dmitri Gruzdyev)
Role: Bluebird *pas de deux* (Princess Florine)
Performances: 5 (Dmitri Gruzdyev)

Role: Lilac Fairy
Performances: 4

The Sleeping Beauty ('In the round')
Choreographer: Derek Deane after Petipa
Composer: Pyotr Tchaikovsky
Role: Lilac Fairy
Debut: 1999/2000 –English National Ballet
Performances: 3 (Robert Marshall)

The Sleeping Beauty
Choreographer: Kenneth MacMillan after Petipa
Composer: Pyotr Tchaikovsky
Role: Aurora
Debut: 2005/6 –English National Ballet
Performances: 15 – 12 (2005/6 Dmitri Gruzdyev); 3 (2008/9 Zdenek Konvalina, Thomas Edur)

The Snow Queen
Choreographer: Michael Corder
Composer: Sergei Prokofiev
Role: Snow Queen
Debut: 2007/8 –English National Ballet
Performances: 11 – 8 (2007/8); 3 (2009/10)

Špaliček
Choreographer: Miroslav Kůra
Composer: Bohuslav Martinů
Role: Butterfly (principal role)
Debut: 1989/90 – Czech National Ballet
Performances: 4

Sphinx
Choreographer: Glen Tetley
Composer: Bohuslav Martinů
Role: Sphinx
Debut: 1997/8 – English National Ballet
Performances: 19 – 6 (1997/8 Robert Marshall, Yat Sen Chang); 9 (1999/2000 Thomas Edur, Dmitri Gruzdyev, Yat Sen Chang); 4 (2001/2 Jurij Slipič, Alexander Katsapov, Jiří Kodym)

Square Dance
Choreographer: George Balanchine
Composers: Antonio Vivaldi and Arcangelo Corelli
Debut: 2000/1 – English National Ballet
Performances: 3 (Dmitri Gruzdyev)

Strictly Gershwin ('In the round')
Choreographer: Derek Deane
Composer: George Gershwin
Debuts: 2007/8 – English National Ballet
Role: Opening Class
Performances: 8 (Dmitri Gruzdyev)
Role: Rhapsody in Blue
Performances: 6 – 4 (2007/8 Friedemann Vogel); 2 (2010/11 Friedemann Vogel)
Role: Summertime *pas de deux*
Performances: 11 (plus 1 as divertissement) 8 (2007/8 Friedemann Vogel); 1 (2009/10 Dmitri Gruzdyev - as a divertissement); 3 (2010/11 Friedemann Vogel)
Role: The Man I Love *pas de deux*
Performances: 5 – 2 (2007/8 Friedemann Vogel); 3 (2010/11 Friedemann Vogel)

Strictly Gershwin ('Proscenium')
Choreographer: Derek Deane
Composer: George Gershwin
Debuts: 2011/12 – English National Ballet
Role: Rhapsody in Blue
Performances: 6 (Vadim Muntagirov)
Role: Summertime *pas de deux*
Performances: 12 (Vadim Muntagirov, Zdenek Konvalina)
Role: The Man I Love *pas de deux*
Performances: 6 (Vadim Muntagirov, Fabian Reimair, Junor Souza)

Suite en Blanc
Choreographer: Serge Lifar
Composer: Edouard Lalo
Roles: Flute solo and *pas de deux*
Debut: 2010/11 –English National Ballet
Performances: 9 – 2 (2010/11 Vadim Muntagirov); 7 (2011/12 Vadim Muntagirov)

Swan Lake
Choreographer: Natalia Dudinskaya/Konstantin Sergeyev after Petipa/Ivanov
Composer: Pyotr Tchaikovsky
Role: *Pas de trois*
Debut: 1990/91 – Czech National Ballet
Performances: 17 – 7 (1990/91 Stanislav Fečo, Jan Nečas); 7 (1991/2 Stanislav Fečo, Petr Šimek); 3 (1992/3 Eugene Vrublevskyj)
Role: Odette/Odile
Debut: 1995/96 – Czech National Ballet
Performances: 5 (Karel Litera, Jiří Horák)

Swan Lake
Choreographer: Galina Samsova after Petipa/Ivanov
Composer: Pyotr Tchaikovsky
Role: Odette/Odile
Debut: 1994/5 – Scottish Ballet
Performances: 17 (Hans Nilsson, Laurent Novis)

Swan Lake
Choreographer: Marius Petipa/Lev Ivanov
Composer: Pyotr Tchaikovsky
Role: Black Swan *pas de deux*
Debut: 1995/6 – Scottish Ballet
Performances: 10 – 1 (1995/6 Simon Gray); 1 (1996/7 Laurentiu Guinea); 1 (1997/8 Stanislav Fečo); 1 (1999/2000 Dmitri Gruzdyev); 1 (2006/7 Dmitri Gruzdyev); 1 (2007/8 Dmitri Gruzdyev); 4 (2011/12 Vadim Muntagirov)
Role: White Swan *pas de deux*
Debut: 1996/7 – English National Ballet
Performances: 35 – 7 (1996/7 Laurentiu Guinea); 2 (1999/2000 Dmitri Gruzdyev); 2 (2001/2 Stanislav Fečo, Dmitri Gruzdyev); 2 (2003/4 Dmitri Gruzdyev); 1 (2005/6 Dmitri Gruzdyev); 3 (2006/7 Dmitri Gruzdyev); 1 (2007/8 Dmitri Gruzdyev); 8 (2008/9 Dmitri Gruzdyev, Esteban Berlanga, Yat Sen Chang); 3 (2009/10 Friedemann Vogel); 6 (2011/12 Vadim Muntagirov, Zdenek Konvalina)
Role: Odette/Odile
Debut: 2007/8 – Czech National Ballet
Performances: 5 – 1 (2007/8 Jan-Erik Wikström); 4 (2008/9 Jan-Erik Wikström, Carlos Phinilos)

Swan Lake
Choreographer: Raisa Struchkova after Petipa/Ivanov

Composer: Pyotr Tchaikovsky
Role: Odette/Odile
Debut: 1997/8 – English National Ballet
Performances: 2 (Dmitri Gruzdyev)

Swan Lake ('Proscenium')
Choreographer: Derek Deane after Petipa/Ivanov
Composer: Pyotr Tchaikovsky
Role: Odette/Odile
Debut: 1998/9 – English National Ballet
Performances: 28 – 7 (1998/9 Dmitri Gruzdyev); 6 (2003/4 Dmitri Gruzdyev); 1 (2005/6 Dmitri Gruzdyev); 6 (2006/7 Dmitri Gruzdyev, Friedemann Vogel); 6 (2007/8 Dmitri Gruzdyev); 2 (2010/11 Vadim Muntagirov)

Swan Lake ('In the round')
Choreographer: Derek Deane after Petipa/Ivanov
Composer: Pyotr Tchaikovsky
Role: Odette/Odile
Debut: 1998/9 – English National Ballet
Performances: 14 – 3 (1998/9 Dmitri Gruzdyev); 3 (2001/2 Dmitri Gruzdyev); 3 (2003/4 Dmitri Gruzdyev); 2 (2006/7 Dmitri Gruzdyev); 3 (2009/10 Vadim Muntagirov)

Swan Lake
Choreographer: Andrei Petrov after Petipa/Ivanov
Composer: Pyotr Tchaikovsky
Role: Odette/Odile
Debut: 2011/12 – Moscow Kremlin Ballet (guest)
Performances: 1 (Vadim Muntagirov)

La Sylphide
Choreographer: Pierre Lacotte after Filippo Taglioni
Composer: Jean-Madeleine Schneitzhoeffer
Role: *Corps de ballet* – sylphs
Debut: 1989/90 – Czech National Ballet
Performances: 1
Role: Peasant *pas de deux*
Debut: 1990/91 – Czech National Ballet
Performances: 6 (Stanislav Fečo)

La Sylphide
Choreographer: August Bournonville
Composer: Hermann Løvenskjold
Debuts: 1995/6 – Scottish Ballet
Role: Effie
Performances: 14 (Vladislav Bubnov)
Role: P*as de deux*
Performances: 1 (Vladislav Bubnov)

Sylvia
Choreographer: Lev Ivanov/Pavel Gerdt
Composer: Léo Delibes
Roles: *Corps de ballet* – nymphs and dryads – solo girl
Debut: 1989/90 – Czech National Ballet
Performances: 3
Role: P*as de deux*
Debut: 1991/2 – Czech National Ballet
Performances: 2 (Jan Němec)

Tančirna: 4 Smyčcový kvartet (String Quartet No 4)
Choreographer: Zdenek Prokeš

Composer: Bohuslav Martinů
Role: *Pas de deux*
Debut: 1990/91 – Czech National Ballet
Performances: 10 – 7 (1990/91 Jiří Horák, Pavel Ďumbala); 3 (1991/2 Jiří Horák, Pavel Ďumbala)

TBA
Choreographer: Christopher Hampson
Composer: Aníbal Troilo
Debut: 2005/6 – Tenerife
Performances: 3

Tchaikovsky Pas de Deux
Choreographer: George Balanchine
Composer: Pyotr Tchaikovsky
Debut: 1999/2000 – English National Ballet
Performances: 24 – 7 (1999/2000 Filip Diaz, Dmitri Gruzdyev); 12 (2001/2 Dmitri Gruzdyev); 2 (2004/5 Dmitri Gruzdyev); 2 (2009/10 Yoel Carreño); 3 (2010/11 Vadim Muntagirov)

That Certain Feeling
Choreographer: André Prokovsky
Composer: George Gershwin
Debut: 1995/6 – Scottish Ballet
Performances: 9 (Vladislav Bubnov)

Three Pieces
Choreographer: Hans van Manen
Composer: Grazyna Basewicz
Debut: 1991/2 – Czech National Ballet
Performances: 4 (Stanislav Fečo)

Three Preludes
Choreographer: Ben Stevenson
Composer: Sergei Rachmaninoff
Debut: 1996/7 – English National Ballet
Performances: 10 – 2 (1996/7 Laurentiu Guinea); 8 (1998/9 Nathan Coppen, John Cavali)

Vue de L'Autre
Choreographer: Van Le Ngoc
Composer: Ludovico Einaudi
Debut: 2010/11 – English National Ballet
Performances: 16 – 15 (2010/11 Vadim Muntagirov, Junor Souza); 1 (2011/12 Vadim Muntagirov)

Voluntaries
Choreographer: Glen Tetley
Composer: Francis Poulenc
Debut: 1999/2000 – English National Ballet
Performances: 7 (Sylvan Bornel, Nathan Coppen, Robert Marshall)

Walpurgisnacht
Choreographer: Veronica Paeper
Composer: Charles Gounod
Debut: 1992/3 – CAPAB Ballet, Cape Town
Performances: 5 (Hisham Omardien, Stanislav Cašov)

Who Cares?
Choreographer: George Balanchine
Composer: George Gershwin
Debut: 1997/8 – English National Ballet
Role: The Man I Love duet

Performances: 6 – 3 (1997/8 Robert Marshall); 3 (2000/1 Dmitri Gruzdyev)
Role: Variation
Performances: 1 (1999/2000)

Workshop Pieces
Choreographer: Vladislav Bubnov & others
Composer: Various
Debut: 1993/4 – Scottish Ballet
Performances: 2 (Vladislav Bubnov)

Z pohádky do pohádky (From fairy tale to fairy tale)
Choreographer: Rudolf Macharovský after Achille Viscusi
Composer: Oskar Nedbal
Role: *Corps de ballet* – insects, *pas de deux*
Debut: 1989/90 – Czech National Ballet
Performances: 11 – 3 (1989/90 Jan Kadlec, David Slobašpycký, Jan Němec); 3 (1990/1 Luboš Hajn, Jan Němec); 4 (1991/2 Jiří Horák, Luboš Hajn); 1 (1992/3 Jiří Horák)

My Top 20 Ballets (by number of performances)

BALLET/ROLES	NO. OF PRODUCTIONS	FULL PERFORMANCES	GALAS
The Nutcracker	6	114	+7
Swan Lake	7	89	+45
The Sleeping Beauty	7	84	+35
Cinderella	2	63	+1
Romeo and Juliet	4	51	+15
Giselle	4	48	+3

Alice in Wonderland	1	42	+ 5
Strictly Gershwin	2	42	
Tchaikovsky *Pas de Deux*	1	24	
La Sylphide	2	21	+1
Coppélia	3	19	+14
Sphinx	1	19	
Apollo	1	18	+1
Anna Karenina	1	18	
A Million Kisses to my Skin	1	16	
Vue De L'Autre	1	16	
Double Concerto	1	14	+6
Chopiniana/Les Sylphides	2	12	
A Midsummer Night's Dream	2	11	+1
The Snow Queen	1	11	
Z pohádky do pohádky	1	11	

Note: Galas are where a *pas de deux* or variation from the ballet has been danced separately. Balanchine's *Tchaikovsky Pas de Deux* has been danced mostly in galas but, since it is a complete piece, it is included here. I have performed the White Swan *pas de deux* 35 times and it would therefore appear in ninth place in this list, but since it is an extract from *Swan Lake* it is not included.

My Top 20 Roles (by number of performances)

BALLET/ROLES	NO. OF PRODUCTIONS	FULL PERFORMANCES	GALAS
Sugar Plum Fairy/ Grown-up Clara	6	83	+4
Odette/Odile	7	72	+45
Aurora	5	45	+35
Ice Queen (*The Nutcracker*)	3	44	
Juliet	3	42	+15
Alice	1	42	+5
Giselle	3	34	+3
Cinderella	2	29	+1
Summer Fairy (*Cinderella*)	2	27	
Princess Florine/Bluebird	3	27	
Tchaikovsky Pas de Deux	1	24	
Summertime Duet	2	23	+1
Swanilda (*Coppélia*)	3	19	+14
Sphinx	1	19	
Pas de trois (*Swan Lake*)	1	17	
Terpsichore (*Apollo*)	1	14	+1
Effie (*La Sylphide*)	1	14	+1
Peasant pas de deux (*Giselle*)	1	14	
Mazurka (*Les Sylphides*)	2	12	
Lilac Fairy (*The Sleeping Beauty*)	3	12	

Note: The role of the grown-up Clara in Wayne Eagling's *The Nutcracker* embraces the choreography traditionally danced by the Sugar Plum Fairy, and therefore I have combined the two roles in this list. On several occasions I danced both the role of the Ice Queen and the Sugar Plum Fairy in the same performance. Galas are where a *pas de deux* or variation in the role has been danced separately and not as a part of the full ballet. Balanchine's *Tchaikovsky Pas de Deux* has been danced mostly in galas, but since it is a complete piece it is included here. The role of Odette in the White Swan *pas de deux* has been performed separately 35 times and would therefore appear in seventh place in this list, but since it is an extract from *Swan Lake* it is not included. 'Role' is extended to include non-narrative parts, which are purely dance.

My Ballet Partners

The total number of performances is given followed by the first and last seasons danced with that particular partner.

NAME	NO. OF PERFORMANCES	SEASON/S
Carlos Acosta	8	2008/9–2009/10
Daniel de Andrante	5	1993/4–1994/5
Alexander Antonievich	1	1997/8
Gary Avis	8	2003/4
Esteban Berlanga	14	2008/9–2011/12
Sylvan Bornel	4	1999/2000
Wim Broexs	1	1993/4
Vladislav Bubnov	103	1993/4–2001/2
Fernando Bufala	1	2007/8
Yoel Carreño	2	2009/10

Stanislav Cašov	5	1992/3
John Cavali	3	1998/9
Paul Chalmer	14	1994/5
Yat Sen Chang	9	1997/8–2009/10
Nathan Coppen	23	1996/7–2000/1
Filip Diaz	24	1999/2000
Pavel Ďumbala	4	1990/1–1991/2
Christian Duncan	1	1998/9
Thomas Edur	18	1999/2000–2008/9
Hubert Essakow	2	1992/3
Stanislav Fečo	54	1990/1–2001/2
James Forbat	2	2011/12
Simon Gray	1	1995/6
Dmitri Gruzdyev	273	1996/7–2009/10
Laurentiu Guinea	39	1996/7–1998/9
Luboš Hajn	6	1989/90–1991/2
Robert Hampton	11	1993/4–1995/6
Jeremy Hodges	3	1992/3
Jiří Horák	23	1989/90–1995/6
Greg Horsman	12	1996/7
Johan Jooste	8	1991/2–1992/3
Francisco Joubert	3	1992/3
Jan Kadlec	6	1989/90
Alexander Katsapov	4	2001/2
Pavel Knole	4	1995/6
Jiří Kodym	2	2000/1–2001/2
Zdenek Konvalina	10	2008/9–2011/12
Karel Litera	7	1995/6
Anton Lukovkin	6	2007/8–2009/10
Campbell McKenzie	2	1994/5
David Makhateli	6	2009/10

Robert Marshall	21	1997/8–1998/9
Ivan Matouš	1	1991/2
Kiril Melnikov	2	1992/3
Vasilij Medvedev	1	1991/2
Nicholas van der Merwe	13	1992/3
César Morales	1	2007/8
Irek Mukhamedov	2	2000/1–2001/2
Vadim Muntagirov	92	2009/10–2011/12
Jan Nečas	6	1989/90–1991/2
Jan Němec	6	1989/90–1991/2
Hans Nilsson	10	1994/5
Laurent Novis	7	1994/5
Alexis Oliveira	1	2001/2
Hisham Omardien	5	1992/3
Roddie Patriczio	26	1993/4
Carlos Phinilos	1	2008/9
Giuseppe Picone	5	1996/7
Pavel Plecháček	1	1990/1
David Pospíšil	1	1991/2
Mario Radačovský	5	1991/2
Fabian Reimair	2	2009/10–2011/12
Jiří Scudlik	2	1989/90
Petr Šimek	5	1989/90–1991/2
Jurij Slipič	4	2001/2
David Slobašpycký	1	1989/90
Tamás Solymosi	4	2008/9–2009/10
Zoltan Solymosi	4	1996/7
Junor Souza	4	2010/11–2011/12
Robert Tewsley	6	1998/9
Arionel Vargas	28	2005/6–2008/9
Friedemann Vogel	33	2006/7–2010/11

Eugene Vrublevskyj	4	1992/3
Max Westwell	1	2011/12
Jan-Erik Wikström	36	2001/2–2008/9

Note: These are the partners with whom I have danced at least a full *pas de deux* as part of a performance. There will be many other dancers with whom I have danced on stage as part of a larger ensemble (for example, in *Manon* I performed a dance with several male dancers, all of whom lifted me into the air) but it is not feasible to list them all here! The number of performances listed concludes at the end of the 2011/12 season.

My Top 20 Dance Partners (by number of performances)

NAME	NO. OF PERFORMANCES	SEASON/S
Dmitri Gruzdyev	273	1996/7–2009/10
Vladislav Bubnov	103	1993/4–2001/2
Vadim Muntagirov	92	2009/10–2011/12
Stanislav Fečo	54	1990/1–2001/2
Laurentiu Guinea	39	1996/7–1998/9
Jan-Erik Wikström	36	2001/2–2008/9
Friedemann Vogel	33	2006/7–2010/11
Arionel Vargas	28	2005/6–2008/9
Roddie Patriczio	26	1993/4
Filip Diaz	24	1999/2000
Jiří Horák	23	1989/90–1995/6
Nathan Coppen	23	1996/7–2000/1
Robert Marshall	21	1997/8–1998/9

Thomas Edur	18	1999/2000–2008/9
Esteban Berlanga	14	2008/9–2011/12
Paul Chalmer	14	1994/5
Nicholas van der Merwe	13	1992/3
Greg Horsman	12	1996/7
Robert Hampton	11	1993/4–1995/6
Zdenek Konvalina	10	2008/9–2011/12
Hans Nilsson	10	1994/5

Note: Out of a total of 75 dance partners these 21 are the only ones to have reached double figures in partnering me! As I prepare this book, I am still dancing with Vadim Muntagirov and we danced our 100th performance together in Wayne Eagling's *The Nutcracker* at the London Coliseum on 28 December 2012. So, by the time you read this, he should have moved into 2nd place in the list. It is interesting that – although I have danced for most of my career in the UK – the three men with whom I have danced the most are all Russian; and the top five are all from Eastern Europe.

Glossary

Note: this is not intended to be extensive but covers only ballet terminology used in the text

Adage/adagio taken from the Italian word *adagio* which means 'at ease'. In ballet it is used to describe slow, graceful technique that has beautiful line and strong and controlled *balances*.

Arabesque the dancer's body is supported on one foot with the other leg extended behind the body and the arms extended. There are several different arm and leg combinations in an *arabesque*.

Balances maintaining strong and controlled balance is a core skill for any ballet dancer, often standing on one foot *en pointe* (as in the Rose Adage in *The Sleeping Beauty*) or *demi-pointe* in *arabesque*; the capability of being able to maintain equilibrium is taught in the ballet class at the *barre*.

Ballet Master a principal coach to dancers in a ballet company.

Barre a horizontal bar at waist height used in ballet class to practice technique. Dancers take class with one hand resting lightly on the *barre* and each class will invariably start with exercises at the *barre* before moving on to centre work.

Battement tendus a *battement* is a beating movement of the leg, which can be exercised to front, side or back. The *battement tendu* is when the extended foot stretches away from the body with the toe touching the floor, sliding forwards or sideways in preparation for elements of technique such as the *pirouette*.

Class the core of any ballet's dancer life. Every dancer takes class in the morning to maintain and improve their technique. Classes can last up to 90 minutes and will contain work at the *barre* and in the centre. Classes are generally taken by a ballet master.

Centre work exercises performed with movement in the centre of the studio. Centre work usually occupies the latter part of a ballet class.

Coda a passage which brings a work to its conclusion in both music and ballet. For example, it describes the final part of the grand *pas de deux* in classical ballet. One of the most famous *codas* is in the Black Swan *pas de deux* in *Swan Lake* in which the ballerina performs 32 *fouettés en tournant*.

Corps de ballet the body of dancers in a ballet company who are not soloists. The *corps de ballet* works as one unit in classical ballets to perform with perfect synchronisation of movement.

Demi-pointe this means 'half' *pointe* and indicates that the dancer is elevating by stretching and standing on the balls of the feet, just beneath the toes.

En pointe a core skill for any ballerina, which means dancing by elevating herself onto the tips of her toes and stepping or balancing in that position.

Flick-flack a sequence of gymnastic, running somersaults, alternating from hands to feet on the ground.

Fouettés en tournant (or Fouettés) a 'whipped' turn made while standing on one leg (the 'supporting' leg) where the 'working' (or turning) leg can pass behind or in front of the supporting leg. There are many types of *fouetté*. The virtuoso *fouetté en tournant* (or *fouetté rond de jambe en tournant en dehors*), in which the dancer throws the working leg out to the side and whips the foot in as she turns is a major element of the classical ballerina's repertoire and she must perform 32 of these turns consecutively in the third act *pas de deux* (known as the Black Swan *pas de deux*) in *Swan Lake*, which is one of the toughest tests for a principal ballerina.

Grand jeté a long, horizontal jump, taking off from one leg and landing on the other. It is usually undertaken moving forward and often involves a full split in mid-air. The key for a dancer is to make the jump appear effortless and long with the full split being achieved at the apex of the jump, which gives an effect of gliding.

Line another core skill in ballet is to achieve graceful positions of the body with harmonious lines being shaped through the carriage of the arms (known as *port de bras*) and their relationship with the lines of the neck, body and legs.

Jeté any jump taking off from one foot to land on the other in which the front leg will seem to be thrown like an arrow in the direction of the movement (front, back or to the side). There are several types of *jetés*.

Manège a term that indicates that the dancer is to travel around the studio or stage in a circle, performing a number of turns, steps or jumps.

Partnering two dancers achieving a harmony of movement so that the audience is unaware of the effort involved in one dancer lifting, catching or carrying another. The dance involving partnering is normally referred to as the *pas de deux*.

Pas a step or a combination of steps that make up a dance.

Pas de bourée a dance of very quick steps with the feet quickly changing positions. A *pas de bourée* may be done *en pointe*.

Pas de chat literally means the 'step of the cat'. The dancer jumps sideways, and while airborne, bends both legs back to touch the feet to the opposite thighs, with the knees kept apart. The famous 'Dance of the Cygnets' in *Swan Lake* involves 16 *pas de chat*, performed by four ballerinas holding hands with their arms interlaced.

Pas de deux a duet, usually for a female and male dancer. Every ballet usually has at least one *pas de deux* as a focal point.

Pas de trois normally a dance for a man and two women (as in the Act *I Swan Lake pas de trois*, for example); a *pas de quatre* is for four dancers and so on.

Pirouette a turn on one leg, which generally begins from a *plié*. Although *pirouettes* can be made in single or multiple turns, professional ballet dancers can turn many times consecutively using the technique of 'spotting', a rapid rotation of the head with the eyes returning to focus on a fixed spot.

Pirouette en dedans a *pirouette* can turn outwards towards the back leg (this is called *pirouette en dehors*) or inwards towards the front leg, which is *pirouette en dedans*.

Plié a smooth, controlled bending of the knees, which maintains turn-out at the hip joints, enabling the knees to be directly above the line of the toes while the heels remain on the floor. A deeper *plié*, where the heels come up from the floor, is known as the *grand plié*.

Pointe shoes *pointe* work is when the dancer is performing steps while on the tips of her toes, using a special *pointe* shoe that has a hardened block at the toes.

Port de bras the carriage of the arms is an essential pre-requisite of classical ballet technique and dancers will perform many exercises at the *barre* during a class to perfect the graceful movement of the arms from one position to another.

Relevé this means 'lifted' and describes the rising of the foot to balance on one or both feet, either with heels off the floor (in what is known as *demi-pointe* or higher onto full *pointe* – balancing on the tips of the ballerina's toes).

Repetiteur a skilled person who supervises rehearsals for ballet performances, teaching the steps and generally working with the dancers in the studio.

Rose Adage the centrepiece of Marius Petipa's *The Sleeping Beauty* where Princess Aurora is presented to four suitors. The choreography requires long-held, exciting *balances en pointe* in the pauses between Aurora taking each suitor's hand in turn. It is one of the major challenges for a classical ballerina.

Split having both legs horizontal to the floor. It can be performed to the left, to the right or facing centrally (commonly known as the box split). It can be performed on the ground; supported on one leg in an *arabesque penchée*; or jumping through the air (in a *grand jeté*).

Split jeté a *jeté* in which the dancer achieves a split position after throwing the leg forward. It is more accurately described as a *grand jeté*.

Tendu a *tendu* means to point or to stretch and it is a common abbreviation of the term *battement tendu*.